J. Kondo (Ed.)

Supercomputing

Applications, Algorithms, and Architectures

For the Future of Supercomputing

With 99 Figures and 11 in Color

Springer-Verlag
Tokyo Berlin Heidelberg
New York London Paris
Hong Kong Barcelona

Editor

Professor Dr. JIRO KONDO
President of The Science Council of Japan, Professor Emeritus
University of Tokyo, 7-22-34 Roppongi, Minato-ku,
Tokyo 106, Japan

Coeditor

TOSHIKO MATSUDA
IBM Japan Ltd., 19-21, Nihonbashi Hakozaki-cho, Chuo-ku,
Tokyo 103, Japan

On the frontcover: Launching of *Akebono* by M-3SII-4 rocket on February 22,
1989 at Kagoshima Space Center. Photograph by permission of the Institute
of Space and Astronautical Science, Ministry of Education, Science, and
Culture.

ISBN-13:978-4-431-68140-3   e-ISBN-13:978-4-431-68138-0
DOI: 10.1007/978-4-431-68138-0

Library of Congress Cataloging-in-Publication Data
Supercomputing: applications, algorithms, and architectures: for the future
of supercomputing/J. Kondo, editor. p. cm. Includes bibliographical
references and index. 1. Supercomputers—Congresses. I. Kondo, Jiro,
1917–   QA76.88.S86   1991   004.1′1—dc20.91-12095

© Springer-Verlag Tokyo 1991
Softcover reprint of the hardcover 1st edition 1991

Typesetting: Asco Trade Typesetting Ltd., Hong Kong

Preface

With the remarkable progress in the development of computer hardware, scientific and/or social problems which are not otherwise amenable to solution can be solved by numerical computation when the mathematical models of the related phenomena have been well established. At the same time, however, it is important that difficult problems to be solved by computers continue to be posed, in order to stimulate the improvement of machine hardware.

Recently, the technology of supercomputing has been making rapid progress. We recognize that, in addition, methodologies for approaching problems have also been developed and linked with much computation experience, in many applications. What enables a final triumph in problem solving? Hardware technology? Software architecture? Approach methodology? Each must be tackled, but that is not enough. Most important is the interdisciplinary participation of experts in related fields and passionate discussion to work toward the solution of problems. What we have attempted is nothing less than this objective. We hope that this book will be a stimulus to scientists involved in supercomputing.

*

This book has its origin in the Computer Application Symposium, held by IBM Japan in 1989. For this symposium, an executive committee was organized, with the following members:

Chairman Prof. Dr. Jiro Kondo	Science Council of Japan
Prof. Dr. Tadahiko Kawai	Science University of Tokyo
Prof. Dr. Yoshio Oyanagi	University of Tsukuba
Prof. Dr. Masaaki Shimazaki	Kyushu University
Prof. Dr. Masatake Mori	University of Tokyo

Speakers and participants were nominated by the committee members, and the speakers submitted papers which are included in this book. In addition, several participants have also contributed papers on their recent research. The two sessions of panel discussion were very interesting, and opportunities arose for discussion from wide-ranging viewpoints. This volume includes selected extracts from these sessions.

We editors would like to express our appreciation to the committee members for their cooperation. We would also like to thank the secretariat staff of IBM Japan for their support of this symposium.

JIRO KONDO
Editor

TOSHIKO MATSUDA
Coeditor

Professor Jiro Kondo was born in Shiga Prefecture, Japan in 1917. He attended the Imperial University of Kyoto and obtained his doctorate of engineering from the University of Tokyo in 1958.

Dr. Kondo was a professor of applied mathematics and gas dynamics in the Department of Aeronautics at the University of Tokyo from 1955 to his retirement in 1977. He then joined the National Institute for Environmental Studies as deputy director and served as director from 1980 to 1985.

Dr. Kondo has served as President of the Science Council of Japan since 1985. He is also a member of the Science Council of the Ministry of Education, Science and Culture and is an ex officio member of the Council for Science and Technology of the Prime Minister's Office. He was appointed President of the Central Council for Environmental Pollution Control in 1988.

Dr. Kondo has received the Ouchi Medal, the Deming Medal, and the Purple Ribbon Medal for his distinguished academic and research activities.

Contents

List of Contributors

Doyama, M. 81
Hijikata, K. 202
Ikeda, K. 174
Iwasaki, Y. 72
Kalos, M.H. 185
Kanada, Y. 199
Kashiwagi, H. 109
Kawai, T. 207

Kikuchi, N. 20, 209
Kobayashi, T. 125
Kondo, J. 3
Miranda Guedes, J. 20
Miyama, S.M. 181
Mori, M. 193
Nakazawa, K. 194

Nomura, O. 155
Oyanagi, Y. 179
Shimazaki, M. 163
Suzuki, K. 20
Tomita, S. 167
Torigaki, T. 20
Yonezawa, F. 141

Color Plates

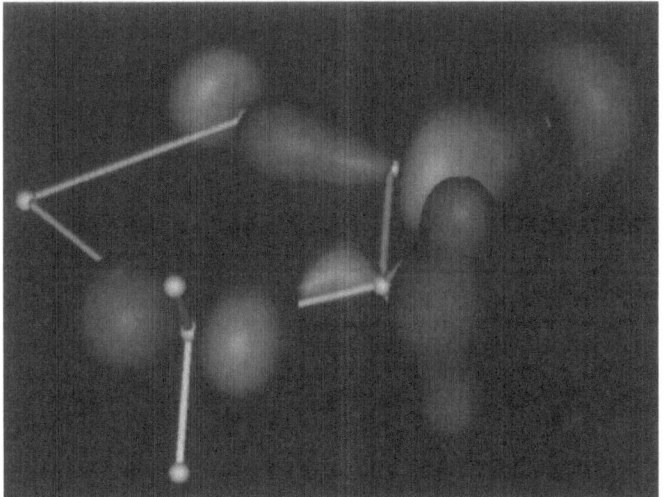

Fig. 5.3a,b. Examples of molecular orbitals. **a** A molecular orbital of a copper-glycine complex. **b** A molecular orbital of an iron-porphyrin-ammonia-oxygen complex, which is a model of the active site of hemoglobin

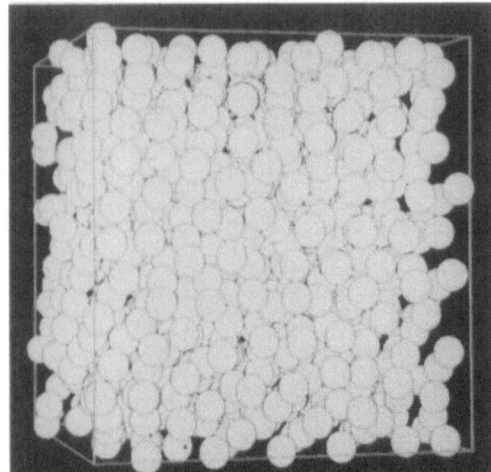

a

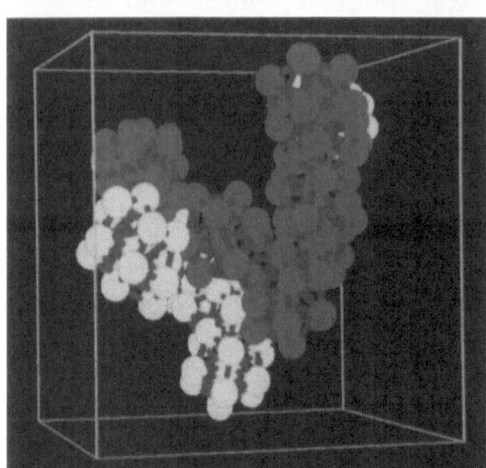

b

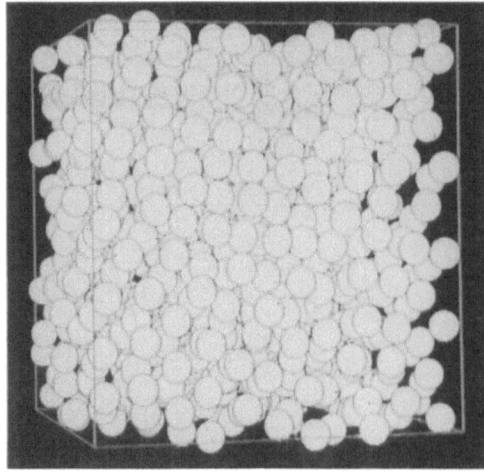

c

Fig. 7.9a–c. The configuration of atoms at some timesteps in the annealing process A. **a** 864 atoms at time step $t = 10,000$; **b** $t = 20,000$, atoms with icosahedral symmetry are *blue* while atoms with cubic symmetry are *white*; *blue clusters* and *white clusters* compete with each other. **c** 864 atoms at $t = 50,000$; the system is still disordered

Fig. 7.10a–f. The configuration of atoms at various timesteps in the annealing process B. **a** 864 atoms at time step $t = 10,000$; **b–e** atoms with icosahedral symmetry are *blue*, while atoms with cubic symmetry are *white*. **b** $t = 29,000$, **c** $t = 39,000$ (*continued*)

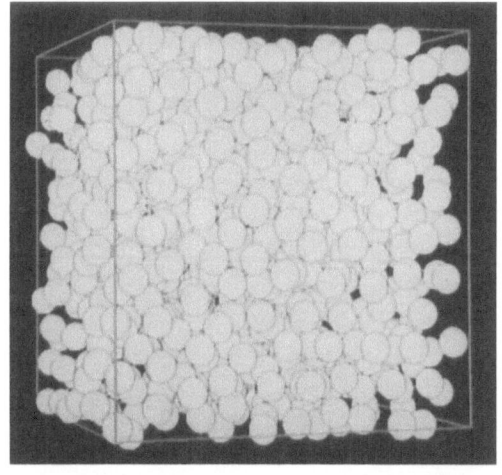

a

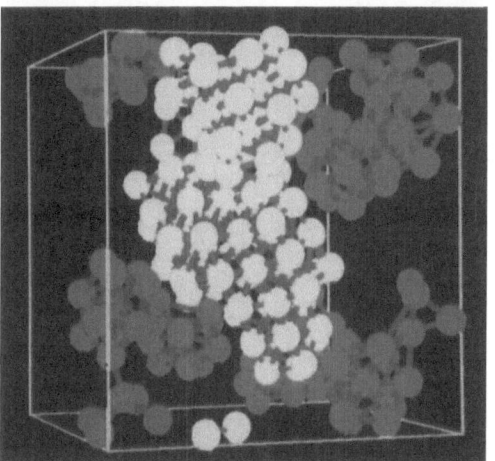

b

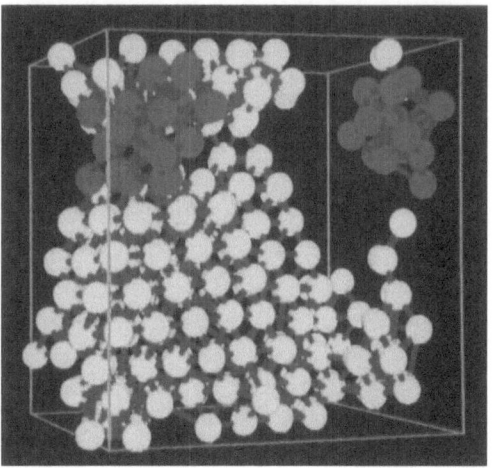

c

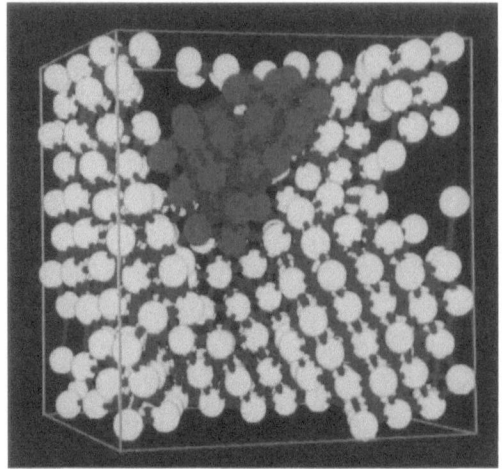

d

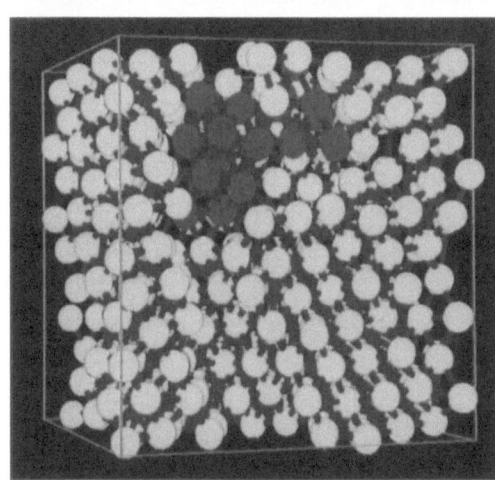

e

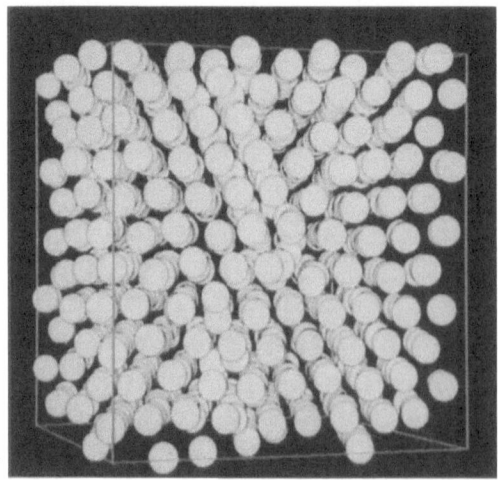

f

Fig. 7.10d–f. d $t = 42,800$, and **e** $t = 46,000$; the white cluster is growing step by step. **f** 864 atoms at $t = 50,000$; the system is almost ordered

Speakers' Papers

1 Scientific Investigations by Supercomputing

Jiro Kondo[1]

Abstract. This paper traces the development of computers and discusses the capability of supercomputers. As examples of the application of a supercomputer, the Global Circulation Model, the consequences of a nuclear war, and climatic change due to the greenhouse effect, each worked out by computer, are discussed. Finally, the transonic flow of a wing body configuration obtained by numerical calculation is presented. Mach number and velocity potential are calculated for every lattice point. Different difference-formulas are applied for subsonic and supersonic flow regions. The location of the shock wave is determined as a curved plane of discontinuity satisfying the shock condition.

1.1 Introduction

Mathematics, like philosophy, is an ancient discipline with great traditions. Having built upon the speculations of outstanding minds over the centuries, it has also been applied extensively to other scientific areas, such as measurement, astronomy, and physics, as well as to commerce and various civic endeavors. Mathematics advanced both in the pursuit of pure theory, as in the case of Niels Henrik Abel (1802–1829) and Karl Weierstrass (1815–1897), and practical applications, as in the case of Isaac Newton (1642–1727) and Paul Adrien Maurice Dirac (1902–1984). There were also many mathematicians, such as Carl Friedrich Gauss (1777–1855), who were active both in pure and applied mathematics.

Apart from these theoretical studies, computations have been deemed important. To this end, John Napier (1550–1617) and Blaise Pascal (1623–1662) developed logarithms and calculating machines, respectively. In 1946, the ENIAC computer, made of vacuum tubes and using the binary algorism, was manufactured. It was quickly followed by a machine devised by John von Neumann (1903–1953), incorporating programming, the so-called "first-generation" computer. Owing to the introduction of semi-conductors and other technological innovations, the computer continued to evolve at an amazing pace, and with increased computing/data pro-

---

[1] President, Science Council of Japan. Professor Emeritus, University of Tokyo.

cessing capability and decreased cost, brought about today's computer age. Now computers are widely used not only by scientists, but also in business and industry.

In the 1990s, the worldwide demand for supercomputers for use in military, pharmaceutical, aerodynamic, and hydromechanic studies and applications in business circles is estimated at over two hundred. In creating a supercomputer, creativity is necessary in addition to semiconductor chips, architectural design, algorithms, and computer language software.

By the late 1980s Japanese manufacturers dominated 90% of the world semiconductor market, and they had caught up with Cray in areas of design and algorithms. The expertise that the United States supercomputer manufacturer accumulated over the past two decades was mastered by Fujitsu, NEC, and Hitachi in a mere 6 years. However, Cray's creativity is still thought to be unsurpassed by their Japanese counterparts.

Having marketed the CDC6600 in 1964 at CDC (Control Data Corporation), Seymour Cray (1925–   ) founded his own supercomputer company in Colorado Springs in 1972. Cray III, their latest model, is capable of 16 billion computations per second. NEC's SX-3, it is said, can perform 22 billion computations per second.

The spread of computers has proven an important stimulus to mathematics through advances in computation. This is reflected in a special section, edited by Dr. P.B. Schneck, on large-scale problems and supercomputing which was published in 1989 [1].

1.2 General Circulation Model

The earth is a big sphere with a diameter of 12,720 km and a surface area of 5.10×10^8 km^2, 70% of which is ocean. The planet is covered with the atmosphere, and 90% of the air mass is found in the troposphere, that is, from the earth's surface to an altitude of about 17 km.

The earth receives thermal rays constantly emitted by the sun. The solar radiation is highest at the equator and decreases gradually towards the north and south poles. The aqueous vapor in the atmosphere is mainly due to the thermal energy from the sun causing sea water to evaporate. Areas of low atmospheric pressure form, which in the northern hemisphere move towards the north. Such atmospheric movements, represented by the Navier-Stokes' equation which takes the compressibility of the air into consideration, are affected by the Coriolis force arising from the earth's rotation. Weather forecasting involves making predictions about atmospheric movements or wind-patterns. The latest models of atmospheric circulation have been developed to such a level of precision that their predictions coincide with observations to a considerable extent. They provide long-range average temperature forecasts for different latitudes. These general circulation models (GCM's) are programmed into supercomputers.

The GCM is still a rough model which uses 500 km grids. It consists of two separate systems. One is a set of equations of motion representing the dynamics of atmospheric circulation, and the other is a set of parameters defining correlations between the atmosphere, the sea, and the land. However, given altitudinal differences of stratospheric density, minute samplings of data by one-kilometer grids on atmospheric density, air pressure, wind patterns, temperature, and moisture would be necessary to make a reliable forecast. This means collecting statistics over approximately 500 million grid points across the earth's surface, each with 20 vertical grid points thereon, that is, a sum-total of 10 billion grid points. Observation of ocean currents would call for more grid points into the sea. Only supercomputers would be capable of processing data and solving equations on such a scale.

One major ecological issue of our time is the rapid rise in the concentration of carbon dioxide in the atmosphere. If its concentration in the air were to reach double the present level of 350 ppm, the planet's atmospheric temperature is predicted to rise by 2–5°C, a phenomenon known as the greenhouse effect. This estimate is provided by the so-called one-dimensional model, that is, the atmosphere on the earth, and is strictly a long-range figure for the entire planet. A more precise three-dimensional model, which takes geographical variability (land and sea) into account, is yet to be developed. At the same time, attempts have been made to utilize a similar model in forecasting weather. It was Lewis Fry Richardson (1881–1953), a British physicist, who first suggested numerical weather forecasts. However, even with the most advanced supercomputers it is still difficult to make accurate forecasts.

In 1986 the International Council of Scientific Unions (ICSU) and the Scientific Committee on Problems of Ecology (SCOPE) produced a two-volume report, entitled *ENUWAR*, on the ecological effects of nuclear war. The report predicted that a military confrontation involving detonation of six billion tons of nuclear warheads would produce 10,000 tons of fallout and that an ensuing nuclear winter would cause acute (fatal) food shortages in the northern hemisphere. The study was based on the computer analysis of the ecological predictions by Carl E. Sagan (1934–), assessing the effects of a nuclear winter on sunshine, climate, precipitation, and crop production. Such an analysis would necessarily require a crop model based on data collected by agricultural scientists in various regions over a period of time. As different regions have different agricultural species with various degrees of susceptibility to climatic factors, precise forecasts are to be made separately for them. Figure 1.1 was arranged after the paper [2] and illustrates the structure of a yield model under the assumptions of a nuclear winter. Using the crop model, the 500-km-grid GCM forecasts regional weather and estimates nuclear effects on food production. However, the current crop model is not reliable enough to provide satisfactory results.

Greenhouse effects upon atmospheric temperature and food production are estimated in much the same way, but there are as many elements of uncertainty in this area of study. Table 1 shows five separate models [3]. Their differences arise from the lack of coincidence on the definitions of parameters, representing inter-actions between the atmosphere, the sea, and the land.

According to S. Manabe of NOAA, there is no model that takes into account the presence of aqueous vapor which can block the sunshine in the form of thick clouds and simultaneously decelerate cooling on the earth's surface.

Also, it is not clear whether the ocean absorbs or decomposes the greenhouse gas. In 1990, ICSU is planning to launch a study called the International Geo-

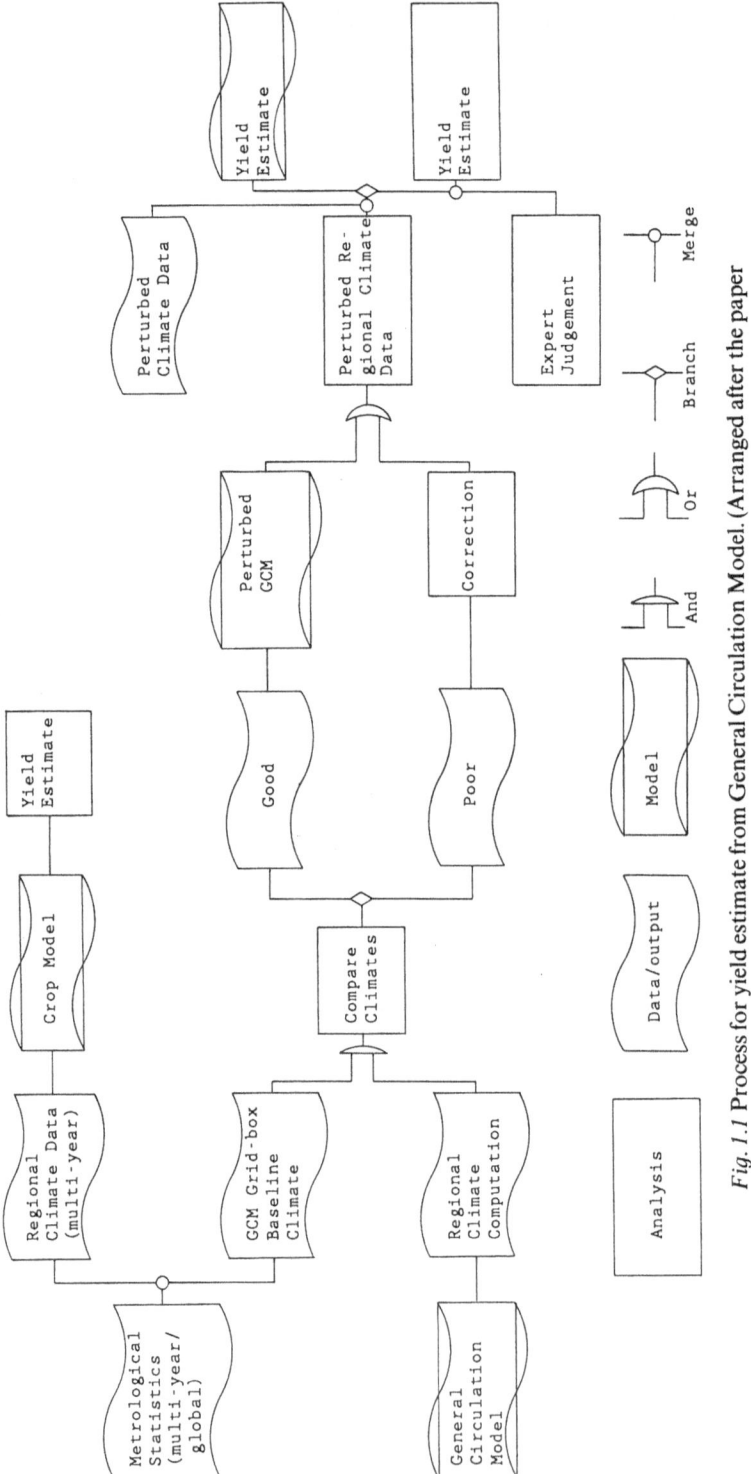

Fig. 1.1 Process for yield estimate from General Circulation Model. (Arranged after the paper of [2])

Table 1.1. Climatic experiments with a 100% increase in CO_2 at equilibrium: cloud distribution forecasting

	GFDL Spectrum R15[1]	GISS Lattice 8 lat × 10 long	NCAR Spectrum R15[1]	UKMO Lattice 5 lat × 7.5 long	MIR Lattice 4 lat × 5 long
Horizontal resolution					
Vertical resolution	9 layers (ground surface 0mb[2])	9 layers (ground surface 10mb)	9 layers (ground surface 0mb)	11 layers (ground surface stratosphere)	5 layers (ground surface 100mb)
Seasonal variation	Not including daily change	Including daily change	Including daily change	Including daily change	Including daily change
Thickness of mixing layer	50 m	Including (<65m)	50 m	60 m	50 m
Heat transfer by sea current	0	Including	0	Including	0
Sea ice model	1 layer no lead[3]	2 layer including lead	1 layer no lead	1 layer no lead	1 layer no lead
Temperature rise on the ground	4.0°C	4.2°C	4.0°C	5.2°C	4.3°C
Increase of precipitation	8.7%	11.0%	7.1%	15.0%	7.4%

lat, latitude; long, longitude; GFDL, NOAA Geophysical Fluid Dynamics Laboratory: Wetherald and Manabe (1986); GISS, NASA Goddard Institute for Space Studies: Hansen et al. (1984); NCAR, National Center for Atmospheric Research: Washington and Meehl (1984); UKMO, United Kingdom Meteorological Office: Wilson and Mitchell (1987); MIR, Meteorological Research Institute; [1] R 15: scalar quantities are expressed approximately by 15 items of a series of spherical functions; [2] mb denotes the unit of the atmospheric pressure, millibar. 1mb = 10^2 Pa = 10^3 dyn/cm^2; [3] lead: a channel of water through a field of ice

graphical Biospheric Program, in which Japan's main focus will be on the interaction of the sea, land, and atmosphere, and to devise an accurate model. Given Japan's location on the western rim of the Pacific, statistical observation of ocean currents would be essential for the development of a reliable model.

1.3 Transonic Flow

Assume there is an acoustic source emitting sound every second. As sound travels through air at sonic speed, that is, approximately 340 meters per second at sea level, the noise produced three seconds ago would have radiated as a spherical wave front with a radius of about 1,000 meters. Similarly, a noise produced two seconds ago would have a spherical wave front with a radius of about 700 meters, or of 340 meters if produced one second ago. However, if the acoustic source is travelling on a straight course, the shapes of wave fronts will vary according to the velocity of the moving source, in general, and in particular as to whether it is faster (supersonic) or slower (subsonic) than the sound velocity. Since the sound source in supersonic motion is invariably outside wave fronts radiating from its sounds, the shape of the wave fronts turns from spherical to conical, forming what is known as the Mach cone. Thus, when a jet plane flies horizontally, an observer standing outside its Mach cone may see the plane but cannot hear its sound. The faster the velocity of the supersonic jet, the smaller the vertical angle of the Mach cone.

As illustrated in Fig. 1.2, supersonic and subsonic wave fronts have distinct characteristics.

It is well known that sound is a pressure wave which alternates an increase and a decrease in air pressure, and travels like a wave. The velocity of the sound wave

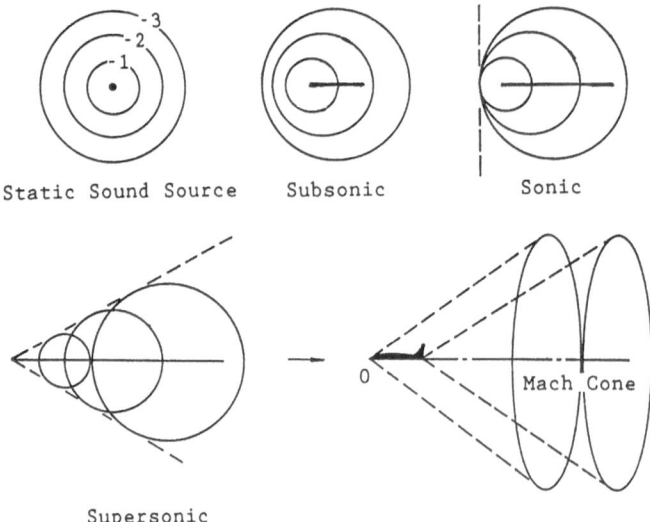

Fig. 1.2. Mach wavefront

is 340 m/s under normal conditions; this is called the sonic speed. When a plane gains velocity, air pressures forming around its body and wings also increase and propagate through air at the sonic speed. As its velocity approaches the transonic zone, the plane is bound to have a myriad of aerodynamic problems collectively identified as the sound barrier.

Figure 1.3 shows values of a wing's drag coefficient C_D at different velocities, assuming that the plane maintains its angle of attack on a straight course. The Mach number is the ratio of the velocity of a moving plane to the velocity of sound. A Mach number smaller than 1 indicates the sound velocity is larger than the plane velocity (subsonic). In the case where the plane velocity is larger than the sound velocity, the Mach number is over 1 (supersonic).

The figure indicates that, as the Mach value approaches 1, the drag coefficient also increases. Thus, in the transonic zone, the control of a plane approaching the velocity of sound would be increasingly difficult, since the lift coefficient decreases and the moment coefficient changes rapidly at the same time.

Due to these aerodynamic problems, scientists and engineers used to believe that breaking the sound barrier was practically impossible. It was the invention of the jet engine, with its greater propulsion, that broke through the barrier.

Shock waves occurring on a wing surface absorb energy and thereby add to the air resistance. Moreover, the high air pressure accompanying shock waves causes air streams to separate from the wing surface and create "shock stall," a phenomenon not dissimilar from stall at low velocity. Shock waves will appear when parts of the flow region around a subsonic jet plane locally surpass Mach 1 and form supersonic regions. Shock waves could appear when the wing as a whole is travelling at subsonic velocity. This is because a supersonic region is produced locally on a convex part of the wing [4].

When a jet plane travels faster than the velocity of sound, parts of the body other than wing surface also begin to suffer shock waves that subtract from its lift and add to air resistance. Moreover, sudden changes in its moment would cause the loss of balance and could sometimes prove fatal [5].

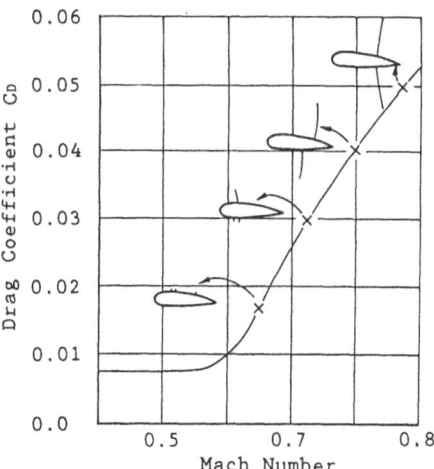

Fig. 1.3. Velocity and drag

1.3.1 The Peaky Wing

Nevertheless, it has recently become possible to design a wing that would delay the formation of shock waves in high-speed flow. Called the *peaky wing*, its profile (Fig. 1.6) is characterized by a fat leading edge, the steep peak in the pressure distribution curve of the upper surface, which is the source of its name. Developed in the United Kingdom, the peaky wing can restore local supersonic airflows on the wing to subsonic levels without forming shock waves, even within the transonic region beginning at about Mach 0.8. Such a wing profile can now be mathematically determined by solving equations describing the properties of high-velocity air streams. Because of their extreme complexity, powerful computers are needed to solve these equations.

However, the performance of the peaky wing depends chiefly on its delicate profile. Even the smallest errors in the manufacturing process and/or the least distortion in the attack angle during transonic flight can trigger the formation of shock waves. Similarly, smooth airflows can be easily destroyed by changes in their Mach value.

The design of a shock-free airfoil profile is still an unconquered frontier. As illustrated in Fig. 1.4, the interference by shock waves to the boundary layer causes the outward separation of the airflow from the convex surface of the airfoil. This phenomenon consists of highly complicated airflow patterns. Accordingly, satisfactory observation of the interactions of airflows necessitates wind tunnel experiments with an airfoil model close to the actual size.

As the boundary layer is extremely thin, precise measurements are essential before the analysis of the shock boundary layer interference can be conducted. Yet it is not.difficult to imagine the enormous cost of constructing a large-scale wind tunnel of high speed.

1.3.2 The Super-Critical Wing

If shock waves were unavoidable in the transonic speed range, it would still be possible to design an airfoil profile that prevented a sudden rise in drag and kept the shock wave drag at an acceptable level. To this end, the National Aeronautical and Space Administration led the research and development of the super-critical wing [6].

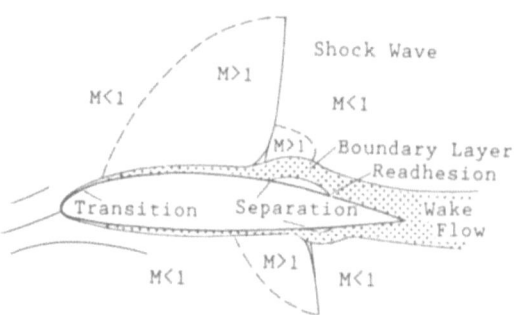

Fig. 1.4. Shockwaves and separation of boundary layer

Shock waves forming at the center of a developed supersonic region are accompanied by severe disruptions in the pressure distribution. It was argued that shock waves could be weakened by somehow containing them near the end of the supersonic region and that pressure distribution patterns could be maintained.

In practice, a flattened upper surface of an airfoil decelerates the development of a supersonic region and affects the pressure distribution below the wing in such a manner that lift is added to the tailing edge.

The performance of a plane is basically determined by the aerodynamic characteristics of its wing profile. Not surprisingly, there is a positive correlation between the velocity and the susceptibility of these characteristics to a distortion in the

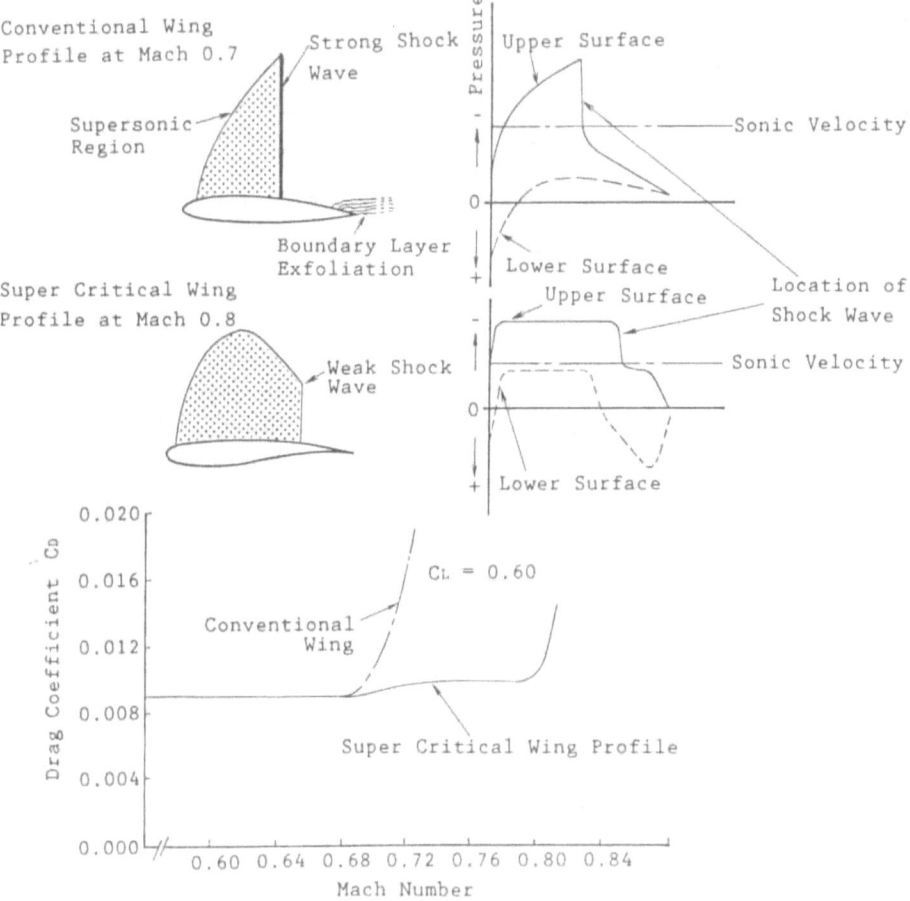

Fig. 1.5. Super-critical wing. The conventional wing suffers shock waves in the most developed part of the supersonic region, whereupon drag increases as the boundary layer separates outward from the surface. The super-critical wing profile, on the other hand, with its flatter upper surface, effectively delays the formation of shock waves. This is confirmed by experimental observation (*top right*) measuring changes in the pressure distribution [7]

profile. In addition, should an airfoil profile be too thin, however satisfactory in experimental aerodynamic characteristics, its design may entail structural deficiencies in strength. Similarly, too complicated a configuration may be practically impossible to manufacture. Thus, the quest for an ideal and practical airfoil profile for high subsonic velocity was an immense challenge for researchers and engineers alike. The super-critical wing developed by NASA, for instance, has a trailing edge thick enough to mount flaps and ailerons.

As is shown in Fig. 1.5, the point at which shock waves occur and the drag coefficient shoots up is called the critical Mach value, which varies with airfoil profiles. Therefore, the development of a wing profile with a high critical Mach value, securing shock-free airflows in the transonic zone, was of major significance in improving optimum aircraft performance.

Modern transport aircraft equipped with powerful jet engines can manage to navigate unfettered by shock waves in transonic flight; however, a large part of the engine power may be consumed by the work done to overcome the drag caused by shock waves. Consequently, the aircraft is not efficient in terms of cost considerations.

Long-range passenger planes, including the DC-10, MD80, L-1011, B747, and European Airbus A320, are all equipped with a wing profile which delays the development of shock waves and prevents a sudden surge in resistance.

1.3.3 Transonic Controversy

When a wing (airfoil profile) is placed in a steady air stream, oving to the convex upper surface, those airflows passing above the wing are faster than those passing below. Therefore, as a wing gradually gains its speed through the air, the airflow first reaches supersonic velocity on the upper region of the wing, thereby developing a supersonic region even though the flow field as a whole is still subsonic.

When shock waves occur within the supersonic region, airflows display extremely complicated patterns as shown in Fig. 1.4 as the boundary layer separates outward. This results in a sudden rise in the drag coefficient known as "shock stall." However, if supersonic air flows can be restored to subsonic velocity, shock stall accompanied by a sudden increase of drag is avoided. Naturally, high-velocity aircraft have much to gain from such a stall-free airfoil profile.

The theoretical evaluation of a given wing profile involves a whole spectrum of technical considerations, mainly because compressibility of the air exhibits a myriad of complex problems in high-velocity air streams. Also, data provided by wind tunnel tests are significantly subject to the aerodynamic interference effects of the tunnel walls. Because of both theoretical and experimental difficulties, studies of the aerodynamic characteristics of an aerofoil at a high speed, in generating supersonic regions on the wing surface, were inadequate.

Yet a great number of specialists found themselves tackling the enigma. The possibility of airflows free of shock waves was first suggested by G.I. Taylor (1886–1948) of Cambridge University in 1928. Theoretical proof for the existence of such supersonic air streams was later provided by a number of aerodynamicists, including S. Tomotika (1903–1964), K. Tamada (1915–), and H.W. Emmons [8, 9].

Nevertheless, for the reasons outlined above, it was impossible to verify the theory in wind tunnel tests. Such prospects seemed quite meagre.

In the meantime, some theoreticians had begun to suspect that smooth supersonic airflows were in fact a rare phenomenon subject to a unique set of variables, easily disrupted by slight changes in the mainstream Mach value and/or distortion in the wing profile. C. Moravetz of New York University mathematically demonstrated in her three essays in 1958 that such airflows can exist only under very special rare conditions and that they disappear with the smallest changes in conditions [10, 11]. Therefore, the problem is not well posed, according to J. Hadamard (1865–1963) [12].

Not surprisingly, Moravetz' conclusive argument discouraged a great majority of aerodynamic theoreticians. But some experimenters continued to seek a wing profile which prevented the formation of shock waves in the transonic zone or contained them by expansion of air due to the convexity of the surface of the aerofoil. They attempted to derive a profile with optimum aerodynamic characteristics.

Those engineers maintained that, since a mathematical model described only a limited aspect of natural phenomena, a mere theoretical proof of the nonexistence of a super-critical aerofoil profile did not automatically imply that such a profile actually did not exist in practice.

In 1960, H.H. Pearcey of the Royal Institute of Physics demonstrated the possibility of an ideal profile, which prevented the formation of shock waves in the transonic range, by producing the so-called peaky wing [13]. Pearcey's profile once again revived scientific interest in the transonic problem. M.J. Lighthill (1924–) of Manchester University soon succeeded in providing the mathematical definitions of the characteristics of the peaky profile (Fig. 1.7). Since the 1960s, NASA has been developing a wing profile that would reduce the hazards of shock waves and the sudden increase of drag [7]. Its major characteristic is its flat upper surface, which allows the formation of shock waves near the tailing edge (Fig. 1.4, 1.5). The three

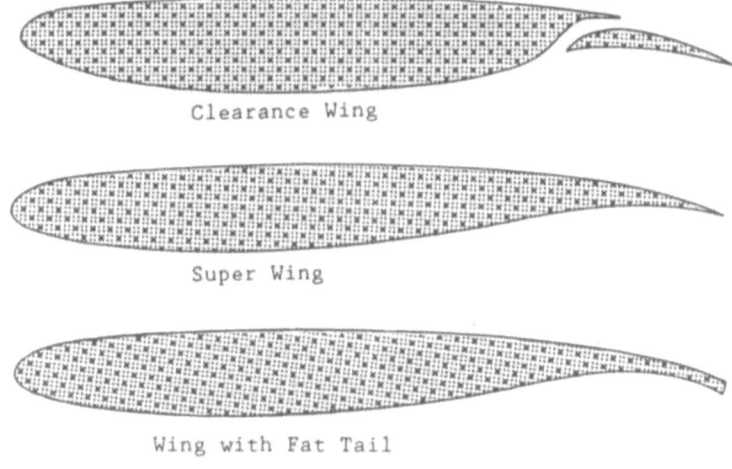

Clearance Wing

Super Wing

Wing with Fat Tail

Fig. 1.6. Super-critical wings. (From [7])

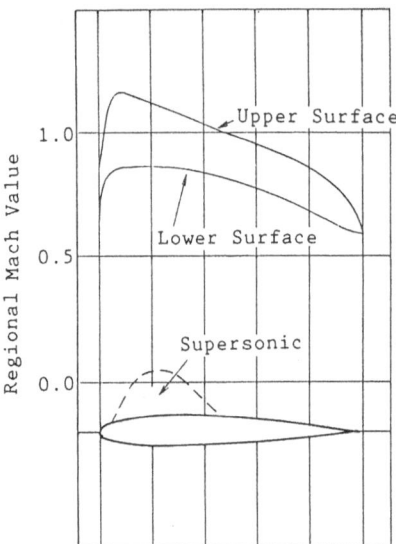

Fig. 1.7. Peaky wing pressure distribution

profile sections (Fig. 1.6) conform to this principle. The thick tailing edge is struc-turally advantageous in mounting flaps and ailerons.

Japan's Aeronautics and Space Research Instutite is now able to design with computers advanced profiles that satisfy specific requirements [14]. It has also been verified that that shock waves could occur even to these super-critical profiles in unfavorable circumstances, but their hazardous effects, including shock stall, remain minimal.

At the same time, it has become possible to build wind tunnels large enough to neutralize the interference of the walls on airstreams therein. They are called transonic wind tunnels.

1.3.4 Numerical Calculation of Subsonic Flows with Shock Waves

The fundamental equation of velocity potential φ of a compressible fluid is

$$(u^2 - a^2)\frac{\partial^2 \varphi}{\partial x^2} + (v^2 - a^2)\frac{\partial^2 \varphi}{\partial y^2} + (w^2 - a^2)\frac{\partial^2 \varphi}{\partial z^2}$$

$$+ 2uv\frac{\partial^2 \varphi}{\partial x \partial y} + 2vw\frac{\partial^2 \varphi}{\partial y \partial z} + 2wu\frac{\partial^2 \varphi}{\partial z \partial x} = 0 \tag{1}$$

where

$$\frac{\partial \varphi}{\partial z} = u, \frac{\partial \varphi}{\partial y} = v, \text{ and } \frac{\partial \varphi}{\partial z} = w \tag{2}$$

represent the velocity components in x, y, and z directions respectively and a denotes the sound velocity [15].

We put

$$D = \begin{vmatrix} u^2 - a^2 & uv & uw \\ vu & u^2 - a^2 & vw \\ wu & wv & w^2 - a^2 \end{vmatrix} = a^4(q^2 - a^2) \tag{3}$$

where q is the velocity of flow and we have

$$q^2 = u^2 + v^2 + w^2 \tag{4}$$

The type of the partial differential equation (1) is hyperbolic, parabolic, and elliptic when $D > 0$, $D = 0$ and $D < 0$, respectively, i.e., supersonic, transonic, and subsonic, by Eq. 3.

For an adiabatic flow

$$a^2 = a_0^2 - \frac{1}{2}(\gamma - 1)q^2 \tag{5}$$

holds, where a_0 denotes the sound velocity at stagnation conditions, and γ means the ratio of the specific heats. From Eq. 5, we have

$$q^2/a_0^2 = M^2\left(1 + \frac{1}{2}(\gamma - 1)M^2\right) - 1 \tag{6}$$

where M stands the local Mach number.

By means of this relation (Eq. 6), Eq. 1 yields

$$\frac{\partial^2 \varphi}{\partial x^2} + \frac{\partial^2 \varphi}{\partial y^2} + \frac{\partial^2 \varphi}{\partial z^2} = \frac{1}{2 + (\gamma - 1)M^2}\left(\frac{\partial M^2}{\partial x}\frac{\partial \varphi}{\partial x} + \frac{\partial M^2}{\partial y}\frac{\partial \varphi}{\partial y} + \frac{\partial M^2}{\partial z}\frac{\partial \varphi}{\partial z}\right) \tag{7}$$

and relation (6) is

$$\left(\frac{\partial \varphi}{\partial x}\right)^2 + \left(\frac{\partial \varphi}{\partial y}\right)^2 + \left(\frac{\partial \varphi}{\partial z}\right)^2 = a_0^2 M^2\left(1 + \frac{1}{2}(\gamma - 1)M^2\right)^{-1} \tag{8}$$

Eqs. 7 and 8 furnish the fundamental system for the numerical analysis of φ and M.

The shock relation is

$$M_2^2 \sin^2(\sigma - \theta) = \frac{M_1^2 \sin^2 \sigma + \dfrac{2}{\gamma - 1}}{\dfrac{2\gamma}{\gamma - 1}M_1^2 \sin^2 \sigma + 1} \tag{9}$$

where σ is the shock angle or the angle between the shock and the direction of the upper flow, and θ is the flow deflection angle or the angle between the down flow and the upper flow of the shock wave. M_1 means the Mach number of the upper stream and M_2 is the Mach number of the down stream.

When a solid body is placed in a uniform flow of u_∞, the boundary conditions are

$$\frac{\partial \varphi}{\partial x} = u_\infty, \frac{\partial \varphi}{\partial y} = 0, \text{ and } \frac{\partial \varphi}{\partial z} = 0 \text{ at infinity} \tag{10}$$

and

$$\frac{\partial \varphi}{\partial n} = 0 \text{ on the body} \tag{11}$$

where n means the normal vector to the surface of the body.

Taking the uniform velocity u_∞ as the unit of air velocity, we assume

$$\varphi = C_0, \frac{\partial \varphi}{\partial x} = 1, \frac{\partial \varphi}{\partial y} = 0, \text{ and } \frac{\partial \varphi}{\partial z} = 0 \tag{12}$$

at a sufficiently long distance from the body, where C_0 denotes a certain constant.

The fundamental system of equations for φ and M can be solved numerically. In the subsonic region the central difference formulae are utilized, while the one-sided difference formulae are used in the supersonic region, since only disturbances within a Mach cone are influential on the point in the down stream, as is shown in Fig. 1.2. E.M. Murman and J.D. Cole obtained a plane steady transonic flows by using this method [12].

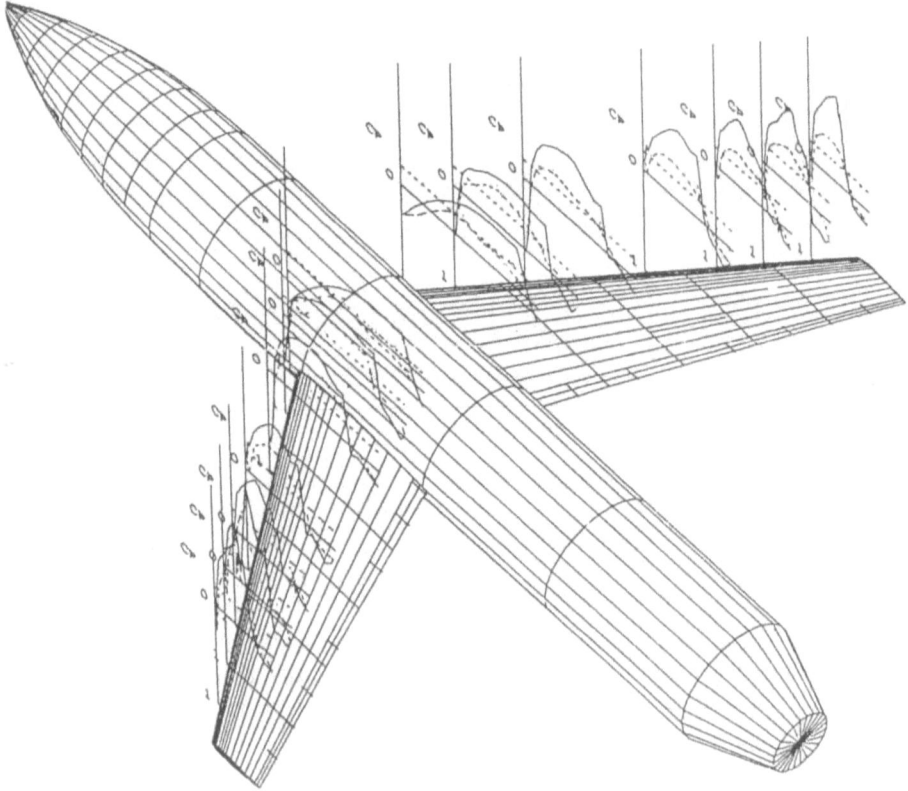

Fig. 1.8. C_p distribution on the wing of the RAE model. $M_\infty = 0.9$; $\alpha = 1°$; C_p, pressure coefficient

In the supersonic region, the flow deflection angle θ and the local Mach number M are constantly calculated. If Eq. 9 holds by assuming the appropriate value of σ, then we conclude that the shock wave passes the stream line at the angle σ. The location and the shape of shock wave are determined in this way. The location of the shock wave might be determined by a variational expression equivalent to Eq. 1. This problem has been considered by the present author [16, 17]. The numerical computations are complicated; however, a supercomputer can work out the flow field around a body [18–21].

M. Nakamura at the National Aerospace Laboratory determined a three-dimensional compressible mixed flow within a shock wave around a wing body configuration (the RAE model). Figure 1.8 is an example of his results [22, 23]. The

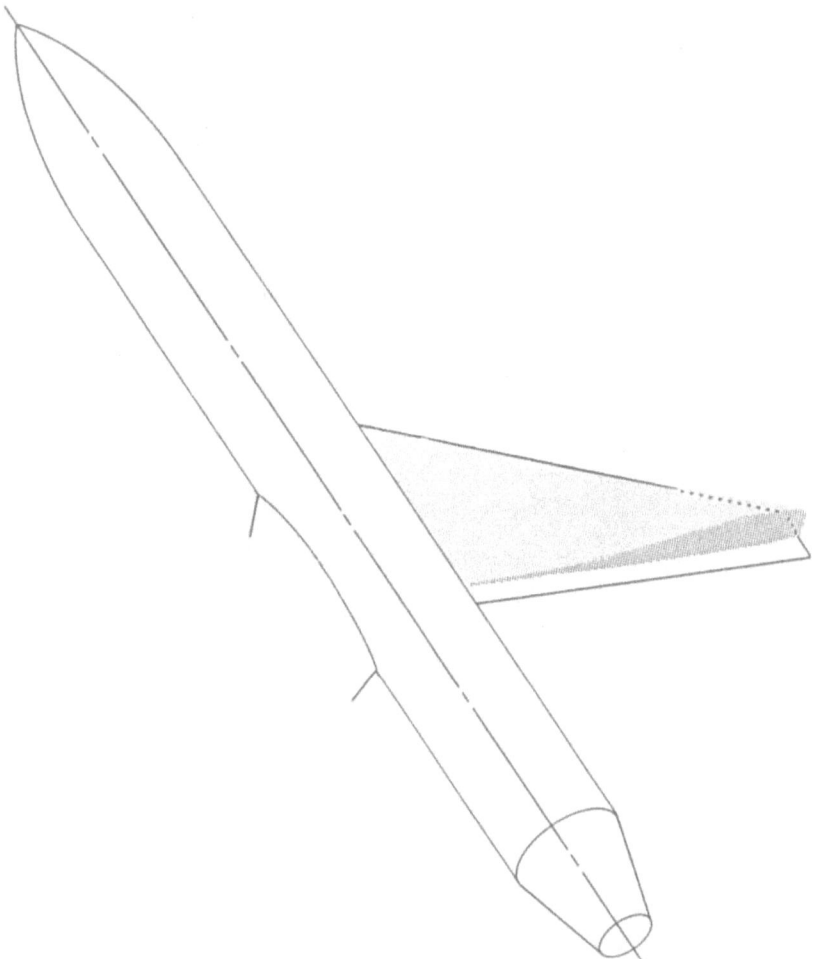

Fig. 1.9. The shock wave and supersonic region on the right wing of the RAE model. $M_\infty = 0.9, \alpha = 1°$

transonic flow around RAE wing 'A' in combination with an axi-symmetric body is carried out [24]. The coincidence with the experiment is satisfactory. The shock wave and the supersonic region on the right wing are sketched in Fig. 1.9.

1.4 Conclusions

Two topics, the prediction of global warming by the greenhouse effect and the transonic flow around an obstacle, are discussed as examples of the application of supercomputers.

In the case of the global modelling, the performance of existing supercomputers is not adequate to carry out the precise prediction of the climate on the earth since the earth is very large. Also, the basic understanding of the interactions among oceans, atmosphere, and continent is not sufficient to establish a satisfactory mathematical model.

In the case of the transonic flow, numerical computations by the difference method can provide satisfactory results. However, the physical characteristics of subsonic or supersonic flows should be considered in order to choose the appropriate difference formulae to converge the numerical calculation.

Supercomputers can solve the problem when the mathematical model is established; however, there is no need to emphasize that the basic understanding of the phenomena is essential. It has been recognized that a supercomputer is a strong tool for scientific investigation [25]. For supercomputing, however, the development of software is most important, in addition to the improvement of hardware. The introduction of new problems by creative scientists will be most useful for the development of hardware.

References

1. Schneck PB (ed) (1989) Special section on large-scale problems and supercomputing. IEEE Proceedings 77 No. 7. Contains the following papers: Lax PD. Science and Computing; Decker JF, Nelson DB, Austin DM. Large-scale problems and supercomputing in the Department of Energy; Peterson VL, Kim J, Holst YL, Deiwert GS, Cooper DM, Watson AB, Bailey FR. Supercomputer requirements for selected disciplines important to aerospace; Lipton RJ, Matt TG, Welsh JD. Computational approaches to discovering semantics in molecular biology; Halem M. Scientific computing challenges arising from space-borne observations
2. Ackerman TP, Cropper WP Jr. (1988) Scaling global climate projections to local biological assessment. Environment 30 (5): 31–34
3. Japan Meteorological Agency (1989) Report on recent climatic change in the world
4. Busemann A, Guderley G (1947) The problem of drag at high subsonic speeds. MOS Reports and Transactions 184
5. Hawker-Siddley (1964) Trident: Aerodynamic design and flying controls. Aircraft Eng 36: 172–175
6. Harris CD, Bartlett DW (1979) Pressure distributions measured on an NASA supercritical-wing research airplane model. AGARD-AR-138

7. Whitcomb RT (1974) Review of NASA supercritical airfoils. ICAS Paper No. 74-10
8. Tomotika S, Tamada K (1951) Studies on two-dimensional transonic flows of compressible fluid. III. Q Appl Math 9: 129–147
9. Emmons HW (1944) The numerical solution of compressible fluid flow problems. NASA TN-932
10. Kuo YH (1951) On the stability of two-dimensional smooth transonic flows. Aero Sci 18: 1–6
11. Morawetz CS (1956–1958) On the non-existence of continuous transonic flows past profiles I, II, III. Commun Pure Appl Math 9: 45–68 (1956); 10, 107–131 (1957); 11: 129–144 (1958)
12. Murman EM, Cole JD (1971) Calculation of plane steady transonic flows. AIAA J 9: 114–121
13. Pearcey HH (1962) The aerodynamic design of section shapes for swept back wings. Adv Aeronautical Sci 3: 277–322
14. Nakamura M (1983) Numerical design of a shockless transonic quasi-aircraft. J Phys Soc Jap 52 (8)
15. Liepman HW, Roshko A (1960) Elements of gas dynamics. Wiley, New York
16. Kondo J (1955) The fundamental equation of transonic flow. Proc 5th Japan Natl Congr Appl Mech, pp 329–332
17. Kondo J (1956) Studies on the low-supersonic flow with a detached shock wave. Proc 6th Japan Natl Congr Appl Mech, pp 253–258
18. Boppe CW (1978) Computational transonic flow about realistic aircraft configurations. AIAA Paper 78-104
19. Carlson LA (1975) Transonic airfoil flow field analysis using Cartesian coordinates. NASA CR-2577
20. Erickson LL, Madson MD, Woo AC (1986) Application of the TRANAIR full-potential code of complete configurations. ICAS-86-1.3.5
21. Nävert UG, Sedin YC (1986) Transonic computations about complex configurations using coupled inner and outer flow equations. ICAS-86-1.3.4
22. Nakamura M (1988) A numerical method for solving transonic flow past aircraft in Cartesian coordinates. National Aerospace Laboratory, TR-1008
23. Nakamura M (1989) A numerical method for solving transonic flow past aircraft in Cartesian coordinates. J Jap Soc Fluid Dynamics 8: 56–70
24. Treadgolf DA, Jones AF, Wilson KH (1979) Pressure distribution measured in the RAE 8ft × 6ft transonic wind tunnel on RAE wing 'A' in combination with an axi-symmetric body at Mach numbers of 0.4, 0.8 and 0.9, AGARD-AR-138
25. Schmitt V, Charpin F (1979) Pressure distributions on the ONERA-M6-WING at transonic Mach numbers. AGARD-AR-138

2 Recent Development of Finite Element Methods in the High-Speed Computing Environment

Noboru Kikuchi[1], Toshikazu Torigaki[1], Katsuyuki Suzuki[1], and Jose Miranda Guedes[1]

Abstract. We shall review how finite element methods have been developed and what subjects researchers in the United States are studying at present in the high-speed computing environment.

2.1 Introduction

The development of computer hardware in the 1980s, especially, introduction of PC (Personal Computers), EWS (Engineering WorkStations), and supercomputers together with LAN (Local Area Networks), enforces definite change of the practice of computational mechanics for design analysis of structures and mechanisms in various engineering fields. More specifically, if the finite element method that is a major method in computational mechanics introduced in the late 1950s, is concerned, its theory and its computer implementation are strictly based on the general purpose computer with a scalar processor in the 1960s and 1970s. Its development has been very parallel to the development of computers. For example, the first systematic computer program of the finite element method was written by Ed. Wilson in 1962 for IBM704 and 7090. There a structure can be modeled by a set of discrete 550, finite elements in which the displacement components are assumed to be linear, and could solve 340 linear equations in the 32K core memory using the SOR method with his special modification. After this publication of a FORTRAN program, further development of the theory of the finite element method and new computing systems enabled us to develop the concept of general purpose FORTRAN programs to analyze structural mechanics and dynamics problems. More specifically, CDC6600/7600 and IBM360 systems were indispensable to raise the project to develop the general purpose standard structural analysis code NASTRAN in NASA in the late 1960s. Based on this project, several commercially available general purpose finite element codes were developed in the 1970s. The introduction of NASTRAN and other commercially available finite element codes

---

[1] Computational Mechanics Laboratory, College of Engineering, The University of Michigan, Ann Arbor, Michigan 49109, USA

made a significant jump of analysis capability of structures and mechanisms both in government organizations and private industries. Another development of the finite element method was derived in the 70s based on the IBM370 system or equivalent to solve various nonlinear problems. The MARC program was such an example. In this sense, most of general purpose finite element analysis programs are based on the scalar processing computer with a large volume of virtual memory. However, after CRAY 1 was introduced in the beginning of 1980s, the concept of the general purpose code became gradually an outdated idea. Indeed, DYNA2D and 3D were developed by John Hallquist at the Lawrence Livermore Laboratory by fully utilizing the vector processor in CRAY 1 to analyze impact problems of structures, and made it possible to bring a new horizon together with a new concept to computational mechanics. They were specialized just for impact problems and did not contain a large library of finite elements and various solution algorithms. That is, they were not general purpose, but were specialized to a very narrow range problem of structural dynamics to optimize the speed of computation. In order to maximize the ability of the vector processing, they had to give up the concept of "general purpose." Without CRAY, DYNA2D and 3D might not have been developed; similarly, without IBM's large scale general purpose mainframe computing systems, general purpose finite element codes such as NASTRAN might not have been developed in the 1970s.

Another significant computer hardware development in the 1980s was the introduction of PCs as well as EWS which effectively merge stand-alone computing capability with very sophisticated interactive graphics, and which are extremely user-oriented. The flexible and easy user interface of PCs and EWS extended the dimensions of the computer both for specialists and nonspecialists. The computer became truly a desktop calculator as well as an intelligent typewriter. It is even more now. As Argyris, who was a pioneer of the finite element method in the 1950s, dreamed in the late 60s, computers are changing our thinking habits. They have a far wider role than a desktop fast calculator and an intelligent typewriter. It should be considered as "an abstract symbol manipulator which leads to an even more valuable notion: artificial intelligence [1]." In 1966 Argyris proudly announced to the community of applied mechanics that he was developing the first general purpose finite element code, ASKA, in Europe because of the installation of UNIVAC 1107 with 64K core memory, 1.5 Mwords drum storage, 11 Mwords mass storage, 2 channels of 120 KC magnetic tape, and seven channels of card, papertape, printer, data collection, and data transmission peripheral equipment. At present a PC which has 2 M random-access memory (RAM) and a 40 M hard disk has become rather standard, and some now have 32 bit processors. Furthermore, because of the invention of the networking of computers, a PC can have access to any other large-scale computer without any difficulty. The communication capability between PCs and the so-called mainframe computer is so user-oriented that data computed in other computers can be easily transferred to a PC at office or at home, and can be postprocessed in a PC to make a report or graphical representation. As Smarr [2] noted, "The user interface for such computers [PCs] is now much more advanced than it is for supercomputers. Market forces are likely to make this software gap grow with time. Therefore, a rational strategy is to integrate the supercomputer into the personal computer software so that the user has the speed advantage of the supercomputer and the ease of use of the PC." This statement indicates that Argyris' 1970 dream [3] of a distributed computer network system and an attache case size computer comparable to CDC7600 in *fifty years' time*, capable of true computer-aided design, has already been realized. Extending his dream, we can choose a "supercomputer" as a host computer, if we wish to do so, from our front-end PCs or EWS which are far more capable than CDC7600 in almost every sense, together with sophisticated but very inexpensive interface software through a network system.

This new situation based on the network which can effectively link various heterogeneous computing facilities gives us a formidable challenge to develop equally capable and equally flexible software for this computer hardware environment. Software in the future, maybe even at this moment, is ideally executable in every computer from PCs, EWS, superminicomputers, mainframes, to supercomputers, and users can choose an appropriate computer for a particular job assigned through a network using a front-end machine which is chosen by a user from a pool of a variety of different PCs or EWS. To this end, a common or at least communicative operating system is required. Such a system is UNIX, which is becoming a major dominant operating system which is widely accepted among scientists and engineers even at present. This indicates that even from now we must quickly act to develop scientific and engineering computer software executable in any computer and which can exploit the advantages of each computer by assuming such an operating system. Most computer software developed in the 1970s must be extensively modified or must be redeveloped in order to utilize the special features of each level of computers, since software was developed based on the concept of the general purpose large-scale computer with a scalar processor and a large amount of virtual memory, and since software was not designed for users who are not exactly experts on a particular area of science or engineering. Nowadays, vector and parallel processing are not for computer science specialists but for "ordinary" engineers who have education in the graduate school. Such new types of computers are widely available even for undergraduate students who are interested in using vector/parallel machines. For example, both undergraduate and graduate students in the College of Engineering in the University of Michigan have access to an IBM3090/600E, ALLIANT FX-8, ARDENT TITAN, STELLAR GS1000, and APOLLO DN10000 through more than 1,000 EWS and over 750 PCs in the CAEN (Computer-Aided Engineering Network [4]) environment which are fully integrated into other various levels of network. It is linked to the University Computing Center's UMnet (which is a part of the State of Michigan's regional Merit Computer Network) and gateways to the Internet (including ARPANET. NSFNET, and CICNet) which extend this connectivity across the country and around the world. Many graduate students and faculty are also using a CRAY 2 and XMP through the Internet; these are located in, for example, NASA Ames, University of California at San Diego, and others. The challenge we face now is to provide concrete ideas to the question of what kind of new education we can provide, fully utilizing these advanced computing facilities, as well as what type of new scientific engineering research areas should be explored, while the accumulated software of the past is integrated into this new environment after appropriate modification and redevelopment.

Naturally, it is impossible to answer all of the issues we face now. Thus, we shall restrict our attention to a specific area of engineering that one of the authors is involved in as his major research area, namely, computational mechanics based on finite element methods. We shall review the present education of finite element methods both in undergraduate and graduate schools as well as the current research into finite element methods, in order to indicate the direction in which we are aiming in this new environment that allows us to use all kinds of computer, especially vector/parallel high-speed computing machines. It is also noted that it is impossible to review everyone's work even in this rather narrow area of engineering. Thus, the following description should have a very strong personal bias and narrow scope.

2.2 Teaching of Finite Element Methods

Because of introduction of vector/parallel computers and EWS, and because of the popularity of integrated software on linear algebra and symbolic and algebraic manipulation software, we now face a very rapid change of contents and style of teaching of courses covering finite element methods, especially in graduate school. Until 1985, there was a very solid understanding of how we should teach this subject. Everybody expected that a general purpose finite element analysis code such as MSC-NASTRAN was executed in the mainframe computer from a terminal, after preparing necessary input data using a pre/post processor, again in the mainframe computer. In this setting, a teaching method was rather simple. In undergraduate courses, we emphasized how to use a general purpose finite element analysis code, i.e., we taught how to make appropriate input data, how to read output, how to post-process the computed result, how to perform design analysis, etc. Once a particular code was chosen, any expert on that program could teach an under-graduate finite element methods course, since it was more or less regarded as a tool to solve design problems. Graduate courses, on the other hand, emphasized the basic theory behind the general purpose code. We had to cover not only shape functions, stiffness matrices, assembling, and support/loading conditions, but also solution methods of a system of linear equations and a generalized eigenvalue problem, since most of the general purpose finite element analysis programs utilized very specially developed solvers just for finite element methods in order to maximize the capability of computers which had, for example, only 128K core memory but a large virtual memory. Furthermore, we had only scalar processing computers. It was not necessary to think much of DO loop structures for vector processors, or of the organization of a program to maximize the utilization of parallel processors. Thus, once we had decided a standard textbook of finite element methods and a targeted general purpose finite element analysis code, a teaching method could be defined very easily. Moreover, it was possible to provide a very standard teaching contents.

However, after 1985, especially after EWS became inexpensive, despite their remarkable capability both for computing and graphic display, courses of finite element methods had to be integrated with computer-aided design (CAD) courses which provided the concepts of geometric modeling and automatic mesh generation for finite element/difference methods. Many such CAD systems are developed for EWS rather than mainframe computers with graphic terminals; that is, they are executable in EWS without using the higher capability of much more expensive and powerful computers unless very special features are required for three-dimensional graphics and animation. For example, SUPERTAB in the I-DEAS CAE system and PATRAN are becoming more and more popular even in university milieu, as are various pre/post processings accompanying general purpose finite element codes. This has resulted in a significant change in the attitudes of students and faculty toward computers. The mainframes sitting in the computer center are becoming less familiar, while EWS or easily accessible (super)minicomputers are more in daily use even for computing. So many students started complaining about the inconvenience of file transfer from EWS to the mainframe where, for example, MSC-NASTRAN is executed. It was natural to demand that if the size of analysis problems is moderately small, finite element analysis should be performed in EWS where all the pre/post processing work takes place. This trend is further accelerated by the popularity of PCs. More and more, students and faculty prefer to solve their assignments in their "personal" computers rather than using a mainframe some-where else, because the PCs have a user-oriented environment with a very sophisticated human interface capability. It is certain that psychology is not the only factor in the new trend. In general, mainframe computers assume the concept of not only time-sharing but also cost-sharing because of their expensive installation cost. This means that despite their fantastic capability, mainframe computers are more expensive to use than EWS, in which one night's continuous execution of a job is reliable and inexpensive. *In fact, one EWS are purchased, their computing cost is, roughly speaking, zero. This feature is very attractive, even for researchers who need vast amount of computing.* In this sense, computers are not very special any more; they are similar to TV/VCR sets. For special high-quality business purposes, we may need sophisticated ones, say STELLAR, TITAN, ALLIANT, VAX, IBM, CRAY, and others, while for daily use, IBM PC2, MAC II, SUN, APOLLO, DEC, HP, and other PCs and EWS are more than sufficient. The software should be fine for all of them in the form of VCR tapes if the operating system is "common."

2.3 Finite Element Methods in a Classroom

Because of a certain mutuality of software development in numerical methods, many FORTRAN libraries such as LINPACK, EISPACK, IMSL, NAS, and others, have been available for a long time for various computers. These have been comple-mented by the rapid development of symbolic and algebraic manipulation software such as MACSYMA, REDUCE, SMP, MATHEMATICA and others. Because of this new software environment, restricting our education to finite element methods using a particular general purpose code does not have much merit. In order to modify or redevelop existing finite element software for future use, it is much better to utilize the available state-of-the-art software which is a common asset for every-body. In this regard, we have to modify the software, integrating finite element methods from different academic disciplines, say numerical analysis, computational linear algebra, and others. In other words, emphasis on special aspects of finite element methods may not be appropriate at present. They should be regarded as generalized tools to solve initial boundary value problems instead of design analysis tools for structural engineers, at least in the graduate school. Programs for finite element methods should consist of mixtures of specialized programs and some standard FORTRAN or C libraries for numerical methods. It is now clear that we face a very different situation from the one before 1985. Textbooks for finite element methods written in the 70s are no longer appropriate, if such integration with computational mathematics is seriously sought. Drastic revision of such textbooks is required, i.e., we have to seek very different teaching of finite element methods, at least in the graduate school, in order to educate engineers so that they can modify existing software and develop new software related to finite element methods.

We shall here briefly introduce a trial made in the University of Michigan in a first year graduate course on finite element methods. As mentioned earlier, we had to spend much time in teaching methods for solving a system of linear equations and a generalized eigenvalue problem using approaches specially developed within the community of researchers on finite element methods. Thus, we could not spend much time in teaching the essence of finite element methods, such as the characteristics of certain finite elements, the methodology for forming element stiffness matrices, the effect of the lumped mass matrix, the best sampling points of fluxes and stresses, and others.

If computational linear algebra software is assumed to be integrated in the course, it becomes possible to discuss details of characteristics of finite elements without much extra effort. For example, suppose that MATLAB [5] software is available for every student on PCs and EWS. MATLAB is an interactive program to provide easy access to matrix software developed by the LINPACK and EISPACK projects, with some graphic capability as well as control flow statements like those found in most computer languages. For example, FOR loops, WHILE loops, IF, and BREAK statements can be used to form a program within MATLAB.

For example, let a 3-dimensional 8-node hexahedron element be considered for stress analysis of a linearly elastic solid in which a displacement component is approximated by a tri-linear polynomial in the parametric coordinates $(\xi, \eta, \zeta) \in$ $]-1, 1[x]-1, 1[x]-1, 1[$. One of important issues even in research is to determine the best integration rule to form the element stiffness matrix $[K^e]$ defined by

$$[K^e]\{d^e\} = \frac{\partial}{\partial\{d^e\}} \int_{\Omega_e} \{\varepsilon\}^T [D] \{\varepsilon\} \, d\Omega$$

where $\{d^e\}$ is the number of degrees of freedom in an element Ω_e, $\{\varepsilon\}$ represents the linearized strains, and $[D]$ is the matrix form of elasticity constants. Using the first derivatives of the shape functions $\{N(\xi, \eta, \zeta)\}$ in the physical coordinate system (x, y, z), the strains $\{\varepsilon\}$ are given by

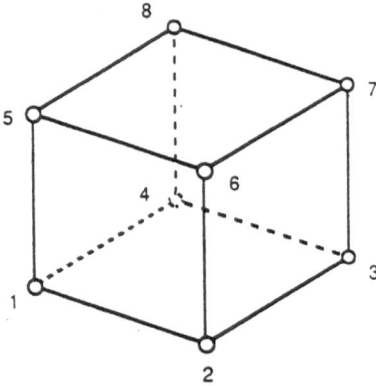

Fig. 2.1. 8 Node hexagonal element

$$\{\varepsilon\} = [B]\{d^e\}$$

where

$$[B] = \begin{bmatrix} \dfrac{\partial N_\alpha}{\partial x} & 0 & 0 \\[2mm] 0 & \dfrac{\partial N_\alpha}{\partial y} & 0 \\[2mm] 0 & 0 & \dfrac{\partial N_\alpha}{\partial z} \\[2mm] 0 & \dfrac{\partial N_\alpha}{\partial z} & \dfrac{\partial N_\alpha}{\partial y} \\[2mm] \dfrac{\partial N_\alpha}{\partial z} & 0 & \dfrac{\partial N_\alpha}{\partial x} \\[2mm] \dfrac{\partial N_\alpha}{\partial y} & \dfrac{\partial N_\alpha}{\partial x} & 0 \end{bmatrix}_\alpha \;, \alpha = 1, 2, \ldots, 8$$

Using the coordinate transformation

$$x = \sum_{\alpha=1}^{8} x_\alpha N_\alpha(\xi, \eta, \zeta), \quad y = \sum_{\alpha=1}^{8} y_\alpha N_\alpha(\xi, \eta, \zeta) \quad and \quad z = \sum_{\alpha=1}^{8} z_\alpha N_\alpha(\xi, \eta, \zeta)$$

where $\{(x_\alpha, y_\alpha, z_\alpha)\}$ are the physical coordinates of nodal points of element Ω_e, the $[B]$ matrix can be computed in terms of the parametric coordinates and the physical coordinates of nodal points, and then the element stiffness matrix $[K^e]$ is computed by applying an appropriate numerical integration method. Depending on the numerical integration method applied, the stiffness matrix $[K^e]$ becomes too stiff to certain deformation patterns. This characteristic can be examined by checking the eigenvalues and eigenvectors of the stiffness matrix $[K^e]$. Thus, after forming

$[K^e]$, its standard eigenvalue problem must be solved. A graphical representation of the eigenvectors should be also required, to identify fundamental deformation modes, since the numeric output of the 24 eigenvectors cannot provide their physical meaning easily. To do this, the following MATLAB program was developed.

```
% HEXA8: A MATLAB Program: 89Fall
%
% Element Stiffness Matrix (Linear Elasticity)
% in the Local Coordinate System
% using Selective Reduced Integration Method
%
% ————————————————————————————————————————
%
% Volumetric Strains {εᵥ} – 1 Point Gaussian Quadrature
% Normal Strains {εₙ}     – 2x2x2 Gaussian Quadrature Rule
% Shear Strains {εₛ}      – 2 point Gaussian along the
%                             Perpendicular Axis
% ————————————————————————————————————————
%
% Physical (Local) Coordinates of a HEXA8 element
hx = 1;hy = 1;hz = 1;                           Define the size of a HEXA
theta1 = 0*3.141592654/180;theta2 = 0*3.141592654/180;
c1 = cos(theta1);s1 = sin(theta1);
c2 = cos(theta2);s2 = sin(theta2);
xe = [ − hx,hx,hx, − hx, − hx,hx,hx, − hx];      Define the xe vector
ye = [ − hy, − hy,hy,hy, − hy, − hy,hy,hy];      Define the ye vector
ze = [ − hz, − hz, − hz, − hz,hz,hz,hz,hz];      Define the ze vector
for i = 1:8
    xei = xe(i);yei = ye(i);zei = ze(i);         Rotate xe, ye, and ze
    xe(i) = (xei*c1-yei*s1)*c2-zei*s2;
    ye(i) = xei*s1 + yei*c1;
    ze(i) = (xei*c1-yei*s1)*s2 + zei*c2;
end
% Elasticity Constants: D Matrix
E = 1;v = 0.3;
D = zeros(6);                                    Zero clear of the matrix
D(1,1) = E*(1 − v)/((1 − 2*v)(H)(1 + v));
D = zeros(6);                                    Zero clear of the D matrix
D(1,1) = E*(1 − v)/((1 − 2*v)*(1 + v));
D(1,2) = D(1,1)*v/(1 − v);
D(1,3) = D(1,2);
D(2,1) = D(1,2);
D(2,2) = D(1,1);
D(2,3) = D(1,2);
D(3,1) = D(1,3);
D(3,2) = D(2,3);
D(3,3) = D(1,1);
D(4,4) = E/(2*(1 + v));
D(5,5) = E/(2*(1 + v));
D(6,6) = E/(2*(1 + v));
% 2x2x2 Gauss Quadrature
a = 1/sqrt(3);                                   Define quadrature points
rgaus = [ − a,a,a, − a, − a,a,a, − a];
sgaus = [ − a, − a,a,a, − a, − a,a,a];
tgaus = [ − a, − a, − a, − a,a,a,a,a];
```

```
% Initialization of the Element Stiffness Matrix
SKE = zeros(24);                                    Zero clear of the stiffness
% Gradient at the 1 Point Gaussian Quadrature
% Volumetric Strain εᵥ                              shape is a "subroutine"
[N0,J0,dNdx0,dNdy0,dNdz0] = shape(xe,ye,ze,0,0,0);
% Numerical Integration (2x2x2 Gauss)
% Normal Strains εₙ (Deviatric Strains)
for int = 1:8
    r = rgaus(int);
    s = sgaus(int);
    t = tgaus(int);
    [N,J,dNdx,dNdy,dNdz] = shape(xe,ye,ze,r,s,t);
    B = zeros(6,24);
    for i = 1:8
        B(1,3*i − 2) = dNdx0(i)/3 + 2*dNdx(i)/3;
        B(1,3*i − 1) = dNdy0(i)/3 −   dNdy(i)/3;
        B(1,3*i   ) = dNdz0(i)/3 −   dNdz(i)/3;
        B(2,3*i − 2) = dNdx0(i)/3 −   dNdx(i)/3;
        B(2,3*i − 1) = dNdy0(i)/3 + 2*dNdy(i)/3;
        B(2,3*i   ) = dNdz0(i)/3 −   dNdz(i)/3;
        B(3,3*i − 2) = dNdx0(i)/3 −   dNdx(i)/3;
        B(3,3*i − 1) = dNdy0(i)/3 −   dNdy(i)/3;
        B(3,3*i   ) = dNdz0(i)/3 + 2*dNdz(i)/3;
    end
    SKE = SKE + B'*D*B*J;                            B' means Bᵀ
end                                                 Matrix product [B]ᵀ[D][B]
% Numerical Integration (2 Point Gauss)
% Shear Strain εᵧ_z
rgau2 = [−a,a];
sgau2 = [0,0];
tgau2 = [0,0];
for int = 1:2
    r = rgau2(int);
    s = sgau2(int);
    t = tgau2(int);
    [N,J,dNdx,dNdy,dNdz] = shape(xe,ye,ze,r,s,t);
    B = zeros(6,24);
    for i = 1:8
        B(4,3*i − 2) = 0;
        B(4,3*i − 1) = dNdz(i);
        B(4,3*i   ) = dNdy(i);
    end
    SKE = SKE + B'*D*B*J*4;
end
% Numerical Integration (2 Point Gauss)
% Shear Strain ε_zx
rgau2 = [0,0];
sgau2 = [−a,a];
tgau2 = [0,0];
for int = 1:2
    r = rgau2(int);
    s = sgau2(int);
    t = tgau2(int);
    [N,J,dNdx,dNdy,dNdz] = shape(xe,ye,ze,r,s,t);
    B = zeros(6,24);
```

```
    for i=1:8
        B(5,3*i−2)=dNdz(i);
        B(5,3*i−1)=0;
        B(5,3*i  )=dNdx(i);
    end
    SKE=SKE+B'*D*B*J*4;
end
% Numerical Integration (2 Point Gauss)
% Shear Strain εxy
rgau2=[0,0];
sgau2=[0,0];
tgau2=[−a,a];
for int=1:2
    r=rgau2(int);
    s=sgau2(int);
    t=tgau2(int);
    [N,J,dNdx,dNdy,dNdz]=shape(xe,ye,ze,r,s,t);
    B=zeros(6,24);
    for i=1:8
        B(6,3*i−2)=dNdy(i);
        B(6,3*i−1)=dNdx(i);
        B(6,3*i  )=0;
    end
    SKE=SKE+B'*D*B*J*4;
end
% Assure Symmetry of SKE
SKE=(SKE+SKE')/2
% Eigenvectors and Eigenvalues of SKE
[X,R]=eig(SKE);                                      call a MATLAB function eig
% Geometric Description of Eigenmodes
xp=zeros(1,14);yp=zeros(1,14);
xo=zeros(1,14);yo=zeros(1,14);
c1=cos(20*3.14/180);s1=sin(20*3.14/180);
c2=cos(10*3.14/180);s2=sin(10*3.14/180);
vx=max(1.4*(c2+c1),1.4*(s2−s1+2));
icont=[1,2,3,4,1,5,6,7,8,5,6,2,3,7];
V=[−vx,vx,−vx,vx];
axis(V)
axis('square')
for i=1:24
    for jj=1:14
        j=icont(jj);
        xo(jj)=ye(j)*c2+xe(j)*c1;
        yo(jj)=ye(j)*s2−xe(j)*s1+ze(j);
        xpj=xe(j)+X(3*j−2,i);
        ypj=ye(j)+X(3*j−1,i);
        zpj=ze(j)+X(3*j,i);
        xp(jj)=ypj*c2+xpj*c1;
        yp(jj)=ypj*s2−xpj*s1+zpj;
    end
    i
    eigenvalue=R(i,i)
    plot(xp,yp,xo,yo)                                call a MATLAB function plot
    title('EigenMode')                              call a MATLAB function title
    xlabel('X')                                     call a MATLAB function slabel
```

ylabel('Y')   *call a MATLAB function ylabel*
pause
end

```
% Function shape: a MATLAB program
%
%
% Define the shape functions for HEXA8
%          their derivatives in (r,s,t)
%          Jacobian Matrix
%          Jacobian
%          their derivatives in (x,y,z)
%
%
% Input:   xe,ye,ze – Nodal coordinates
%          r,s,t     – Parametric coordinates
% Output: N          – Shape functions
%          J          – Jacobian
%          dNdx      – Derivatives of N in x
%          dNdy   –                        y
%          dNdz   –                        z
%
%  ————————————————————————————————————————
%
function [N,J,dNdx,dNdy,dNdz] = shape(xe,ye,ze,r,s,t)
%
N = [(1 − r)*(1 − s)*(1 − t)/8;
     (1 + r)*(1 − s)*(1 − t)/8,
     (1 + r)*(1 + s)*(1 − t)/8,
     (1 − r)*(1 + s)*(1 − t)/8,
     (1 − r)*(1 − s)*(1 + t)/8,
     (1 + r)*(1 − s)*(1 + t)/8,
     (1 + r)*(1 + s)*(1 + t)/8,
     (1 − r)*(1 + s)*(1 + t)/8]';
dNdr = [ −(1 − s)*(1 − t)/8,
          (1 − s)*(1 − t)/8,
          (1 + s)*(1 − t)/8,
         −(1 + s)*(1 − t)/8,
         −(1 − s)*(1 + t)/8,
          (1 − s)*(1 + t)/8,
          (1 + s)*(1 + t)/8,
         −(1 + s)*(1 + t)/8]';
dNds = [ −(1 − r)*(1 − t)/8,
         −(1 + r)*(1 − t)/8,
          (1 + r)*(1 − t)/8,
          (1 − r)*(1 − t)/8,
         −(1 − r)*(1 + t)/8,
         −(1 + r)*(1 + t)/8,
          (1 + r)*(1 + t)/8,
          (1 − r)*(1 + t)/8]';
dNdt = [ −(1 − r)*(1 − s)/8,
         −(1 + r)*(1 − s)/8,
         −(1 + r)*(1 + s)/8,
         −(1 − r)*(1 + s)/8,
          (1 − r)*(1 − s)/8,
          (1 + r)*(1 − s)/8,
          (1 + r)*(1 + s)/8,
          (1 − r)*(1 + s)/8]';
jacmat = [dNdr*xe',dNdr*ye',dNdr*ze';
```

```
          dNds*xe',dNds*ye',dNds*ze';
          dNdt*xe',dNdt*ye',dNdt*ze'];
jacinv = inv(jacmat);                          call a MATLAB function inv
J = det(jacmat);                               call a MATLAB function det
dNdx = jacinv(1,1)*dNdr + jacinv(1,2)*dNds + jacinv(1,3)*dNdt;
dNdy = jacinv(2,1)*dNdr + jacinv(2,2)*dNds + jacinv(2,3)*dNdt;
dNdz = jacinv(3,1)*dNdr + jacinv(3,2)*dNds + jacinv(3,3)*dNdt;
```

This demonstrates that a program similar to BASIC and FORTRAN can be developed in a MATLAB session using various ready-made functions (which are the same as subroutines in FORTRAN) without specifying the dimensions of arrays. Since most of the elementary mistakes in FORTRAN programming are related to dimensioning of arrays in the main and subroutine programs, this feature of MATLAB is very helpful when we use it in a classroom. Furthermore, transferring a program in MATLAB to a usual FORTRAN or BASIC program is very straight-forward because of the similarity of flow control commands. Thus, after developing the logic and a bone structure of a program in MATLAB, it can be transferred to a FORTRAN code without much effort using the editing capability of PCs and EWS. If we execute the program listed, we can obtain, for example, the following response:

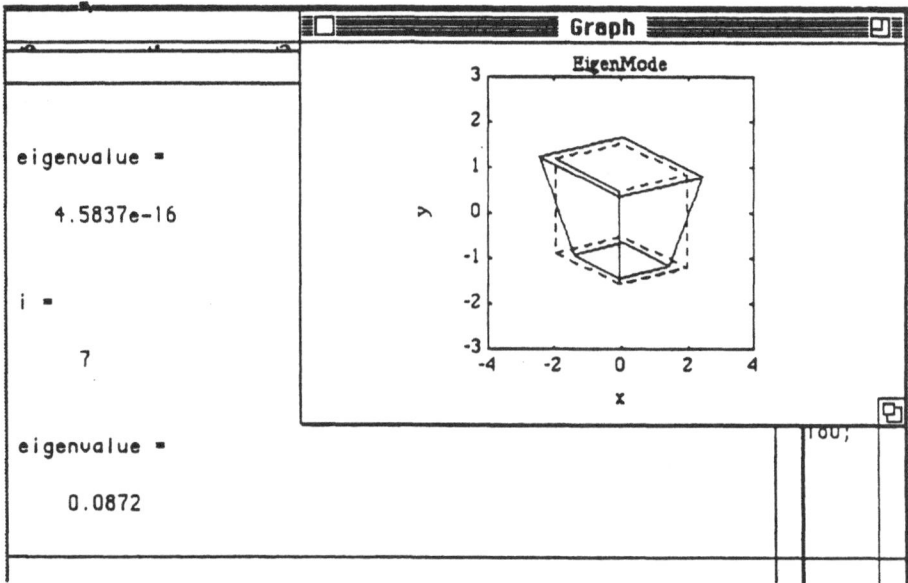

Fig. 2.2. Screen output of MATLAB program

In this example, a 24×24 matrix SKE is computed by applying quadrature rules to the integrand $[B]^T[D][B]J$, where J is the determinant of the coordinate trans-formation matrix. Matrix multiplication and obtaining the determinant of a matrix are very simple in MATLAB. They are simply $[B]'*[D]*[B]*J$ and $J = \det(jacmat)$ in MATLAB. It is also noted that an eigenvalue problem is solved for the matrix

SKE just by calling a MATLAB function [X, R] = eig(SKE). This means that after solving the eigenvalue problem, X is assigned to be the matrix consisting of the eigenvectors while R contains the eigenvalues. For understanding the physical meaning of the eigenvectors, their graphical display is useful. To this end we can use the plot command in MATLAB.

It is clear that there are lots of advantages in MATLAB for studying the characteristics of a finite element. This is merely an example of the utilization of linear algebra software. Although this particular feature is not directly related to supercomputers, it is important to think about this direction of utilization of software in order to integrate all computers available with a variety of software of general applicability.

2.4 Utilization of Vector/Parallel Processing

Another factor we must consider in a classroom is the availability of vector/parallel processing computers, even for instruction. This means that instructors of finite element methods are required to introduce methods for utilizing such processors to optimize computation, and to extend the existing scope of finite element methods to accommodate such special processors. Software developed in the 1970s was not specialized for vector/parallel processing. To modify such software, it is necessary for many engineers to know how to modify programs for scalar processing to use them optimally in both scalar and vector/parallel processing.

A basic approach to develop a program for such computers is not to avoid long and complicated line statements but to avoid complicated program structures such as nested lines and multiple do loops. Simple line statements cannot be written without multiple do loops and a simple program structure is not possible without using long line statements, especially for matrix and vector operations which are essential to finite element methods. An ideal program for those computers is written in the form of a series of single do loops which has length of the longest array. To write such a program, it is unavoidable to have long explicit expressions of equations which cannot easily be written by hand. Instead, symbolic manipulation software such as REDUCE can be used, which generates explicit expressions of complicated equations in FORTRAN with very simple input data.

There is another reason to use the symbolic manipulation software. If element vectors and matrices, which are usually sparse, are precalculated in symbolic level, all the "zero addition/multiplication" operations can be avoided in later computation. For example, the three-dimensional elasticity tensor $\mathbf{E}$ of isotropic materials is given as

$$\mathbf{E} = \begin{bmatrix} E_{11} & E_{12} & E_{13} & & & \\ E_{21} & E_{22} & E_{23} & & & \\ E_{31} & E_{32} & E_{33} & & & \\ & & & E_{44} & & \\ & & & & E_{55} & \\ & & & & & E_{66} \end{bmatrix}$$

in the *contracted* notation, and the gradient matrix **B** of the three-dimensional solid elements is also given as

$$\mathbf{B} = [\ \mathbf{B}_\alpha \mid \alpha = 1, LN\ ], \qquad \mathbf{B}_\alpha = \begin{bmatrix} B_{11}^\alpha & \\ B_{21}^\alpha & B_{23}^\alpha \\ & B_{33}^\alpha \\ & B_{42}^\alpha\ B_{43}^\alpha \\ B_{51}^\alpha & B_{53}^\alpha \\ B_{61}^\alpha\ B_{62}^\alpha & \end{bmatrix}$$

where LN is the total number of nodes in an element. In these, shaded portions show zero components. To show how inefficient ordinary matrix operations are, two FORTRAN programs are shown to calculate $\mathbf{B}_\alpha^T \mathbf{E} \mathbf{B}_\alpha$:

```
      DO 100 I=1,6
      DO 100 J=1,3
      A(I,J)=0
      DO 100 K=1,6
  100 A(I,J)=A(I,J)+E(J,K)*B(K,I)
      DO 200 I=1,3
      DO 200 J=1,3
      K(I,J)=0
      DO 200 K=1,6
  200 K(I,J)=K(I,J)+B(K,J)*A(K,I)
```

is the conventional program, which has couple of matrix multiplication triple do loops.

```
K(1,1)=B61**2*E66+B51**2*E55+B11**2*E11
K(1,2)=B62*B61*E66+B22*B11*E12
K(1,3)=B53*B51*E55+B33*B11*E13
K(2,1)=B62*B61*E66+B22*B11*E21
K(2,2)=B62**2*E66+B42**2*E44+B22**2*E22
K(2,3)=B43*B42*E44+B33*B22*E23
K(3,1)=B53*B51*E55+B33*B11*E31
K(3,2)=B43*B42*E44+B33*B22*E32
K(3,3)=B53**2*E55+B43**2*E44+B33**2*E33
```

is the program generated by REDUCE. In the conventional program, the total number of operations, including addition, multiplication, and substitution, totals 513. On the other hand, only 63 operations are necessary in the latter program, in which all zero additions/multiplications are eliminated. In general, precalculation of such sparse matrices can drastically improve the efficiency of computer programs.

Equations to Be Programmed. In finite element analysis, all equations are classified into two groups. One is the group of equations expressed in the global system, and the other is that expressed in the local element level. Using upper-case characters for variables in the global system and lower-case characters for those in the element level, basic equations of the explicit time integration finite element analysis of solid/structural dynamics can be written as

1. Displacement increment and update: $\Delta U = \Theta(\Delta t)$, $U^n = U^{n-1} + \Delta U$
2. Stress update: $\sigma^n = \Psi(\sigma^{n-1}, \Delta u)$
3. Internal load vector: $p^n = \nabla \sigma^n$
4. Dynamic equation: $\ddot{U}^n = M^{-1}(F^n - P^n)$

where all equations are very simplified. Notations appearing in these equations are defined by

> Variables
>> U: Displacement   Ü: Acceleration
>> ΔU, Δu: Displacement Increment   M: Diagonal mass matrix
>> F: External load vector   P, p: Internal load vector
>> Δt: Time increment   σ: Stress
>> Superscript(n): Iteration number
>
> Method, law and operator
>> Θ: Central difference time integration method
>> Ψ: Material constitutive law ∇: Divergence operator

Equations in 1 and 4 are expressed in the global system while equations in 2 and 3 are in the element level. Let NEQ denote the total number of degrees of freedom in the global system, and NELX denote the total number of finite elements. In the global system, the longest do loop is from 1 to NEQ, while for the element-level equations, it ranges from 1 to NELX.

Program Structures. Assuming acceleration as a primal variable, a dynamic equation is solved by just addition and multiplication of arrays in the explicit time integration scheme. Velocity and displacement are obtained in a similar manner by definition of the central difference method. Thus, for equations in 1 and 4, it is simple to program in the ideal form for vector/parallel type computers such that

```
    DO 10 N=1,NEQ
 10 ....
    DO 20, DO 30, ................, DO 80
    DO 90 N=1,NEQ
 90 ....
```

For equations in 2 and 3, all variables are computed, in element-by-element and independently. If the program can be written in the form of a series of single do loops whose length is NELX, it may be computed very efficiently in vector/parallel type computers. To do this, additional memory space is required since two kinds of arrays are necessary to keep the same variables, one in the global system and the other in the element level. For a two-dimensional QUAD4 element, U(NEQ) and u1(NELX), u2(NELX), ..., u8(NELX) must be used for the displacement where un(NEL) denotes the displacement of the n-th local equation number of the NEL-th element. However, this requirement may be acceptable for recent computers which tend to have big memory capacity. The other thing to ensure is that all equations must be expressed explicitly to be included in single do loops whose length is NELX. In other words, all element-level equations must be precalculated using symbolic manipulation software. As an example of such explicit expressions, the special gradient matrices B^s and B^t are obtained by using REDUCE:

```
REDUCE Input:
OFF EXP; ON GCD; ON FORT; OFF ECHO;
MATRIX XA,YA,LS,LT,H,BX,BY,GA,GB,GC,GD $
OPERATOR XE1,XE2,XE3,XE4,XE5,XE6,XE7,XE8,DJ $
OPERATOR G1,G2,G3,G4,G5,G6,G7,G8,
            G9,G10,G11,G12,G13,G14,G15,G16 $

XA:= MAT( (XE1(NEL)),(XE3(NEL)),(XE5(NEL)),(XE7(NEL)) ) $
YA:= MAT( (XE2(NEL)),(XE4(NEL)),(XE6(NEL)),(XE8(NEL)) ) $
 LS:= MAT( ( − 1/4),(1/4),(1/4),( − 1/4) ) $
 LT:= MAT( ( − 1/4),( − 1/4),(1/4),(1/4) ) $
 H  := MAT( (1/4),( − 1/4),(1/4),( − 1/4) ) $
 BX:= (     LS*(TP(LT)*YA) − LT*(TP(LS)*YA) )/DJ(NEL) $
 BY:= (   − LS*(TP(LT)*XA) + LT*(TP(LS)*XA) )/DJ(NEL) $
GA:=(H − BX*(TP(H)*XA)
       − BY*(TP(H)*YA))*(   TP(LS)*XA) $
GB:=(H − BX*(TP(H)*XA)
       − BY*(TP(H)*YA))*( − TP(LT)*XA) $
GC:=(H − BX*(TP(H)*XA)
       − BY*(TP(H)*YA))*( − TP(LS)*YA) $
GD:=(H − BX*(TP(H)*XA)
       − BY*(TP(H)*YA))*(   TP(LT)*YA) $
 G1 (NEL):= GA(1,1); G2 (NEL):= GA(2,1); G3 (NEL):= GA(3,1); G4
    (NEL):= GA(4,1);
 G5 (NEL):= GB(1,1); G6 (NEL):= GB(2,1); G7 (NEL):= GB(3,1); G8
    (NEL):= GB(4,1);
 G9 (NEL):= GC(1,1); G10 (NEL):= (2,1); G11 (NEL):= GC(3,1);
    G12 (NEL):= GC(4,1);
 G13 (NEL):= GD(1,1); G14 (NEL):= GD(2,1); G15 (NEL):= GD(3,1);
    G16 (NEL):= GD(4,1);
 END;
```

where XEn, DJ, and Gn show the coordinates, the determinant of the Jacobian matrix, and 16 independent non-zero components of $\mathbf{B}^s$ and $\mathbf{B}^t$, respectively.

```
REDUCE Output (FORTRAN Code):
      DO 100 NEL = 1,NELX
      G1(NEL)= −(((XE8(NEL) − XE6(NEL) + XE4(NEL) − XE2(NEL))*(XE7
     . (NEL) − XE3(NEL)) − (XE8(NEL) − XE4(NEL))*(XE7(NEL) − XE5(
     . NEL) + XE3(NEL) − XE1(NEL)) + 8.*DJ(NEL))*(XE7(NEL) − XE5(
     . NEL) − XE3(NEL) + XE1(NEL)))/(128.*DJ(NEL))
      G2(NEL),G3(NEL),G4(NEL),G5(NEL),G6(NEL),G7(NEL),G8(NEL)......
     . . . G9(NEL),G10(NEL),G11(NEL),G12(NEL),G13(NEL),G14(NEL),G15(NEL)
      G16(NEL)=(((XE8(NEL) − XE6(NEL) + XE4(NEL) − XE2(NEL))*(XE5
     . (NEL) − XE1(NEL)) − (XE7(NEL) − XE5(NEL) + XE3(NEL) − XE1(NEL)
     . )*(XE6(NEL) − XE2(NEL)) − 8.*DJ(NEL))*(XE8(NEL) + XE6(NEL)
     . − XE4(NEL) − XE2(NEL)))/(128.*DJ(NEL))
      100 CONTINUE
```

To calculate those matrices in the conventional way, multiple do loops are required for such complicated matrix and vector operations. As we pointed out, matrices or vectors obtained from the finite element equation contain lost of zeros. Because of this, the output shows that the explicit expressions are not very long while the input equations are complicated.

Also for this type of nonlinear finite element problem, programs may have several branches which usually produce FORTRAN IF statements which are not suitable for vector/parallel type computers. The following example shows a part of the radial return process to deal with plasticity, where an IF statement is avoided by using the FORTRAN AMAX1 function.

```
        DO 100 NEL=1,NELX
        SPL=AMAX1(0.,VNYS(NEL)−RYL(NEL))/(1.+HPL(NEL)/(3.*GNU(NEL)))
        ST1(NEL)=ST1(NEL)−SPL*VNY1(NEL)
        ST2(NEL)=ST2(NEL)−SPL*VNY2(NEL)
        ST3(NEL)=ST3(NEL)−SPL*VNY3(NEL)
  100 ST4(NEL)=ST4(NEL)−SPL*VNY4(NEL)
```

where STn, VNYn, VNYS, RYL, HPL, and GNU denote stress components, components of the deviation trial stress, its size, the radius of the yield surface, the plastic tangent, and the shear moduli, respectively.

In summary, an ideal program structure for such element-by-element local equations must look like

```
        DO 10 NEL=1,NELX
   10....
        DO 20, DO 30, ............, DO 80
        DO 90 NEL=1,NELX
   90....
```

The remaining part of the program is assembling and disassembling. The former assembles local variables computed in equations in 2 and 3 into the global ones, while the latter disassembles global variables computed in the equations in 1 and 4 to the local ones. For example,

$$p1(NELX), ..., pn(NELX)... \text{assemble} \rightarrow P(NEQ)$$

and

$$\Delta U(NEQ)... \text{disassemble} \rightarrow \Delta u1(NELX), ..., \Delta un(NELX).$$

Thus, an ideal structure for the whole of the program is expressed in the form of a series of single do loops with assembling and disassembling routines such that

```
      1 DO 10 N=1,NEQ, ..., DO nn N=1,NEQ,
        [Disassembling routine]
        DO 10 NEL=1,NELX, ..., DO nn NEL=1,NELX,
        [Assembling routine]
        GO TO 1
```

Assembling and Disassembling. Although programming of these routines is very simple, it must be done carefully, since it may consume a considerable part of the total computing time. The CPU(s) accesses a memory storage very randomly in these routines. This part may occupy 1% of the total lines in a program, but it may consume nearly 35% of the total computing time in some computers.

In general, the element connectivity which keeps all node numbers related to a element is used for these purposes. Here, the element connectivity keeps equation numbers instead of node numbers, to simplify the program. The global equation number is defined by 2*(node number $-1) + j$, $j = 1$ and 2 in two-dimensional problems, and the local equation number is also defined in a similar manner. An example of such element connectivity for two-dimensional QUAD4 elements is shown in the following where JKLn(NEL) denotes the element connectivity and presents the equation number corresponding to the *n*-th local equation of the NEL-th element:

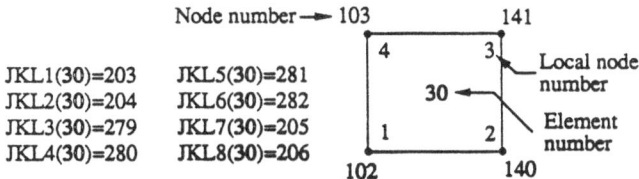

JKL1(30)=203   JKL5(30)=281
JKL2(30)=204   JKL6(30)=282
JKL3(30)=279   JKL7(30)=205
JKL4(30)=280   JKL8(30)=206

Fig. 2.3. Element connectivity for two-dimensional QUAD4 elements

The disassembling routine for two-dimensional QUAD4 elements is, thus, written as

```
     DO 100 NEL=1,NELX
     VE1(NEL)=V(JKL1(NEL))
     ....
 100 VE8(NEL)=V(JKL8(NEL))
```

where VEn and V denote local and global variables respectively, and all statements are computed independently of NEL although they access memory storage very randomly.

If the same element connectivity is used for the assembling routine, such a statement appears in a do loop as

$$V(JKLn(NEL)) = V(JKLn(NEL)) + VEn(NEL),$$

which is inadequate for vector/parallel type processors, since the same global variable is modified at several different subscript NWLs. To obtain a similar do loop for the disassembling routine, the equation connectivity is introduced, in which all element numbers related to an equation are kept. In contrast to the element connectivity, the total number of such elements is not fixed; however, it may be fixed by introducing a null element so that a program may be executed systematically. An example of the null element is shown in the following, as a two-dimensional model with QUAD4 elements:

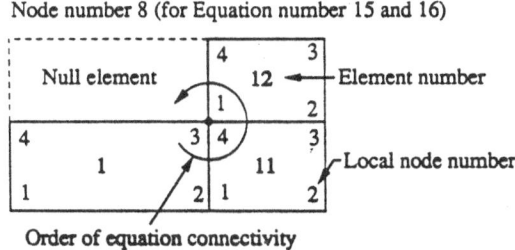

Fig. 2.4. Null element in a two-dimensional model with QUAD4 elements

Using the model shown in Fig. 2.4, an example of the equation connectivity may be defined by

$$
\begin{array}{ll}
\text{LKJ11(15)} = 0 \qquad & \text{LKJ31(15)} = 12 \\
\text{LKJ12(15)} = 0 \qquad & \text{LKJ32(15)} = 0 \\
\text{LKJ13(15)} = 1 \qquad & \text{LKJ33(15)} = 0 \\
\text{LKJ14(15)} = 0 \qquad & \text{LKJ34(15)} = 0 \\
\text{LKJ21(15)} = 0 \qquad & \text{LKJ41(15)} = 0 \\
\text{LKJ22(15)} = 0 \qquad & \text{LKJ42(15)} = 0 \\
\text{LKJ23(15)} = 0 \qquad & \text{LKJ43(15)} = 0 \\
\text{LKJ24(15)} = 11 \qquad & \text{LKJ44(15)} = 0
\end{array}
$$

where LKJnn denotes the the equation connectivity, LKJnn(15) = LKJnn(16) and the maximum element number related to an equation is taken to be 4. Using this equation connectivity, the assembling routine may be written as

```
      DO 100 N=1,NEQ-1,2
100 V(N)=VE1(LKJ11(N))+VE3(LKJ12(N))+VE5(LKJ13(N)) +VE7(LKJ14(N))
     .      +VE1(LKJ21(N))+VE3(LKJ22(N))+VE5(LKJ23(N))+VE7(LKJ24(N))
     .      +VE1(LKJ31(N))+VE3(LKJ32(N))+VE5(LKJ33(N))+VE7(LKJ34(N))
     .      +VE1(LKJ41(N))+VE3(LKJ42(N))+VE5(LKJ43(N))+VE7(LKJ44(N))
      DO 200 N=2,NEQ,2
200 V(N)=VE2(LKJ11(N))+VE4(LKJ12(N))+VE6(LKJ13(N)) +VE8(LKJ14(N))
     .      +VE2(LKJ21(N))+VE4(LKJ22(N))+VE6(LKJ23(N))+VE8(LKJ24(N))
     .      +VE2(LKJ31(N))+VE4(LKJ32(N))+VE6(LKJ33(N))+VE8(LKJ34(N))
     .      +VE2(LKJ41(N))+VE4(LKJ42(N))+VE6(LKJ43(N))+VE8(LKJ44(N))
```

where $VEn(0) = 0$. Here, another problem arises. Although all statements can be computed independently of N, this routine increases the total number of operations greatly, due to many zero additions, and each operation accesses memory storage very randomly. Sometimes, such an increase of random access to the memory storage obscures the merit of vector/parallel processors. Using the same model, another type of equation connectivity may be defined by

$$
\begin{array}{ll}
\text{KLI(15,1)} = 1 \qquad & \text{LIJ(15,1)} = 5 \\
\text{KLI(15,2)} = 11 \qquad & \text{LIJ(15,2)} = 7 \\
\text{KLI(15,3)} = 12 \qquad & \text{LIJ(15,3)} = 1 \\
\text{KLI(15,4)} = 0 \qquad & \text{LIJ(15,4)} = 1 \\
\\
\text{KLI(16,1)} = 1 \qquad & \text{LIJ(16,1)} = 6 \\
\text{KLI(16,2)} = 11 \qquad & \text{LIJ(16,2)} = 8 \\
\text{KLI(16,3)} = 12 \qquad & \text{LIJ(16,3)} = 2 \\
\text{KLI(16,4)} = 0 \qquad & \text{LIJ(16,4)} = 1
\end{array}
$$

where two arrays $KLI(n, m)$ and $LIJ(n, m)$ are used, which keep element and local equation numbers respectively for the n-th equation, while m is the order of the equation connectivity and counts up to the maximum element number among all equations. If local variables are transformed into a two-dimensional array such as $VEn(NEL) = VE(NEL, n)$, the assembling routine may be written with less instructions such that

```
      DO 100 N=1,NEQ
100 V(N)=VE(KLI(N,1),LIJ(N,1))+VE(KLI(N,2),LIJ(N,2))
             +VE(KLI(N,3),LIJ(N,3))+VE(KLI(N,4),LIJ(N,4))
```

where $VE(0, 1) = 0$. Transformation of the local variables is trivial in computation. Both of the assembling routines are not general. If the maximum element number associated with an equation is other than 4, a different routine has to be written. However, to pursue generality is sometimes harmful in writing an efficient program for vector/parallel type computers.

Basically, only one-dimensional arrays have been used to make programming more understandable in the present examples. Arrays of more than two-dimensions may be used to make a simpler program. In this case, however, the most inner do loop must have a length of NEQ or NELX, and more consideration for the architecture of a specific computer is required.

Actual Program and Computation. A program was written based on the ideal structure for the program, except for some parts of the boundary conditions which are trivial in the whole computation. Using this program, computing time is measured for the example of a rod impact problem. Results are shown for three cases with two computers, namely, the ALLIANT FX/8 without vector and parallel options, the ALLIANT FX/8 with vector and parallel options, and the CRAY2. Percentages of computing time used for the assembling and the disassembling are compared for two cases; one employs only the element connectivity and the other employs both the element and equation connectivities. We defined two kinds of the equation connectivities; however, only the latter one is used to solve the example, since the former increases assembling time from several percent to nearly 100 percent in comparison with the assembling with the element connectivity for some test problems. In contrast, the latter type of equation connectivity decreases assembling time by a great amount.

A cylindrical rod is impacted against a rigid foundation. Axisymmetry is assumed for this problem. The rod is modeled using 250 QUAD4 elements, and 12418 time steps are counted to reach the final shape, shown in Fig. 2.5, $80\mu s$ after the impact. Material properties of the rod are given in Fig. 2.6, where E is Young's modulus, v is Poisson's ratio, σ_y is the yield stress, E_t is the plastic tangent modulus, ρ is the mass density, $\bar{\sigma}$ is the effective stress, and $\ln(L/L_0)$ is the true strain in a uniaxial tension test. Table 2.1 shows the computing time in seconds, and the percentage of this time used for the assembling and the disassembling routines, where ASelm and Asequ denote the assembling by the element connectivity and the equation connectivity, respectively, and ALvp and ALno denote the ALLIANT FX/8 computer with and without vector/parallel options, respectively.

The performance ratio of ALvp to ALno is 21.4; this ratio may show how the programs utilize vector and parallel processors. According to the ALLIANT computer manual, program optimization typically increases the execution speed by a factor approaching the number of CPU for parallelization, or by 2–4 for vec-

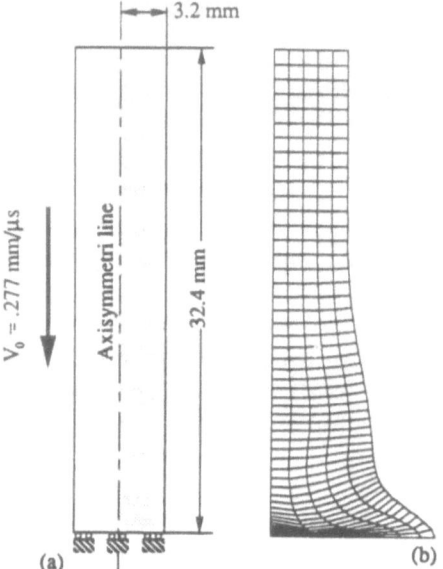

(a)   (b)

Fig. 2.5**a,b**. Rod impact problem, initial setting (**a**) and deformed shape (**b**)

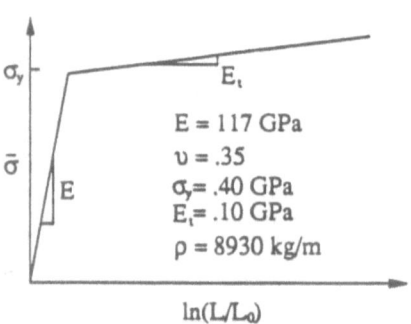

$E = 117$ GPa
$\upsilon = .35$
$\sigma_y = .40$ GPa
$E_t = .10$ GPa
$\rho = 8930$ kg/m

Fig. 2.6. Material properties of the impacted rod

Table 2.1. Computing time and the percentage of time percentage of time used for the assembling and disassembling

	Computer					
	CRAY2		ALvp		ALno	
Method	ASelm	ASequ	ASelm	ASequ	ASelm	ASequ
Computing time (s)	48.74	41.37	831.2	726.9	15422.8	15554.7
% of time used for assembling and disassembling	33.9	22.1	16.2	4.1	6.0	6.8

torization; thus, 16 to 32 times in the present case. The example shows the good performance of the program, although it was not optimized for ALLIANT computers. The performance ratio of CRAY2 to ALvp is 17.6. The assembling routine using equation connectivity greatly contributed to program efficiency, especially for ALLIANT computers.

2.5 Adaptive Finite Element Methods

One of the most active research subjects in finite element methods in the 1980s is the implementation of an adaptive method that can control the total amount of approximation error starting from an arbitrary finite element model, without requesting any human interface during the execution of a program. By implementing this capability, we can assure the quality of finite element solutions as well as a significant reduction in the effort required for modeling and analysis. The demand for such an automated method is motivated by the popularity of finite element methods in science and engineering. At first, finite element methods had been used only by structural engineers who were involved in program development. Thus, it could be expected that users of the methods were familiar with the underlying theory as well as their programs, and well recognized their limitations and strengths. However, after the introduction of general purpose finite element analysis codes even users who were not specialists in structural mechanics/dynamics could use the codes without spending much time to fully understand the methods. Furthermore, the popularity of computer-aided engineering (CAE) systems including geometric modeling and automatic mesh generation capability, leads users to generate finite element models using such computer software. It is noted that both geometric modeling and mesh generation depend only on the geometry of a given structure, but they are independent of the loading and support conditions. It is clear that the solution of a stress analysis problem is a function of the boundary conditions. Since the finite element model is defined solely by geometry, it might not be the best. However, if the adaptive method is applied, the software can provide an appropriate refinement of the finite element model initially introduced, by examining the distribution of estimated approximation error. Because of automation of the refinement process, users may obtain an approximated solution based on the finite element model that is very different from the original one, but nevertheless optimized. It could be ten times refined from the original without additional human effort.

There are two major steps in the adaptive finite element method: estimation of the approximation error and automatic refinement of a finite element model. After the work of Babuska and Rheinboldt [6], several error estimation methods have been introduced. Here we shall introduce Bank's method [7] as an example. Let a boundary value problem

$$\sum_{i,j=1}^{n} -\frac{\partial}{\partial x_i}\left(k_{ij}\frac{\partial u}{\partial x_j}\right) + c_i\frac{\partial u}{\partial x_i} + k_0 u = f \quad in \quad \Omega \quad and \quad u = 0 \quad on \quad \Gamma$$

be considered for given functions k_{ij}, c_i, k_0, and f on the domain Ω in the n-dimensional Euclidian space. The weak form of the above problem is then given by

$$u \in H_0^1(\Omega): \sum_{i,j=1}^{n} \int_{\Omega} \left\{ \frac{\partial v}{\partial x_i} k_{ij} \frac{\partial u}{\partial x_j} + c_i v \frac{\partial u}{\partial x_i} + v k_0 u \right\} d\Omega = \int_{\Omega} v f \, d\Omega \qquad \forall v \in H_0^1(\Omega)$$

where $H_0^1(\Omega)$ is the Sobolev space that is the completion of the space of infinitely continuously differentiable functions with compact supports in Ω with respect to the H^1 norm h.

$$\|v\| = \sqrt{\sum_{i=1}^{n} \int_{\Omega} \left\{ \left(\frac{\partial v}{\partial x_i} \right)^2 + v^2 \right\} d\Omega}.$$

Let V_h be a finite element approximation of $H_0^1(\Omega)$, where h indicates the size of finite elements covering the domain Ω. For simplicity, assume that the domain is exactly covered by finite elements Ω_e, $e = 1, \ldots, E$. Then the finite element approximation of the above problem is stated by

$$u_h \in V_h: \sum_{e=1}^{E} \sum_{i,j=1}^{n} \int_{\Omega_e} \left\{ \frac{\partial v_h}{\partial x_i} k_{ij} \frac{\partial u_h}{\partial x_j} + c_i v_h \frac{\partial u_h}{\partial x_i} + v_h k_0 u_h \right\} d\Omega$$

$$= \sum_{e=1}^{E} \int_{\Omega_e} v_h f \, d\Omega \qquad \forall v_h \in V_h.$$

If the approximation error e_h is defined by $e_h = u - u_h$, the weak form and its finite element approximation yield

$$\sum_{e=1}^{E} \sum_{i,j=1}^{n} \int_{\Omega_e} \left\{ \frac{\partial v_h}{\partial x_i} k_{ij} \frac{\partial e_h}{\partial x_j} + c_i v_h \frac{\partial e_h}{\partial x_i} + v_h k_0 e_h \right\} d\Omega$$

$$= \sum_{e=1}^{E} \int_{\Omega_e} v_h r_h^e \, d\Omega + \int_{\partial \Omega_e} v_h \sum_{i,j=1}^{n} n_i k_{ij} \frac{\partial u_h}{\partial x_j} \, d\Gamma \qquad \forall v_h$$

where $\partial \Omega_e$ is the boundary of Ω_e, n is the unit vector outward normal to $\partial \Omega_e$, and r_h^e is the residual of the finite element approximation u_h in Ω_e defined by

$$r_h^e = f + \sum_{i,j=1}^{n} \frac{\partial}{\partial x_i} \left(k_{ij} \frac{\partial u_h}{\partial x_j} \right) - c_i \frac{\partial u_h}{\partial x_i} - k_0 u_h \qquad in \qquad \Omega_e,$$

after applying the divergence theorem in each finite element. Since every inner boundary of elements is shared with two adjacent elements, the second integral term in the right-hand side of the weak form for the approximation error is nothing but the jump of the approximated flux across element boundaries. Therefore, the approximation error e_h is the solution of the weak form and is generated by the residual r_h^e and flux jumps across element boundaries. This result is not a surprise, given the work of applied mathematicians in the 1970s and 1980s. If we go back to the original paper on finite element methods, Clough's paper [8] published in the middle 1960s, we find the statement "In general, equilibrium will not be maintained along element boundaries, and similarly there is no necessity that the assumed displacement functions maintain equilibrium within the elements. The lack of equilibrium represents the extent of the approximation which has been made." That is, this result was predicted in the original theory. Most of the works on the adaptive method in the 1970s and 1980s were more or less restatements of Clough's idea, and of the extension that makes it possible to quantify the approximation error.

Since the divergence theorem is applied in each finite element, an arbitrary function v_h in the weak form for the approximation error e_h need not be in V_h nor be continuous along the element boundaries. Thus, it is possible to assume v_h is "disjointed" in each finite element. If this is assumed, the weak form of the approximation error e_h is solved on each finite element Ω_e "independently" from other elements. If e_h is obtained in Ω_e by solving

$$\sum_{i,j=1}^{n} \int_{\Omega_e} \left\{ \frac{\partial v_h}{\partial x_i} k_{ij} \frac{\partial e_h}{\partial x_j} + c_i v_h \frac{\partial e_h}{\partial x_i} + v_h k_0 e_h \right\} d\Omega$$

$$= \int_{\Omega_e} v_h r_h^e \, d\Omega + \sum_{i,j=1}^{n} \int_{\partial \Omega_e} v_h n_i k_{ij} \frac{\partial u_h}{\partial x_j} d\Gamma \; \forall v_h$$

then the amount of the approximation error in each finite element Ω_2 is estimated by

$$E_e = \sqrt{\sum_{i=1}^{n} \int_{\Omega_e} \left\{ \left(\frac{\partial e_h}{\partial x_i} \right)^2 + e_h^2 \right\} d\Omega}.$$

If the total amount of the approximation error e_h should be less than $\alpha\%$ of the H^1 norm of the finite element solution u_h, the estimated error E_e in each finite element must satisfy the relation

$$\sqrt{\sum_{e=1}^{E} E_e^2} \leq 0.01\alpha \|u_h\|.$$

The simplest requirement may then be stated as

$$E_e \leq \frac{\alpha \|u_h\|}{100\sqrt{E}},$$

where E is the total number of finite elements in a model.

Another major issue in the adaptive method is how a given finite element model is refined to meet the error criterion. To do this, there are three methods: r-, h-, and p-methods. The r-method relocates nodal position optimally to reduce the amount of approximation error by increasing error in the portion where it is considerably small. Thus, it is sometimes unable to reduce the amount of error until the desired one unless the total number of nodes is increased. In general, in this method, the total numbers of nodes and elements are fixed during the adaptation. The h-method refines elements by subdividing into smaller ones. Thus the number of elements is increased. The p-method stays in the initial discrete, finite element geometrically, but the degrees of polynomials for the shape functions are increased to reduce the amount of the approximation error. Typical finite element models which are adapted by the r- and h-methods are shown in the following:

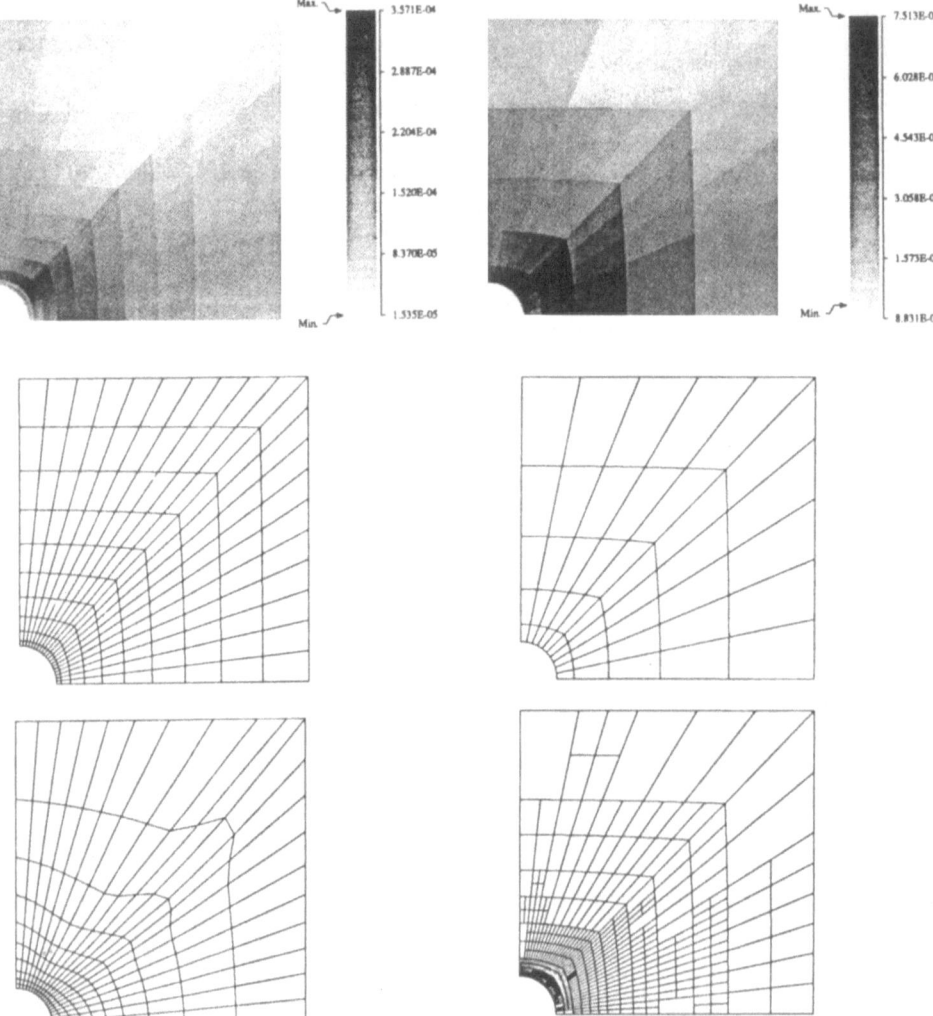

Fig. 2.7. Approximation error distribution, initial and adapted finite element models. (From [9] with permission)

We shall now briefly review present research on the adaptive finite element method.

Oden, J.T./Texas Institute for Computational Mechanics. The major activity of the group lead by Oden, Texas Institute for Computational Mechanics in the University of Texas at Austin, is a development of the adaptive method in computational fluid dynamics [9]. More specifically, their interest is to solve time-dependent compressible Navier-Stokes equations:

$$\frac{\partial U}{\partial t} + \frac{\partial E}{\partial x_1} + \frac{\partial F}{\partial x_2} + \frac{\partial G}{\partial x_3} = divS$$

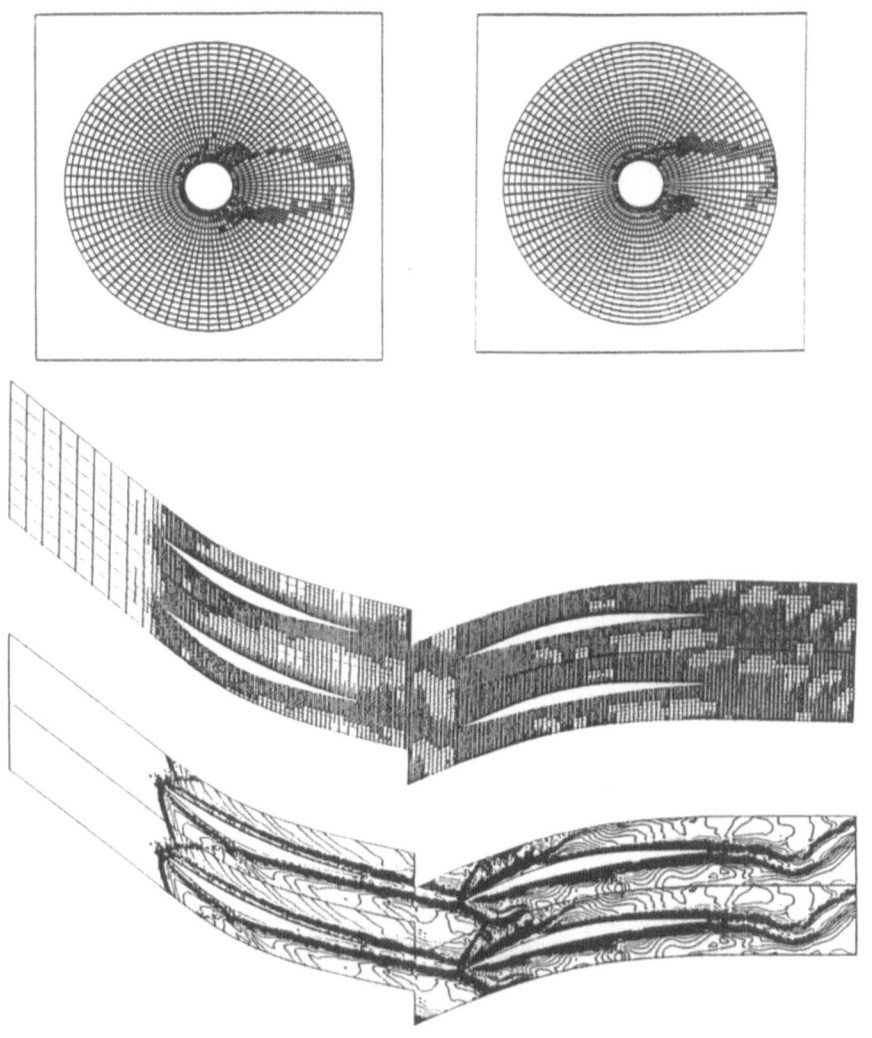

MACH   CONTOURS   MIN = 0.172 +00   MAX = 0.327 +01   INTERVAL= 0.107 +00

Fig. 2.8. Adapted finite element meshes by Oden for computational fluid dynamics applications. (From [9] with permission)

$$U = \left\{ \begin{array}{c} \rho \\ \rho u_1 \\ \rho u_2 \\ \rho u_3 \\ \rho e \end{array} \right\} \quad E = \left\{ \begin{array}{c} \rho u_1 \\ \rho u_1^2 + p \\ \rho u_1 u_2 \\ \rho u_1 u_3 \\ (\rho e + p)u_1 \end{array} \right\} \quad F = \left\{ \begin{array}{c} \rho u_2 \\ \rho u_1 u_2 \\ \rho u_2^2 + p \\ \rho u_2 u_3 \\ (\rho e + p)u_2 \end{array} \right\} \quad G = \left\{ \begin{array}{c} \rho u_3 \\ \rho u_1 u_3 \\ \rho u_2 u_3 \\ \rho u_3^2 + p \\ (\rho e + p)u_3 \end{array} \right\}.$$

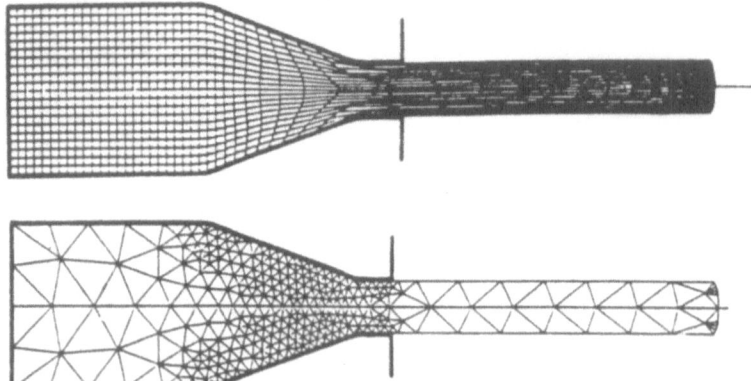

a

Fig. 2.9. Adapted finite element meshes and metal flow for analysis of metal forming process and computational fluid dynamics application by Zienbiewicz et. al.

$$
divS = \left\{ \begin{array}{c} 0 \\[2mm] \dfrac{\partial \tau_{11}}{\partial x_1} + \dfrac{\partial \tau_{12}}{\partial x_2} + \dfrac{\partial \tau_{13}}{\partial x_3} \\[3mm] \dfrac{\partial \tau_{21}}{\partial x_1} + \dfrac{\partial \tau_{22}}{\partial x_2} + \dfrac{\partial \tau_{23}}{\partial x_3} \\[3mm] \dfrac{\partial \tau_{31}}{\partial x_1} + \dfrac{\partial \tau_{32}}{\partial x_2} + \dfrac{\partial \tau_{33}}{\partial x_3} \\[3mm] \tau \nabla u + divq \end{array} \right\}
$$

where ρ is the mass density, u is the velocity, p is the pressure, τ is the viscous stress, e is the total energy, and q is the heat flux. Applying two-step Taylor-Galerkin/Lax-Wendroff algorithms with artificial viscosity for shock waves, they solve the problem of discretion. The h-, h-p, and h-r methods are applied for adaptation. Some of the results are shown in Fig. 2.8.

Zienkiewicz, O.C./Institute for Numerical Methods in Engineering. The group of Zienkiewicz, Institute for Numerical Methods in Engineering, University College of Swansea, SA28PP, Wales, U.K., has spent the last 10 years establishing an adaptive method that is sound in engineering. Ken Mogan, especially, has been very active in computational fluid dynamics. They established a h-method accompanied by an automatic mesh generation capability [10]. Since most of the adaptive schemes applied so far are restricted to the initial finite element model, when adaptation processes are applied repeatedly to solve time-dependent or nonlinear problems, the adapted model generates very irregular refinement. Furthermore, especially for solving large deformation nonlinear problems, the domain to be analyzed has large deformation. Thus, the initial finite elements are very distorted and are still the basis for the adaptation. It is clear that this situation is not appropriate in many engineering applications. In this regard, they made a significant

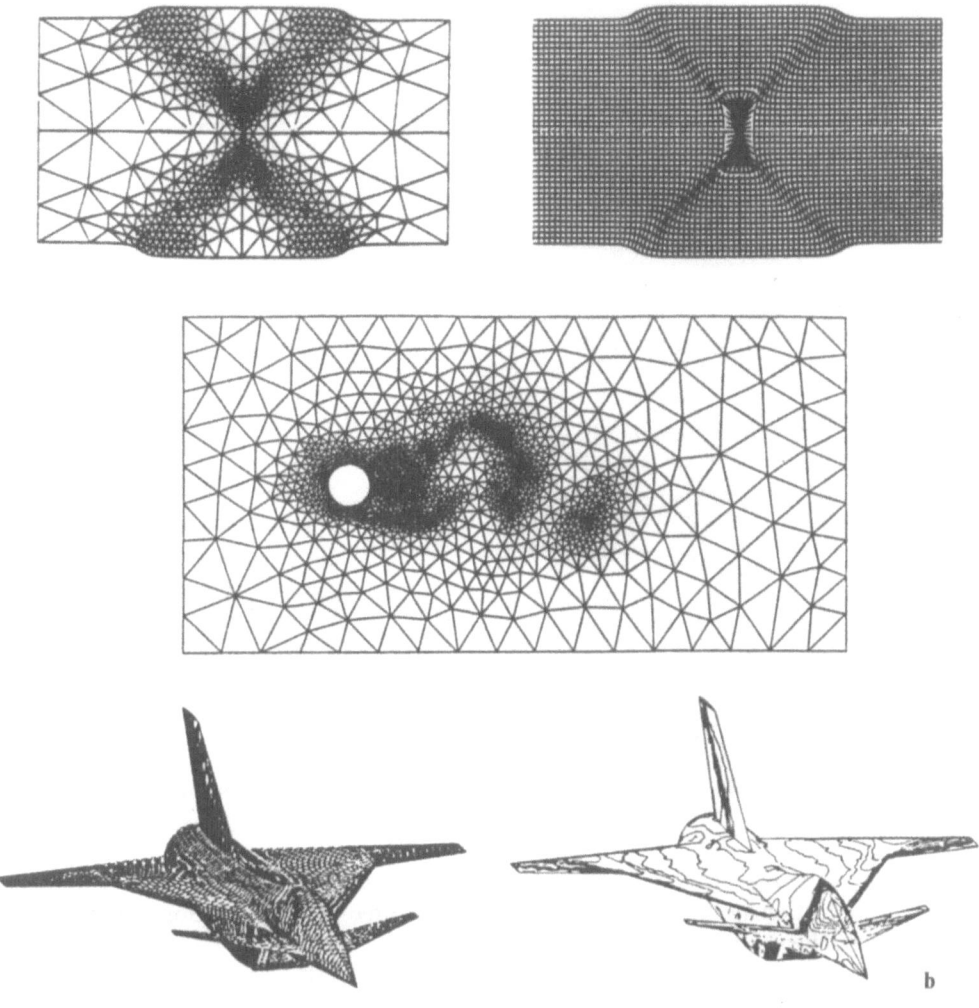

Fig. 2.9 *continued*

contribution in the method of adaptation. This adaptive remeshing method has been applied to stress analysis [11] and analysis of metal forming [12]. Some examples are shown in Fig. 2.9 to illustrate their results on the adaptive method.

Shephard, M.S./Rensselaer Design Research Center. A key method for the adaptive scheme is not the method of error estimation but the method of automatic mesh generation as far as engineering applications are concerned. As did Zienkiewicz' group, Shephard and colleagues also adapted the remeshing scheme for adaptation. That is, the adaptive scheme had to be combined with automatic mesh generation and error estimation on variable domains as also proposed by Tezuka and Kikuchi [13]. The first success of this approach was reported by Bennett and Botkin [14] who solved shape-optimization problems of elastic structures. In this regard the activity of Mark Shephard in Rensselaer Polytechnic Institute, Troy, NY must be

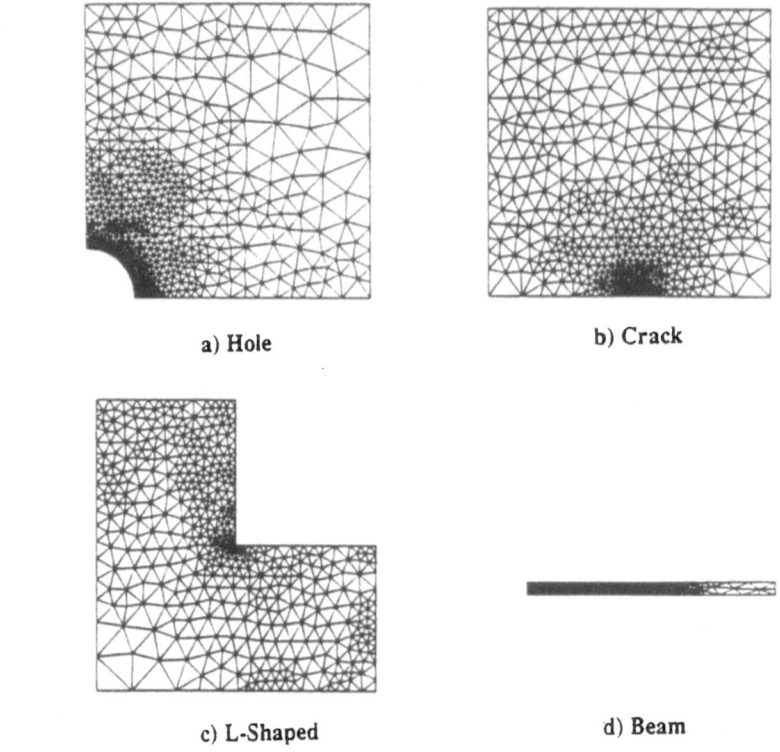

a) Hole

b) Crack

a

c) L-Shaped

d) Beam

Fig. 2.10. Adapted finite element meshes by Shephard for structural mechanics. (From [16] with permission)

specially acknowledged. He has spent more than fifteen years to establish automatic mesh generation methods [15] both for two- and three-dimensional domains. Some results published by them are shown in Fig. 2.10.

Szabo, B.A./Center for Computational Mechanics. A pioneer of the p-adaptive method, B.A. Szabo, Center for Computational Mechanics, Washington University, St. Louis, MO 63130, is now working toward finite element analysis of structural connections using the h-p approach for aerospace industry, after previous work on plates and shells [17]. He is a close collaborator of I. Babuska [18], Institute for Physical Science and Technology, University of Maryland, College Park, MD, who basically introduced and established the mathematical theory of the adaptive method. It is also noted that Szabo is marketing the PROBE code [19] for the h-p adaptive method which will be an option of MSC-NASTRAN.

Belytschko. T./Northwestern University. Another approach [20] to increase the accuracy of finite element approximation, where a very high gradient of the solution is expected in a narrow range of the domain, is proposed by Belytschko, Northwestern University, Evanston, IL 60208. His approach is, in some sense, similar to the p-method, but the conventional finite element approximation need not be

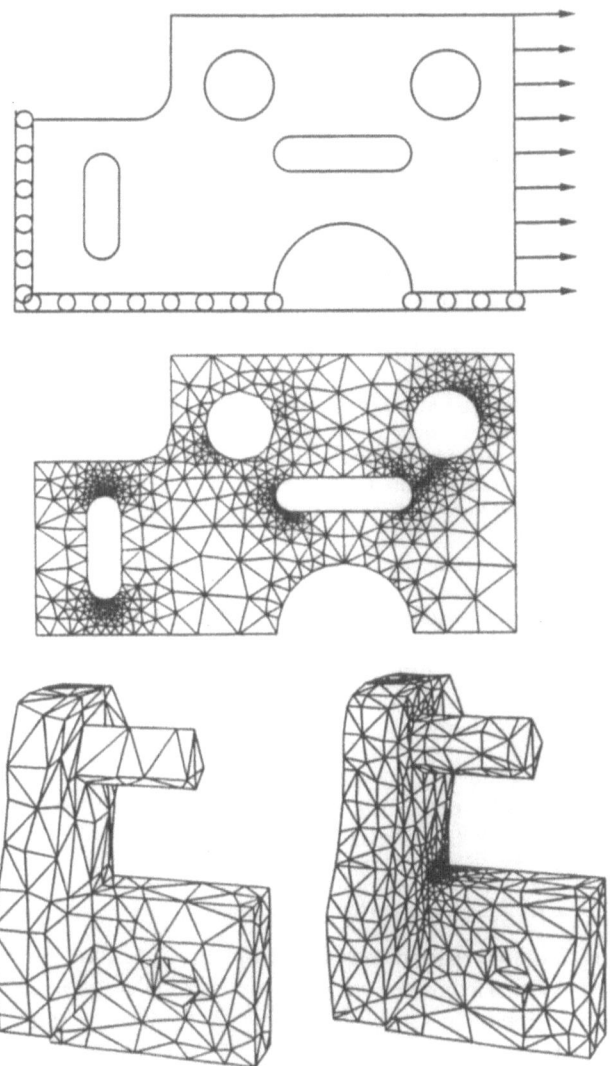

Fig. 2.10 continued. (From [16] with permission)

modified to increase the degree of polynomials of the shape functions in each finite element. The finite element model initially introduced is not modified at all, but the spectral approximation [21] is superimposed on the original finite element approximation over a spectral patch which is placed over the region of large gradients. In other words, this approach combines the best two methods to solve boundary value problems: the generality of the finite element method with regards to complex geometry and boundary conditions, and the spectral method possessing an infinite order convergence property. This approach is applied to solve the localization problem [22] of deformation of solids with finite strain elastic-plasticity or elastic viscoplasticity.

The most recent research activity on the adaptive finite element method can be found in the Workshop on Reliability in Computational Mechanics, organized by J.T. Oden, at the Texas Institute for Computational Mechanics, The University of Texas at Austin, October 26–28, 1989. The following is the list of workshop speakers:

Bathe KJ, Quality assessment of mathematical modeling in engineering analysis, I
Brezzi F, Inf-Sup condition and related practical aspects
Ewing R, A-posteriori error estimation technique
Roach P, The need for control of numerical accuracy
Flaherty J, Parallel computations with adaptive methods for partial differential equations
Zienkiewicz OC, Error estimation and adaptivity in context of engineering practice
Meissner U, A least-square principle for the a-posteriori computation of finite element approximation error
Desai CS, Discussion of various factor for reliable computer solutions with hierarchical single surface constitutive models
Babusuka I, Quality assessment of mathematical modeling in engineering analysis, II
Szabo B, Use of a-priori information in engineering analysis
Oden JT, A posteriori error estimation and adaptive h-p methods in computational fluid dynamics
Wheeler M, Mixed finite element methods for second order hyperbolic equations
Stein E, Accuracy and adaptivity in the numerical analysis of thin-walled structures
Belytschko T, Expert system and error estimations for time steps in structural dynamics
Atluri S, Reliability of integral equation methods
Arnold D, Mixed finite element methods for elliptic problems
Johnson C, Adaptive finite element methods for parabolic and hyperbolic problems
Bank R, Adaptive local mesh refinement for the Stokes equations
Noor AK, Assessment of computational models for multi-layered composite shells
Carey G, Research on adaptive and parallel computing
Park KC, Symbolic analysis for element evaluation and discretization guide
Jirousek J, A FE formulation for adaptive solution in presence of multiple load cases – an approach easy to implement into the existing FE codes
Goldak J, Dynamic meshing for computational weld mechanics
Lee JK, Sheet metal forming analyses/Benchmark testing.

Participants in the workshop were invited from the United States, Europe, and South America. As seen from the speakers' titles, the majority of researchers in finite element methods joined to establish reliable computational methods which can control the approximation error automatically so that it can be used even by nonspecialists with confidence.

Since the adaptive method requires several iterations to reach to the final finite element model, even with linear problems, it is recommended that a program be developed that fully utilizes the advantages of vector/parallel processing. Because the adaption is based on the estimation of the error using the finite element solution, a parallel algorithm is applicable to each major step in the adaptive finite element method. It consists of the following three major steps:

1. Finite element analysis
    1.1 Setting up the necessary input data such as nodal coordinates, element connectivities, boundary conditions, material characterization
    1.2 Forming the element and global stiffness matrices

If steps 1, 2, and 3 are largely independent, then the adaptation of the vector/parallel algorithm is applicable to these major steps. It should be applied at substages such as formation of the lement stiffness matrices, solving a system of linear equations, computing flux, strain, stress in elements, and error estimation in elements. Details of this can be found in Section 3.

Hughes, T.J.R./Stanford University. One significant development in this direction can be found in Hughes, Ferencz, and Hallquist [23]. These authors established a vectorized element-by-element preconditioned conjugate gradient method for solving a system of linear equations. The objective of their work was to speed up the NIKE3D code that Hallquist developed in the Lawrence Livermore National Laboratory for large scale nonlinear finite strain solid and structural dynamics calculations using an unconditionally stable time-integration scheme and quasi-Newtonian equilibrium iteration. The application of iterative methods is very sensible because the norm of the correction at each Newton's iteration is in general small and also, the increment of the state variables in a time-integration step is also sufficiently small. Thus, the application of the direct elimination procedure to solve a system of linear equations is not very attractive. However, during Newton's iteration or a time increment, the stiffness of a certain number of degrees of freedom may drastically change due to plasticity, geometric instability, and other mechanical responses, while irregular size and shape of finite elements must also be expected to build up a finite element model for practical applications. Thus, since most iterative methods provide rapid convergence for well-conditioned regular matrices, many poor results were reported in the past prior to the introduction of preconditioning. Because of this, iterative methods to solve a system of linear equations were not popular in finite element methods, despite their frequent application in the early stage of development of the finite element method. As mentioned in the Introduction, the first published finite element program, by Wilson, employed the SOR (Successive Over-Relaxation) method to solve a system of linear equations in order to save storage space for the stiffness matrix and to effectively apply this to solve nonlinear problems using a step-by-step incremental procedure.

There are several choices for an appropriate preconditioner B, but the basic idea is that B^{-1} is an approximation of A^{-1} for $Ax = b$, while retaining a computationally efficient structure. Hughes *et al.* [23] proposed the choice of B as the Crout element-by-element preconditioner defined by the product decomposition

$$B = W^{1/2} \prod_{e=1}^{E} L^e \prod_{e=1}^{E} D^e \prod_{e=1}^{E} U^e W^{1/2}$$

where $W = \text{diag}(A)$, and L^e, D^e, and U^e are the assembled elementwise ${}^eL$, ${}^eD$, and ${}^eU$ which are the LDU decomposition of the regularized element (stiffness) matrix

^eA defined by

$$^eA = I + W|_e^{-1/2}(A^e - W^e)W|_e^{-1/2}$$

Here $W|_e$ is the restriction of $\mathrm{diag}(A)$ which are rearranged to the same nodal ordering to A^e, $W^e = \mathrm{diag}(A^e)$, and A^e is the element (stiffness) matrix of Ω_e, i.e. element Ω_e's contribution to the global one A.

As a benchmark example, Hughes et al. [23] solved a three-dimensional linear elasticity problem with a $24 \times 24 \times 24$ finite element grid which yields 45,000 linear equations. Using a CRAY XMP/48, the direct elimination method requires 3387 CPU seconds while the element-by-element preconditioned conjugate gradient method provides the solution within 61.9 CPU s using approximately 1/10 of the storage of the global and element (stiffness) matrices A and A^e.

As shown previously, significant improvement can be obtained by changing equation-solving methods which are appropriately vectorized or parallelized. If such ideas are extended into other substeps and modules of finite element analysis, the computing time required can be dramatically reduced. This reduction is indispensable to utilize the adaptive finite element method in engineering practice.

2.6 Computational Aspects of Nonlinear Composite Materials

Despite rapid progress and the development of high-performance high-temperature composites in material science, there is still limited application of newly developed composites in real structures and machine components. The main reason for this delay of application in the real world strongly depends on the large gap between science and engineering. More precisely, the necessary information related to material characterization, on both mechanical and thermal aspects of highly heterogeneous composite materials, is not properly transferred to structural engineers who analyze designed structures. It is also true that detailed information on stresses and strains in the microstructure of composite materials is not transferred to the material scientists who are developing or have developed those materials. If materials scientists could have more information on the stresses and strains in the microstructure of composite materials, when they are used for structures to carry loads in a given temperature range, then there would be a greater chance for improvement by the utilization of newly developed composites, or for the development of other composite materials to carry certain stresses and strains in a given environment. Furthermore, precise information on stress and strain fields in the microstructure is indispensable for the analysis of processing of composite materials, for example, cutting, drilling, grinding, surface finishing, and others, as well as the manufacturing processing of such materials. To this end, the thermal/stress analysis of composite materials, both in the microstructure and macrostructure, is very important for the utilization of them as structural components. However, there has been little progress in the development of a mechanics theory of general composite materials applicable for a computer program which could be used not only by specialists in composite mechanics but also by structural engineers, design engineers, processing engineers, and material scientists. In other words, it is now necessary to develop computational methods and computational mechanics for analyzing composite materials, to exploit fully the existing capability in thermal/stress analysis of structures, for example, by finite element methods, and to emphasize aspects of the structural mechanics and dynamics of composite materials. The resulting methods must also be capable of solving various problems encountered in the use of composite materials, both in the material development stage by material scientists, and in the design stage of structures by structural engineers. To do this, the following issues must be considered:

1. Development of means to construct macroscopic constitutive equations for composite materials which are used in the thermal/stress analysis of structures, and which precisely reflect the microstructure of the composite materials, *with as little as possible laboratory work.*
2. Development of means to compute stress and strain fields at an arbitrary point in the microstructure, as well as in the macrostructure, when structures made of composite materials are stressed thermally or mechanically.
3. Development of means to reflect possible local damage of the microstructure of composites caused by decohesion, debonding, breakage, or other factors, in the macroscopic constitutive equations of the overall structure.
4. Development of the capability to simulate the mechanics behavior of the interfaces of fibers/whiskers/particle inclusions and matrices in the microstructure, to study decohesion, debonding, breakage, and other damage processes at these interfaces.

Overview of the Research

To solve these problems, the homogenization method for general composite materials should be applicable for both linear and nonlinear cases. As already indicated, composite materials are characterized by their high degree of very refined microscale heterogeneity that presents difficulties in structural analysis, if stress and strain fields must be computed at every point of highly heterogeneous media. In other words, enormous efforts are required to compute stresses and strains, both in the matrix and in fibers/whiskers/inclusions of composite at any arbitrary point of the macroscopic structure. The usual procedure to overcome this difficulty is to define some equivalent material properties characterizing the composite overall mechanical behavior which reflect the heterogeneity and details of the microstructure. Using such "averaged" mechanical and thermal properties, called "macroscopic constitutive relations," over the neighborhood of a given point, displacement, strain, and stress fields are computed in the "average" sense. Now, the remaining step is to establish a method for transferring these mechanical quantities, averaged over the matrix and any fibers, whiskers, or inclusions, to the actual values in the microstructure at an arbitrary point; this is, how the average quantities are transferred to the nonaveraged true values. Much research in engineering and material science fields has been focusing on ways to determine these equivalent properties, and several methods have been proposed. A survey of these methods can be found in Hashin [24]. It is, however, noted that there are few works on the second aspect, i.e., on developing a systematic method to transfer the averaged quantities into the nonaveraged ones in true heterogeneous media, especially in the mechanics field. An answer to this question comes from a research group in applied mathematics in France.

When considering composite materials with a periodic microstructure, the equivalent material properties can be rigorously computed using the homogenization theory, a mathematical theory that started its development in the 1970s, and stress and strain fields can also be predicted precisely, both in the microstructure and in the macrostructure of composite materials. If materials do not possess an exactly periodic microstructure, they are idealized to be periodic in the vicinity of a point considered in the macrostructure. This idealization provides a means to deal with composite materials by varying the microstructure in an approximate sense. The fundamentals of this theory can be found, among others, in the works of Benssousan, Lions, and Papanicoulau [25] Sanchez-Palencia [26], Duvaut [27], Lene [28], and Murat and Tartar [29]. Also, a recent review by Kohn [30] provides a good insight into the actual status of these mathematical methods. Several numerical implementations of the homogenization method exist, and one may mention, in addition to the previous references, the work of Begis *et al.* [31] at INRIA in France.

The research we are performing in the University of Michigan is to show how the homogenization method can be used to study both the global (macroscopic) and the local (microscopic) behavior of composite materials, and how it can be helpful for designing the microstructure of composite materials. To this end the following issues have been studies [32]:

1. Extension of the homogenization theory for linear elasticity to encompass decohesion of particulates from the matrix as well as slippage of fibers, whiskers, and inclusions from the matrix, following Lene's approach.
2. Extension of the homogenization method to large-deformation finite strain elastic-plasticity using the rate formulation, so that plastic deformation of, for example, a matrix can be considered.
3. Development of sensitivity analysis of the homogenization method to have reliable macroscopic constitutive equations, so that the uncertainty of material constants of constituents is taken into account.
4. Establishment of reliability analysis of finite element methods for determining constitutive equations of composite materials so that adaptive methods are applicable to improve the accuracy of predictions using constitutive equations.

Homogenization Theory. Here we shall briefly describe the homogenization method. Consider the body characterized by the domain Ω, fixed on the boundary Γ_d, subjected to body forces $\mathbf{f}$ in Ω, tractions $\mathbf{t}$ on the boundary Γ_t, and made of composite materials. We assume that these composite materials are formed by the *spatial repetition of a unit base cell Y* whose typical dimensions are of order ε compared to those of Ω, and where the properties of the material can change and/or there is applied internal traction $\mathbf{p}$. If the microstructure does not possess an exact periodic nature, we may idealize it so that a periodic structure is assumed. Note that the unit cell describing the microstructure of composite materials can consist of several different materials as well as voids, while a distributed traction is also

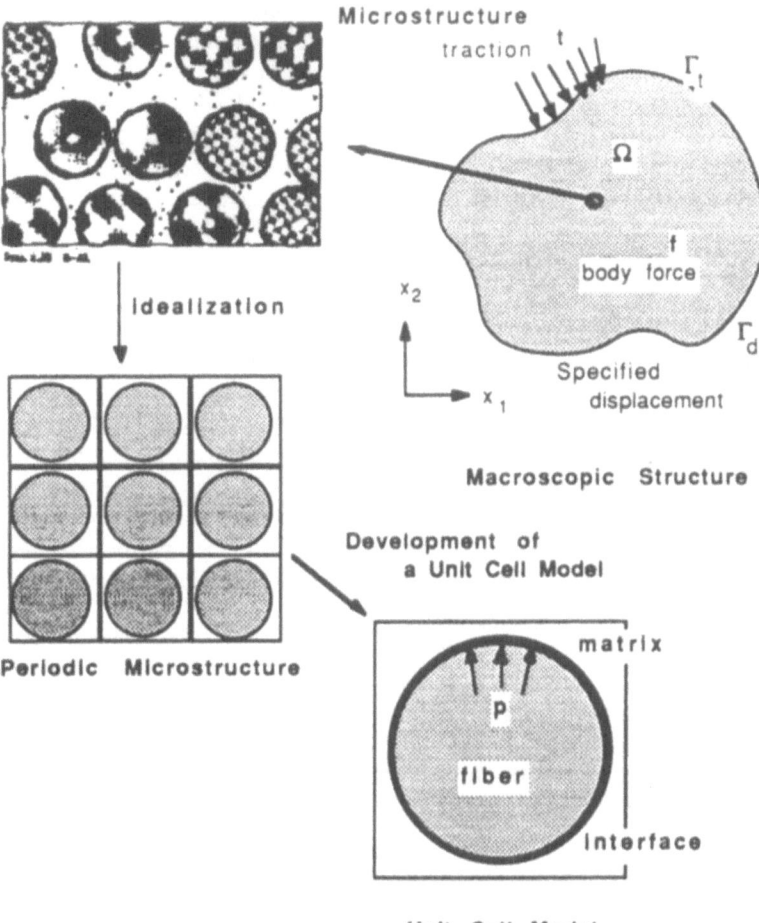

Fig. 2.11. Macroscopic domain, the microstructure, idealization, and a unit cell model

applicable along the interface of two different materials in order to simulate the situation of a partial debonding (i.e., failure) of the interface. Since the material properties may change in the vicinity of the interface, we should have the capability for modelling such a layer. Furthermore, if the failure process of the interface is of interest, such a modeling capability becomes important.

From the global viewpoint, the composite material presents a high degree of heterogeneity. These heterogeneities have to be taken into account if this problem is to be solved either analytically or numerically. As is well known, analytical solutions, when existing, are usually restricted to a particular set of geometries that quite often lack the generality necessary for practical applications. On the other hand, when attempting to use numerical methods, to fully characterize these heterogeneities by, say, a finite element procedure would be almost impossible. Therefore, the natural way of overcoming this difficulty is to, somehow, evaluate some equivalent material properties of the composite material that represent its overall behavior but would not contain heterogeneities. A possible method to obtain this equivalent material, making the assumption of spatial repetition of Y (Y-periodicity), is to use the homogenization method. Moreover, this method will also provide the first approximation of the local response of Ω, i.e, the solution in the unit cell Y so that stresses and strains can be computed, even in a microstructure which is non-averaged. This feature turns out to be extremely useful in order to analyze the microscopic behavior of composite materials, and it provides a tool that can help in the study and understanding of the effects that can trigger local degradation of composite materials.

Mathematical Procedure of the Homogenization Method. Let Ω be an open subset of the three-dimensional space R^3 with a smooth, say, Lipschitz, boundary Γ, and let Y be an open rectangular parallelepiped in R^3 (see Fig. 2.11) defined by $Y =]0, y_1^0[\times]0, y_2^0[\times]0, y_3^0[$, let ϑ be an open subset of Y with the boundary $\partial\vartheta = S$, and let $\mathbf{Y} = Y \backslash \bar{\vartheta}$, where $\mathbf{Y}$ is the solid part of the cell, $\bar{\vartheta}$ denotes the closure of ϑ, and Y represents the base cell of the composite microstructure. If one defines $\Theta(\mathbf{y}) = 1$ if $\mathbf{y} \in \mathbf{Y}$ and $= 0$ if $\mathbf{y} \notin \mathbf{Y}$, and extend Θ to R^3 by ε periodicity, i.e., repeat the base cell in all the three directions, the solid part of the domain of the composite material is characterized by, $\Omega^\varepsilon = \left\{ \mathbf{x} \in \Omega : \Theta\left(\dfrac{\mathbf{x}}{\varepsilon}\right) = 1 \right\}$. Also define $S^\varepsilon = \overset{\text{all cells}}{\underset{\alpha=1}{\bigcup}} S_\alpha$, and consider the following hypothesis: (1) Ω^ε is a connected domain, (2) the hole(s) ϑ has sufficiently smooth boundary(ies) S, and (3) none of the holes S intersect the boundary Γ of Ω. Now let V^ε be the space of all admissible displacements satisfying the essential boundary condition $\mathbf{v}|_{\Gamma_d} = \mathbf{0}$, where $\mathbf{v}|_{\Gamma_d}$ represents the value of $\mathbf{v}$ on the boundary Γ_d. Then, the problem of the deformation of a body Ω^ε subjected to body forces $\mathbf{f}$ and tractions $\mathbf{t}$ on the boundary Γ_t together with tractions $\mathbf{p}$ inside the holes S, and prescirbed displacement on Γ_d (with $\Gamma = \Gamma_t \cup \Gamma_d, \Gamma_t \cap \Gamma_d = \varnothing, \dot{\Gamma}_d \cap S^\varepsilon = \varnothing, \Gamma_t \cap S^\varepsilon = \varnothing$), can be stated by using the principle of virtual displacement as:

$$u_i = g_i \qquad \text{on } \Gamma_d$$

and

$$\sum_{i,j,k,l=1}^{2 \text{ or } 3} \int_{\Omega^\varepsilon} E_{ijkl}^\varepsilon \frac{\partial u_k^\varepsilon}{\partial x_l} \frac{\partial v_i}{\partial x_j} d\Omega^\varepsilon = \sum_{i=1}^{2 \text{ or } 3} \int_{\Omega^\varepsilon} f_i^\varepsilon v_i \, d\Omega^\varepsilon + \int_{\Gamma_t} t_i v_i \, d\Gamma + \int_{S^\varepsilon} p_i^\varepsilon v_i \, dS^\varepsilon$$

$$\text{for } v \text{ s.t. } v_i = 0 \text{ on } \Gamma_d$$

Here, it is assumed that

Strain – displacemnt relation

$$\varepsilon_{ij}^\varepsilon = \frac{1}{2}\left(\frac{\partial u_i^\varepsilon}{\partial x_j} + \frac{\partial u_j^\varepsilon}{\partial x_i}\right)$$

Stress – strain relation

$$\sigma_{ij}^\varepsilon = \sum_{k,l=1}^{2 \text{ or } 3} E_{ijkl}^\varepsilon \varepsilon_{kl}^\varepsilon$$

Elasticity tensor

$$E^\varepsilon_{ijkl} = E^\varepsilon_{jikl} = E^\varepsilon_{ijlk} = E^\varepsilon_{klij}$$

$$\exists\alpha > 0 \ s.t. \ \sum_{i,j,k,l=1}^{2 \ or \ 3} E^\varepsilon_{ijkl} X_{kl} X_{ij} \geq \alpha \sum_{i,j=1}^{2 \ or \ 3} X_{ij} X_{ij}, \qquad \forall X_{ij} = X_{ji}$$

The superscript ε is used to indicate dependence on the microstructure, i.e., the unit cell.

Since the body forces $\mathbf{f}$, the tractions $\mathbf{p}$, and the elastic constants vary within a microscale cell of the composite, i.e., they are functions of both $\mathbf{x}$ and $\mathbf{y} = \dfrac{\mathbf{x}}{\varepsilon}$, the solution $\mathbf{u}_\varepsilon$ should also depend both on $\mathbf{x}$ and $\dfrac{\mathbf{x}}{\varepsilon}$, that is, $\mathbf{u}_\varepsilon(\mathbf{x}) = \mathbf{u}_\varepsilon(\mathbf{x}, \mathbf{y}), \mathbf{y} = \dfrac{\mathbf{x}}{\varepsilon}$. The dependence of the solution $\mathbf{u}^\varepsilon$ in the macroscopic and microscopic levels makes it reasonable to assume that $\mathbf{u}^\varepsilon$ can be expressed as an asymptotic expansion with respect to the parameter ε (a measure of the microscopic/macroscopic dimension ratio), i.e.,

$$\mathbf{u}^\varepsilon(\mathbf{x}) = \mathbf{u}^0(\mathbf{x}, \mathbf{y}) + \varepsilon\mathbf{u}^1(\mathbf{x}, \mathbf{y}) + \varepsilon^2\mathbf{u}^2(\mathbf{x}, \mathbf{y}) + \cdots, \mathbf{y} = \dfrac{\mathbf{x}}{\varepsilon}$$

where $\mathbf{u}^j(\mathbf{x}, \mathbf{y})$ is defined in $(\mathbf{x}, \mathbf{y}) \in \Omega \times \mathbf{Y}$ and $\mathbf{y} \to \mathbf{u}^j(\mathbf{x}, \mathbf{y})$ is $Y-$ periodic. Note that for a Y-periodic function $\Psi(\mathbf{y})$,

$$\frac{\partial}{\partial x_i}\Phi\left(x, y = \frac{x}{\varepsilon}\right) = \frac{\partial\Phi}{\partial x_i} + \frac{1}{\varepsilon}\frac{\partial\Phi}{\partial y_i}$$

$$\lim_{\varepsilon \to 0^+} \int_{\Omega^\varepsilon} \Psi\left(\frac{x}{\varepsilon}\right) d\Omega = \frac{1}{|Y|}\int_\Omega \int_Y \Psi(y)\, dY\, d\Omega$$

$$\lim_{\varepsilon \to 0^+} \varepsilon \int_{S^\varepsilon} \Psi\left(\frac{x}{\varepsilon}\right) d\Omega = \frac{1}{|Y|}\int_\Omega \int_S \Psi(y)\, dS\, d\Omega$$

where $|Y|$ stands for the volume (or area, for a two-dimensional domain), of the cell. Introducing the expansion into the principle of virtual displacement, considering the terms associated with the different powers of ε, choosing properly the function v, and taking the limits when $\varepsilon \to 0^+$, one can show that

1. $\mathbf{u}^0$ is only a function of $\mathbf{x}$, i.e., $\mathbf{u}^0 = \mathbf{u}^0(\mathbf{x})$
2. $\mathbf{u}^1$ is the solution of the following local problem in the unit cell:

$$\sum_{i,j,k,l=1}^{2 \ or \ 3} \int_\mathbf{Y} E_{ijkl}\left(\frac{\partial u^0_k}{\partial x_l} + \frac{\partial u^1_k}{\partial y_l}\right)\frac{\partial v_i}{\partial y_j} d\mathbf{Y} = \sum_{i=1}^{2 \ or \ 3} \int_S p_i v_i\, dS \qquad for \ \forall v \in V_\mathbf{Y}$$

where x is considered as a parameter and $V_\mathbf{Y} = \{v \text{ smooth enough}, v \text{ is } Y\text{-periodic}\}$
3. $\mathbf{p}$, the applied traction inside the holes S, has to be self-equilibrating:

$$\int_S p_i(x, y)\, dS = 0 \qquad for \ i = 1, 2, 3$$

and the moments in each cell due to $\mathbf{p}$ have also to be zero.

4. u^0 is then the solution of the global problem in the macroscopic scale structure:

$$\sum_{i,j,k,l=1}^{2\ or\ 3} \int_\Omega \left[\frac{1}{|Y|} \int_Y E_{ijkl} \left(\frac{\partial u_k^0(x)}{\partial x_l} + \frac{\partial u_k^1}{\partial y_l} \right) d Y \right] \frac{\partial v_i}{\partial x_j} d\Omega$$

$$= \sum_{i=1}^{2\ or\ 3} \int_\Omega \left(\frac{1}{|Y|} \int_Y f_i\, d Y \right) v_i\, d\Omega + \int_{\Gamma_i} t_i v_i\, d\Gamma \qquad \forall v \in V_\Omega$$

where $V_\Omega = \{v(x)$ defined in $\Omega;\ v|_{\Gamma_a} = 0;\ v$ smooth enough$\}$

5. Similarly, equations for the higher-order terms of the expansion in ε could be derived. However, the first two terms of the expansion are sufficient to obtain the information necessary for our study.

Consequence of the Perturbation Analysis. Noting that the equation for the microscopic problem in u^1 is linear, and that x is considered as a parameter, we define the characteristic deformations χ^{kl} and the residual stress ψ which can reflect the microstructure of composite materials by the solutions of the following problem defined on the unit cell Y:

$$\sum_{i,j,m,n=1}^{2\ or\ 3} \int_Y E_{ijmn} \frac{\partial \chi_m^{kl}}{\partial y_n} \frac{\partial v_i}{\partial y_j} d Y = \sum_{i,j=1}^{2\ or\ 3} \int_Y E_{ijkl} \frac{\partial v_i}{\partial y_j} d Y \qquad \forall v \in V_Y$$

and

$$\sum_{i,j,k,l=1}^{2\ or\ 3} \bigg|_Y E_{ijkl} \frac{\partial \psi_k}{\partial y_l} \frac{\partial v_i}{\partial y_j} d Y = \sum_{i=1}^{2\ or\ 3} \int_S p_i v_i\, dS \qquad \forall v \in V_Y.$$

Using the characteristic deformations and the residual stress in the unit cell, the solution u^1 of the problem in the unit cell can be written as

$$u_i^1(x, y) = -\sum_{k,l=1}^{2\ or\ 3} \chi_i^{kl}(x, y) \frac{\partial u_k^0}{\partial x_l} - \psi_i(x, y) \qquad i = 1, 2, 3$$

within arbitrary additive constants in y. The introduction of this result yields the following global equilibrium equation for the macroscopic structure:

$$\sum_{i,j,k,l=1}^{2\ or\ 3} \int_\Omega D_{ijkl} \frac{\partial u_k^0}{\partial x_l} \frac{\partial v_i}{\partial x_j} d\Omega = \sum_{i,j=1}^{2\ or\ 3} \int_\Omega \tau_{ij} \frac{\partial v_i}{\partial x_j} d\Omega + \sum_{i=1}^{2\ or\ 3} \int_\Omega b_i v_i\, d\Omega + \int_{\Gamma_i} t_i v_i\, d\Gamma$$

Here

Homogenized elasticity tensor

$$D_{ijkl}(x) = \frac{1}{|Y|} \sum_{m,n=1}^{2\ or\ 3} \int_Y \left(E_{ijkl}(x, y) - E_{ijmn}(x, y) \frac{\partial \chi_m^{kl}}{\partial y_n} \right) dY$$

Homogenized residual stress

$$\tau_{ij}(x) = \frac{1}{|Y|} \sum_{k,l=1}^{2\ or\ 3} \int_Y E_{ijkl}(x, y) \frac{\partial \psi_k}{\partial y_l} dY$$

Homogenized body force

$$b_i(x) = \frac{1}{|Y|} \int_Y f_i \, dY$$

It is noted that the macroscopic homogenized constitutive relations for composite materials can be determined by the characteristic deformations and the residual stresses computed in the unit cell, independently of the homogenized macroscopic problem, because of the linearity of the problem considered. If nonlinear material characterization, such as elastic-plasticity, is considered, these problems would be coupled. That is, the homogenized material constants cannot be determined without knowing the stress fields of the macroscopic structure. However, if linearity is assumed, these can be decoupled, and the homogenized constitutive equations are determined in the unit cell. Indeed, the homogenized constitutive relations are given by

$$\sigma_{ij}^H(x) = \sum_{k,l=1}^{2 \text{ or } 3} D_{ijkl}(x) \varepsilon_{kl}^0(x) - \tau_{ij}(x) \qquad \text{for } i, j = 1, 2, 3$$

As shown previously, the homogenized elasticity tensor $\mathbb{D}$ is *not the simple average* of the elasticity tensors of composite constitutents with respect to their volume ratios. It is clear that the homogenized elasticity tensor $\mathbb{D}$ has a strong contribution from the microstructure through the characteristic deformation χ defined in the unit cell. Because of the traction $\mathbf{p}$ assumed in the microstructure, the initial stress τ appears in the homogenized constitutive equations. Furthermore, the displacement and stress fields are evaluated at every point of a composite material as follows:

$$u_i^\varepsilon(x) = u_i^0(x) - \varepsilon \left(\sum_{k,l=1}^{2 \text{ or } 3} \chi_i^{kl}(x, y) \frac{\partial u_k^0}{\partial x_l} + \psi_i(x, y) \right) + o(\varepsilon^2)$$

and

$$\sigma_{ij}^\varepsilon(x) = \sum_{k,l=1}^{2 \text{ or } 3} \left(E_{ijkl}(x, y) - \sum_{m,n=1}^{2 \text{ or } 3} E_{ijmn}(x, y) \frac{\partial \chi_m^{kl}}{\partial y_n}(x, y) \right) \frac{\partial u_k^0}{\partial x_l}(x)$$
$$- \sum_{k,l=3}^{2 \text{ or } 3} E_{ijkl}(x, y) \frac{\partial \psi_k}{\partial x_l}(x, y) + o(\varepsilon)$$

Using the characteristic deformations and the residual stress in the unit cell, the stress fields are computed for everywhere that is not averaged over a certain volume. We can extract precise pointwise information and can evaluate the stress fields both in the matrix and in any fibers, whiskers, or inclusions. Therefore, in order to study failure of composite materials, it may not be necessary to determine the failure function using the averaged stress fields over a certain volume. If averaged values are used for the failure function, we have to conduct a large number of experiments to determine the form of the failure function for each individual composite material. However, if the homogenization method is applied, the stress fields are computed at every point. Thus, if the failure function is known for each constituent and for each interface of composite materials, it becomes possible to predict whether a failure will occur in the matrix, fibers, or their interface. This feature of the homo-genization method should be recognized.

Application of Parallel-Processing Algorithms. If there is only one microstructure to be considered in a structure to be analyzed, it may not be necessary to introduce a special hierarchical parallel algorithm to exploit the advantage of many parallel processors. Vectorization and standard parallelization for do loops can save a large amount of computing time, but if several portions of a program can be executed separately, such independence should be utilized by introducing a hierarchical parallel algorithm. In fact, if several different microstructures are involved in the analysis, such a hierarchical parallel algorithm can be easily implemented in a program for the homogenization method, since the cell problem is independently defined in each microstructure while the homogenized elasticity tensor is computed using all of the characteristic deformations of all the microstructures.

Extension to Nonlinear Composites. Although in most studies in mathematics the homogenization theory is restricted linear problems, it can formally extend to large-deformation large-strain nonlinear mechanics of composites. We have obtained this extension for the case of elastic-plasticity. If nonlinearity is involved, the problem in the microstructure is not independent of the stress fields in the macrostructure at all. In other words, they are highly coupled. This means that the homogenized tensor characterizing material behavior cannot be computed as it can for linear problems. Furthermore, the homogenized tensor is obtained by using quite a large number of samples of different microstructures. Therefore, we have the following special parallel structure in this nonlinear homogenization method:

1. Coupling of the macro and microstructures
2. Stress analysis of the macrostructure
3. Characteristic deformations for the microstructures
   Sampling point 1, Sampling Point 2, ..., Sampling Point N

This structure again suggests that a hierarchical parallel algorithm may be intro-duced to develop an efficient computer program. To emphasize this necessity, we

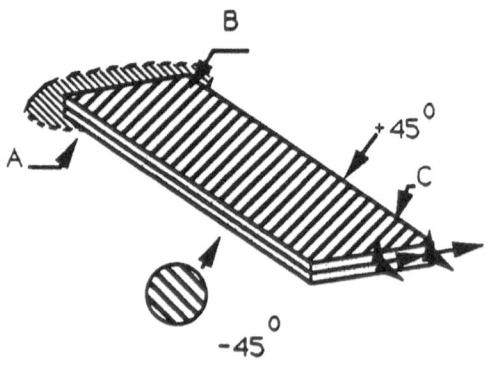

Fig. 2.12a. A fiber reinforced laminate. (From [16] with permission)

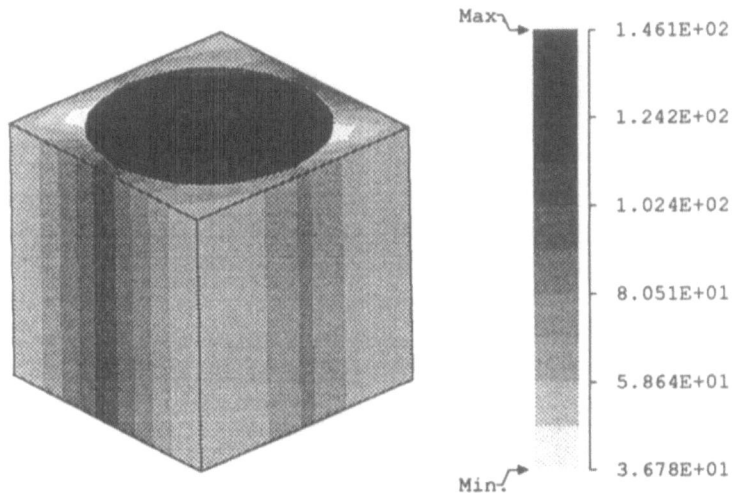

Max ↘

	1.461E+02
	1.242E+02
	1.024E+02
	8.051E+01
	5.864E+01

Min ↗   3.678E+01

*Fig. 2.12*b. Stress distribution in the microstructure at A

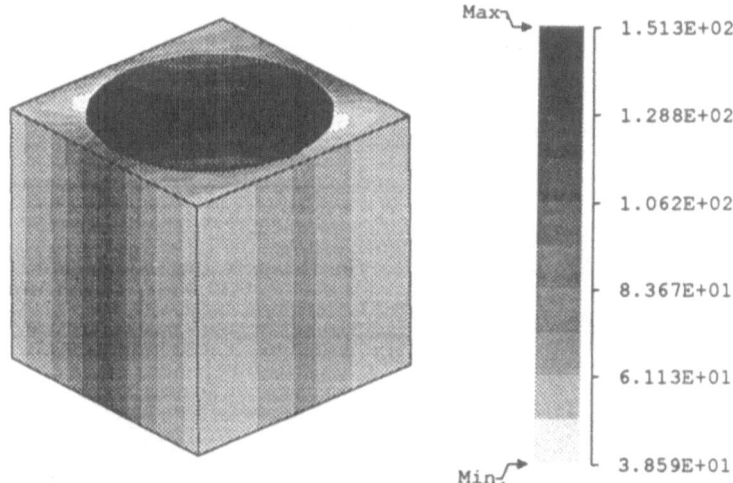

Max ↘

	1.513E+02
	1.288E+02
	1.062E+02
	8.367E+01
	6.113E+01

Min ↗   3.859E+01

*Fig. 2.12*c. Stress distribution in the microstructure at B

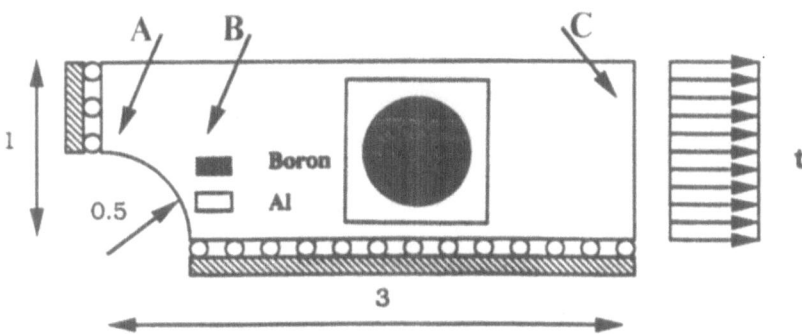

*Fig. 2.12*d. A notched composite plate subject to a large tensile stress. (From [16] with permission)

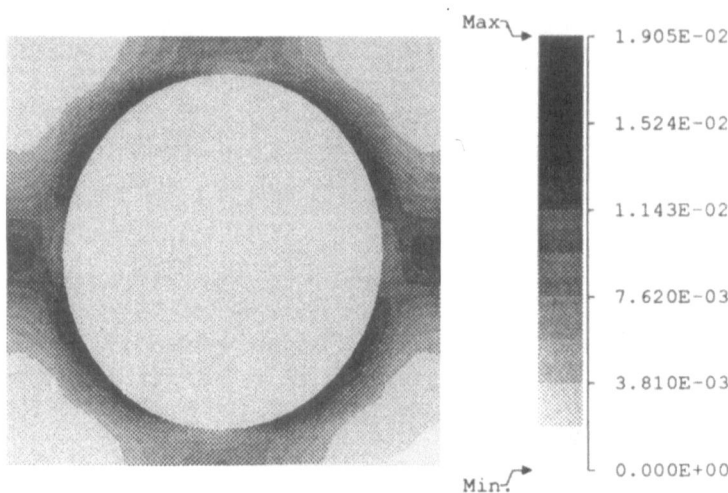

Max ⌐ 1.905E-02

1.524E-02

1.143E-02

7.620E-03

3.810E-03

Min ⌐ 0.000E+00

*Fig. 2.12*e. Accumulated plastic strain in the microstructure at point A

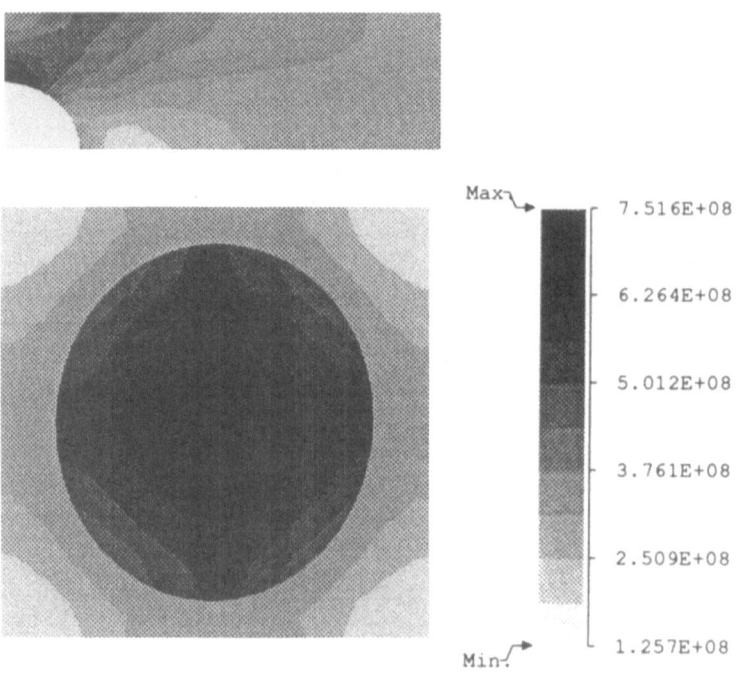

Max ⌐ 7.516E+08

6.264E+08

5.012E+08

3.761E+08

2.509E+08

Min ⌐ 1.257E+08

*Fig. 2.12*f. Accumulated mises stress in the microstructure at point A. (From [16] with permission)

shall note that the result shown in the following was obtained after 6 hours' execution of the APOLLO DN3500. Here 352 degrees of freedom were introduced for the macroscopic problem while 642 degrees of freedom were used for each microstructure. Fifteen sampling points of the microstructure were assumed. Only ten increments were taken to reach to the final loading stage because of limited computing resources. There, the possibility of elastic-plasticity was assumed both for matrix and fibers. It is clear that the degrees of freedom in the present example both for the microstructure and microstructure are far from those that would yield sufficiently accurate finite element approximations.

2.7 Shape and Topology Optimization for Elastic Structures

Structural optimization has recently received wide-ranging attention in computer-aided design. One reason is the rapid development of sophisticated but inexpensive engineering workstations with graphics capabilities, multi-windows, and high-speed computation. The other reason is the acceptance of various computer-aided engineering systems including reliable analysis capabilities such as finite element, finite difference, and boundary element methods which are supported by geometric modeling capability employing automatic mesh generation methods. The notion of structural optimization was widely discussed by structural engineers in the early 1970s right after the rapid development of finite element methods. However, it could not provide the practical means to design structures except in aeronautical engineering, because of the lack of flexible geometric modeling and handy interactive graphics display capabilities at that time. Since most of the structural design of machine parts involves heavily their geometric representation, in other words, their shape, structural design must deal with shape optimization, while most aeronautical applications are based on frame structures with shell reinforcements which need only the concept of sizing optimization – dealing with, for example, the sizes of the cross sections of frames as well as the thickness of shells. It is clear that geometric representation of the structural configuration is not required in sizing optimization, and thus, its development may not be bounded by the capability of geometric modeling.

2.7.1 Brief Review of Present Research

A modern theory of structural optimization based on mathematical programming and sensitivity analysis was developed by Schmit and Fox in the early 1960s, although the concept of fully stressed design was widely applied in design practice without solid mathematical justification but with engineers' intuition. Prager and Taylor produced a justification of the fully stressed design for a class of structural optimization problems by deriving their optimality criteria, whose direct use in constructing optimization algorithms lead to the so-called optimality criteria method in contrast to the mathematical programming method, using variational methods such as Lagrange multipliers and calculus of variations. Structural optimization in the 1960s was restricted mostly to sizing problems of frame structures, despite the fact that layout problems were also solved by Prager [33] for a very restricted class of structures as an extension of the concept of Michell trusses [34]. A layout problem may be formulated by finding the best possible layout of frames in a design domain, to transmit applied forces to given supports by minimizing an objective function while design constraints are satisfied. In general, the size of the cross section of frames is fixed in layout problems, while the location of joints and the length of frames are design variables. On the other hand, the sizes of cross sections become design variables in sizing problems, while the location of joints and the length of frames are fixed. There have been few computational works using finite element methods related to layout problems. Most layout problems of frames have been solved analytically based on Prager's approach. Thus, the range of area covered is necessarily very restricted.

Sizing problems for static frames can be solved straightforwardly at present by using sensitivity analysis and an appropriate mathematical programming method for optimization, since a strong tie to geometric modeling with automatic mesh generation is not required when finite element methods are applied to obtain displacements and stresses. For the fixed geometry, i.e., for the fixed nodal location and element connectivity, finite element analysis must be performed repeatedly only by varying the cross-sectional properties of frames to reach the optimum. Thus, research on sizing problems has been concentrated on optimization algorithms and methods to compute sensitivity; see, for example, Fleury [35].

Shape optimization problems were solved by Zienkiewicz and Campbell [36] in 1973, and extensive works have been published since then. Details of such publications are well surveyed in Haftka and Gandhi [37]. The difficulty of shape problems arises from the fact that the geometry of a structure is the design variable. This means that a finite element model associated with a structure must be changed in a process of optimization. If such change is sufficiently small, the problem can be solved easily by applying sensitivity analysis and an appropriate optimization method, since such a change of the location of control points of the boundary shape or nodal points on the design boundary can be proportionally transferred to internal nodes of the finite element model so that the convexity of each finite element is well preserved. However, if a design change becomes large, it becomes difficult to vary the finite element model without introducing excessively distorted elements which imply large amount of approximation error in the computation of stress. Generating well "designed" finite element models by varying the location of nodal points is, in general, a too demanding task if an automatic remeshing capability is not embedded in a shape optimization program. In this sense, as we mentioned before, the approach taken by Botkin and Bennett is a natural choice; that is, an automatic mesh generation method is combined with the shape optimization program in order to deal with any amount of design change despite additional cost in computation.

Most shape optimization problems are restricted to the case that topology of the design domain is maintained in an optimization process. In other words, the initial topology of a structure is same as the final one. However, there are many cases in which internal holes can be introduced to reduce the weight of a structure without violating design constraints. Automatic generation of holes in a design domain is, at this moment, impossible, even though automatic remeshing capabilities are embedded, because such capabilities cannot yet manage automatic topological change of the domain. Thus, if the topology of the design domain is to be changed to make internal holes, it is necessary to terminate the optimization process and then to restart after modifying the finite element model by generating holes. This means that varying the shape of the domain is insufficient for optimization involving topology. To overcome this limitation, an intuitive approach may be considered using a "fixed" finite element model in which less-stressed finite elements are assigned artificially as very soft material so that holes can be approximately realized. This approach, however, possesses difficulties which need to be accounted for. For example, algorithms to identify less-stressed elements which are "removed" from the design are not uniquely defined, and their convergence may strongly depend on the finite element models applied. That is, there is too much ambiguity in this intuitive approach. To sophisticate this naive idea, Bendsoe and Kikuchi [38] introduced a homogenization method that utilizes infinitely many microscale holes in a design domain rather than removing the whole of a finite element.

By solving these various problems, it is shown that the present method can solve not only shape optimization problems but also topology optimization problems for a linearly elastic structure using a fixed finite element model. In other words, layout problems in a generalized sense can be solved computationally for any type of linearly elastic structure.

2.7.2 Generalized Layout Problem by the Homogenization Method

As already mentioned, the main idea of solving a class of shape optimization problems involving varying topology, which is called a generalized layout problem, is that infinitely many microscale voids (holes) are introduced to form a possibly porous medium that yields a linearly elastic structure in some sense [39]. An optimization problem for the generalized layout problem is defined by solving the optimal porosity of the medium identified with a design domain. If a portion of porous medium consists of only voids, structure is not placed over that region. On the other hand, if no porosity is realized at another portion, "solid" structure must be placed there. If porosity is not at the lower limit value, a porous medium is generated. In this sense, "solid" material consisting of a structure is optimally distributed in a specified region so that a certain objective function is minimized under a set of constraints.

Suppose that the volume of microscale voids is specified in a given design domain Ω; that is, the volume Ω_s of "solid" material distributed in the design domain is specified. For simplicity, the design domain is planar so that plane stress analysis is sufficient to compute displacements and stresses, while the shape of microscale voids is assumed to be rectangular as shown in Fig. 2.13.

Rectangular holes are chosen because they can realize the complete void ($a = b = 1$) and solid ($a = b = 0$) as well as a generalized porous medium ($0 < a < 1, 0 < b < 1$). Since holes are rectangular in the unit cell that characterizes the microstructure of a generalized porous medium for the layout problem, their orientation is important in the macroscopic problem for stress analysis. Indeed, the anisotropic elasticity tensor in the macroscopic problem strongly depends on the orientation of microscale holes. Thus, the sizes a and b and the orientation θ of microscale rectangular holes are the design variables of the generalized layout problem.

Suppose that a, b, and θ are functions of the position $\mathbf{x}$ of an arbitrary point of a macroscale domain of a linearly elastic "porous" structure Ω in the two-dimensional Euclidean space $\mathbb{R}^2$: $a = a(\mathbf{x})$, $b = b(\mathbf{x})$, and $\theta = \theta(\mathbf{x})$. Functions a, b, and θ may not be so smooth, i.e., it could be true that $a \in L^\infty(\Omega)$, $b \in L^\infty(\Omega)$, and θ maintains smoothness equivalent to the angle θ_p of the principal coordinates of the stress tensor $\sigma(\mathbf{x})$, i.e., θ may be continuous in Ω except for a finite number of points. However, we shall assume that they are sufficiently smooth, for example, $a, b, \theta \in H^1(\Omega)$. Assuming that a periodic microstructure characterized by $a(\mathbf{x})$, $b(\mathbf{x})$, and $\theta(\mathbf{x})$ exists in a small neighborhood of an arbitrary point $\mathbf{x}$ in Ω, and assuming that such a microstructure at $\mathbf{x}$ need not be the same as one at a different point $\mathbf{x}^*$ (see Fig. 2.14 which shows a schematic setting of varying microstructures) a homogenized elasticity tensor $\mathbb{E}^H(\mathbf{x})$ is computed in order to solve a macroscopic stress analysis problem for a "porous" structure.

The homogenized elasticity tensor is computed by solving the homogenization problem defined in the unit cell in which a rectangular hole is placed. Since the sizes $\{a, b\}$ of rectangular holes are functions of the position $\mathbf{x}$, the homogenized elasticity tensor $\mathbb{E}^H$ varies in Ω. This means that the characteristic deformations must be obtained everywhere in the design domain Ω. Solving the unit cell problem for every cell is unrealistic. Thus, we shall solve it for several sampling points $\{a_i, b_j: i, j = 1, \ldots, n\}$ of the sizes $\{a, b\}$ of rectangular holes, where $0 \le a_i \le 1$ and

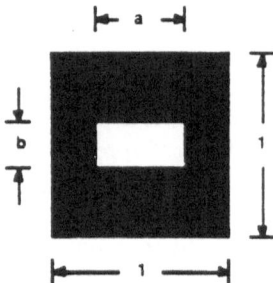

Fig. 2.13. Design variables in the microstructure

Fig. 2.14. A schematic description of a continuously perforated plate

$0 \le b_j \le 1$, and we shall form a function $\mathbb{E}^H = \mathbb{E}^H(a, b)$ by an appropriate interpolation. The last step for the elasticity tensor $\mathbb{E}^G$ for stress analysis of the macroscopic "porous" structure is the rotation of $\mathbb{E}^H$ by the angle θ. It is clear that $\mathbb{E}^G$ is a function of the sizes $\{a, b\}$ and the rotation θ of microscale rectangular holes.

Now, let us define an optimization problem for the generalized layout that involves the shape and topology of a structure. Since the purpose of the present section is the examination of the homogenization method, we shall define the problem using the simplest objective function, the mean compliance of the structure, without any other side constraints:

$$\underset{\substack{a, b, \text{ and } \theta \\ subject\ to \\ equilibrium\ equations \\ and \\ \int_\Omega (1-ab)\,d\Omega \le \Omega_s}}{Minimize} \quad \sum_{i=1}^{2} \int_\Omega f_i u_i \, d\Omega + \sum_{i=1}^{2} \int_{\Gamma_T} t_i u_i \, d\Gamma$$

Here $\mathbf{u}$ is the solution of the principle of virtual displacement, and Ω_s is the total volume of "solid" material forming the "porous" structure. In general, Ω_s is smaller than Ω, that is, the domain of the structure containing the design domain Ω_d, i.e., $\Omega_s < \Omega_d$. It is noted that the design variables a and b are restricted by $0 \le \alpha(x)$, $\beta(x) \le 1$. As shown in the following, if there is a sufficient amount of "solid" material, the optimal structure is singly connected without having holes.

Example. Consider a "triangular" design domain as shown in Fig. 2.15. Applying the symmetry condition, only 1/6 of the design domain is modeled by the finite element method. The boundary condition and physical dimensions are specified. The domain is made discrete by 40 × 40 meshes which are not orthogonal. Using this example, we shall examine the transition from the shape optimization to the topology optimization that forms more or less truss-like structures. To do this, the volume of "solid" material is varied in a wide range from 50 cm² to 180 cm², while the area of the 1/6 of the original domain is inside of the domain. The shape obtained is very smooth, and of almost same quality as the one obtained by the boundary

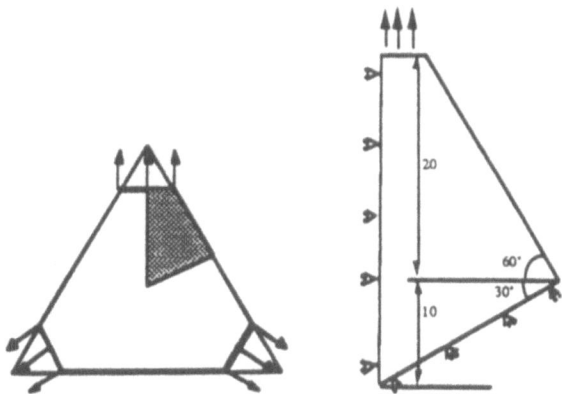

Fig. 2.15. A shape design problem of a triangular thin plate

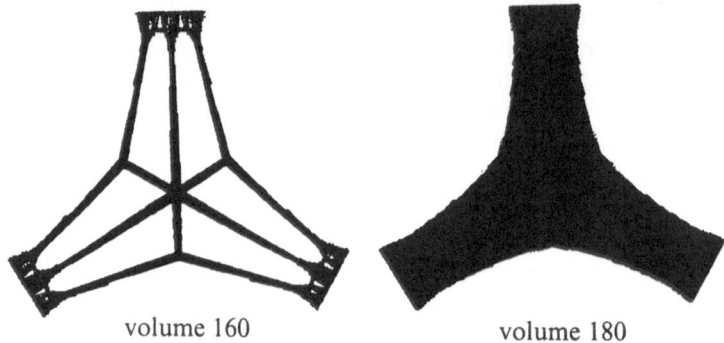

volume 160   volume 180

Fig. 2.16. Optimized layouts of a structure with different material volume

variation method which is traditionally applied to solve the shape optimization problem. When the amount of "solid" material volume is reduced, holes start appearing in the interior of the domain. It is also noted that the loading portion becomes porous when the amount of "solid" material is really small in order to disperse the applied traction uniformly in all directions, while the three compressed link bars in the 30°, 150°, and 270° directions, are also porous. Thus, if these porous bars are replaced by solid bars maintaining the "solid" material volume, the size of bars becomes very small. Thin solid bars, which are under tension, are allocated in the 90°, 210°, and 330° directions in the optimal structure. The otuer frames are completely solid.

Necessity of High-Speed Computing. The result shown in Fig. 2.16 was obtained by the SUN 3/60 after a 5-hour execution, while if the CRAY 2 was used, it could be computed within 5 minutes. The problem involves 3,362 degrees of freedom for stress analysis, and 4,800 design variables for the optimization. We have developed the same capability for three-dimensional shell structures. In this case, if the discretion of the same finite element is assumed, 10,086 degrees of freedom are generated for stress analysis while 9,600 design variables define the optimization problem. Until this level, we can manage using our existing computing capability. However, if the full three-dimensional extension is considered (in fact, we have developed a program already, but it is too expensive to execute for a decent discretization model) with $40 \times 40 \times 40$ meshes, 413,526 degrees of freedom must be introduced for stress analysis while 384,000 design variables define the optimization problem. This is, at this moment, unrealistic!

2.8 Concluding Remarks

It is evident that high-speed computing capability opens the way to development of an adaptive finite element method that can control the amount of approximation error without any additional human interface. Even for linear problems, this method requires several iterations to reach the level of accuracy we desire, because of the error estimation for the adaptation of the finite element model initially set up. This means that in order to be realistic in practical application, it is necessary to reduce the necessary computing time as much as possible. This article gave a general indication of how to use vector/parallel processing, with an example on impact problems of solids and structures. Since we have to extensively modify programming methods to utilize these new devices and since the rapid development of software for computational linear algebra, the teaching contents and methods must be also modified for courses covering finite element methods. Furthermore, because of the capability of the computers we have now, new subjects in computational mechanics can be explored. These increased capabilities have allowed the recent development of computational mechanics for composite materials, or more generally, for material science, as well as the solution of generalized layout problems of structural design by very different ways from those existing. These developments are only possible under the high-speed computing environment. As stated in Sect. 2.7, the present capability is not sufficient to solve design problems of structures in three-dimensional space. Definitely, much faster and much larger computers are required, but they must be inexpensive. The computer is not special any more.

Acknowledgments. The authors are supported by ONR, N-00014-88-K-0637, NASA Lewis Research Center, NAG 3-661, RTB Corporation, Ann Arbor, and Quint Corp., Tokyo. They sincerely appreciate this support.

References

1. Argyris JH, Patton PC (1966) Computer-oriented research in a university milieu. Appl Mech Rev 19: 1029–1039
2. Smarr L (1988) The computational science revolution: technology, methodology, and sociology. In: Wilhelmson RB (ed) High-speed computing: scientific applications and algorithm design. University of Illinois Press, Urbana Chicago, pp 12–33
3. Argyris JH (1970) The impact of the digital computer on engineering sciences. Parts I and II, Aeronautical J Aeronautical Soc, pp 13–41, 111–127
4. Bruner M, Gordon A, Vonk B (1989) Computer aided engineering network. College of Engineering, University of Michigan
5. Moler C, Herskovitz S, Little L, Bangert S. MATLAB, The Math Works, Inc., 20 North Main St, Suite 250, Sherborn, MA 01770, USA, phone (617) 653-1215; E-mail: na.mathworks@score.stanford.edu
6. Babuska I, Rheinboldt WC (1978) Error estimates for adaptive finite element computations. SIAM J Numer Anal 15: 736–754
7. Bank RE (1984) Locally computed error estimates for elliptic equations. Proceedings international conference on accuracy estimates and adaptive refinements in finite element computations. Arantes e Oliveira ER et al. (eds) Lisbon, Portugal, Vol 1 pp 21–30
8. Clough RW (1965) The finite element method in structural mechanics. In: Zienkiewicz OC, Holister GS (eds) Stress analysis. Wiley
9. Oden JT (1989) Progress in adaptive methods in computational fluid dynamics. In: Flaherty JE et al. (eds) Adaptive methods for partial differential equations. SIAM, Philadelphia

10. Peraire J, Vahdati M, Morgan K, Zienkiewicz OC (1987) Adaptive remeshing for compressible flow computations. J Comput Phys 72: 449–463
11. Zienkiewicz OC, Zhu JZ, Liu YC, Morgan K, Peraire J (1988) Error estimates and adaptivity from elasticity to high-speed compressible flow. In: Whiteman JR (ed) MAFELAP IV. Academic, London, pp 483–512
12. Zienkiewicz OC, Huang GC (1989) Adaptive modelling of transient coupled metal forming processes. In: Thompson EG et al. (eds) NUMIFORM89 Numerical methods in industrial forming processes. Balkema, Rotterdam, pp 3–10
13. Tezuka A, Kikuchi N (1989) H-adaptation in finite element analysis with global mesh refinement. Report 89-4, Department of Mechanical Engineering and Applied Mechanics, University of Michigan, Ann Arbor
14. Bennett JA, Botkin ME (1985) Structural shape optimization with geometric problem description and adaptive mesh refinement. AIAA J 23: 458–464
15. Bachmann PL, Wittchen SL, Shephard MS, Grice KR, Yerry MA (1987) Robust geometrically based automatic two-dimensional mesh generation. Int J Numer Methods Eng 24: 1043–1078
16. Shephard MS, Niù Q, Baehmann P (1989) Some results using stress projections for error indication and estimation. In: Flaherty JE et al. (eds) Adaptive methods for partial differential equations. SIAM, Philadelphia, pp 83–99 (Chap. 7)
17. Szabo B, Sharmann CJ (1988) Hierarchic plate and shell models based on p-extension. Int J Numer Methods Eng 26: 1855–1881
18. Babuska I (1988) The p- and h-p versions of the finite element method: the state of the art. In: Dwoyer DL et al. (eds) Finite elements: theory and application. Springer-Verlag, New York, pp 199–239
19. Szabo BA (1985) PROBE: theoretical manual. Noetic Technologies Corporation, St. Louis, Missouri
20. Belytschko T, Fish J, Bayliss A (to be published) The spectral overlay on finite elements for problems with high gradients. Comput Methods Appl Mech
21. Patera AT (1984) Spectral element method for fluid dynamics. Laminar flow in a channel expansion. J Comput Phys 54: 468–488
22. Ortiz M, Leroy Y, Needleman (1988) A finite element method for localization failure analysis. Comput Methods Appl Mech Eng 61: 189–214
23. Hughes TJR, Ferencz RM, Hallquist JO (1988) Experience with an element-by-element iterating strategy for solid mechanics on a CRAY XMP/48. In: Wilhelmson RB (ed) High-speed computing: scientific applications and algorithm design. University of Illinois Press, Urbana Chicago, pp 180–195
24. Hashin Z (1970) Theory of composite materials. In: Wend FW, Liebowitz H, Perrone N (eds) Mechanics of composite materials. Pergamon, Oxford
25. Benssousan A, Lions JL, Papanicoulau G (1978) Asymptotic analysis for periodic structures. North Holland, Amsterdam
26. Sanches-Palencia E (1980) Non homogeneous media and vibration theory. Lecture Notes in Physics 127. Springer-Verlag, Berlin
27. Duvaut G (1976) Analyse functionelle et mécanique des milieux continueu applications à l'etude de matérieux composites elastiques à structure périodiques. Homogénéisation. In: Koiter WT (ed) Theoretical and applied mechanics. North Holland, pp 119–132
28. Lene F (1984) Thése de Doctorat d'Etat, Université Pierre et Marie Curie, Paris
29. Murat F, Tartar L (1985) Calculs des variations et homogénéization. In: Les methodes de l'homogenéization: theory et applications en physique. Coll. de la Dir. de Etudes et Recherches d'Electricité de France, Eyrolles, p 319

30. Kohn R (1988) Recent progress in the mathematical modeling of composite materials (preprint). Courant Institute, New York
31. Begis I, Dinari S, Duvaut G, Hassim A, Pistre F (1978) Modulef and composite materials (preprint). INRIA, Rocquencourt, Les Chesnay
32. Guedes JM (1989) A computational method for mechanics of nonlinear composites. PhD thesis, University of Michigan, Ann Arbor, MI 48109
33. Prager W (1974) A note on discretized Michell structures. Comput Mech Appl Mech Eng 3: 349–355
34. Michell AGM (1904) The limits of economy of material in framed structures. Philos Mag 6: 589–597
35. Fleury C (1979) Structural weight optimization by dual methods of convex programming. Int J Numer Meth Eng 14: 1761–1783
36. Zienkiewicz OC, Campbell JS (1973) Shape optimization and sequential linear programming. In: Gallagher RH, Zienkiewicz OC (eds) Optimum structural design Wiley, New York, 109–126
37. Haftka RT, Gandhi RV (1986) Structural shape optimization-A survey. Comput Mech Appl Mech Eng 57: 91–106
38. Bendsoe MP, Kikuchi N (1988) Generating optimal topologies in structural design using a homogenization method. Comput Mech Appl Mech Eng 71: (1988) pp. 197–224
39. Suzuki K, Kikuchi N (1989) Shape and topology optimization for generalized layout problems using the homogenization method. To appear in 1991. Comput Methods Appl Mech Eng, Technical Report 89-06. Computational Mechanics Laboratory, Department of Mechanical Engineering and Applied Mechanics, The University of Michigan, 1989, Ann Arbor, Michigan, 48109, USA.

3 Lattice Quantum Chromo Dynamics (QCD) and the Dedicated Computer QCDPAX

YOICHI IWASAKI[1]

Abstract. Lattice QCD (Quantum ChromoDynamics) is believed to be the fundamental law for quarks and gluons, which constitute particles such as protons, neutrons, and pions. QCDPAX is a local memory MIMD parallel computer designed for simulations in lattice QCD. Processing units (PU's) are connected in a toroidal two-dimensional nearest-neighbor mesh. We have completed construction of the computer made of 240 PU's (7 GFLOPS peak speed) and we will complete construction of the final QCDPAX made of 480 PU's (14 GFLOPS peak speed) by the spring of 1990. The program is written in terms of a C-like language, psc (parallel scientific C), and the tuning is possible at an assembly language, qfa (quick floating assembler), developed for the purpose of optimizing the object code. The link update time is evaluated.

3.1 Introduction

Hadrons are particles which constitute the nucleus, such as protons, neutrons, and pions. They were first thought to be elementary particles which could not be divided into smaller particles. However, it later turned out that they consist of more fundamental particles, quarks and gluons. QCD (Quantum ChromoDynamics) is believed to be the fundamental law for quarks and gluons.

QCD resembles QED (Quantum Electromagnetic Dynamics) in the sense that both are gauge theories; their actions are of similar form. However, the perturbation theory cannot be applied to QCD to calculate physical quantities such as the mass of the proton, while it is applicable to QED for the calculation of physical quantities such as the anomalous magnetic moment of the electron.

Therefore, one has to formulate the theory of QCD without depending upon the perturbation theory. Lattice QCD is such a theory defined nonperturbatively. It is difficult or impossible to calculate analytically physical quantities from lattice QCD.

---

[1] Institute of Physics, University of Tsukuba, Ibaraki, 305 Japan

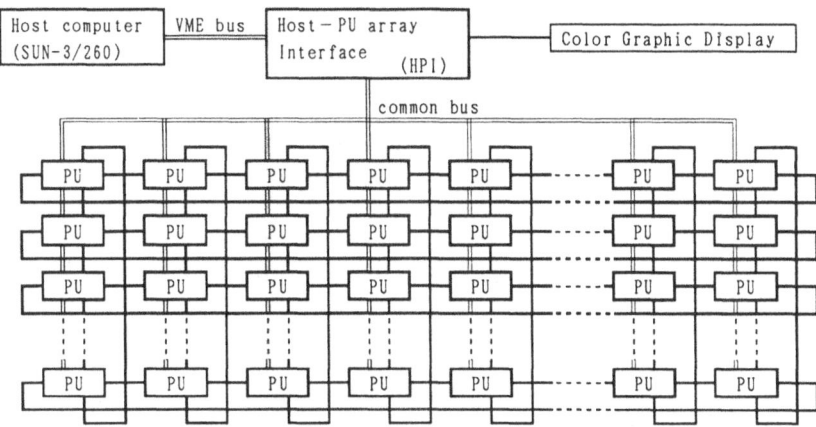

Fig. 3.1. System configuration of the QCDPAX

Numerical methods using computers are very powerful for the derivation of physical quantities from lattice QCD. To do so, we need computers with a speed of more than 10 GFLOPS and a memory greater than 1 Gbyte.

For this purpose, we started a project, QCDPAX[1], in 1987, as a joint collaboration of the physical sciences and the computer sciences groups mainly at University of Tsukuba. PAX stands for Parallel Array eXperiment and QCDPAX is the fifth of the PAX series [2]. A more detailed technical description is in [3].

The global architecture of QCDPAX is shown in Fig. 3.1. There are 480 (at present 240) identical processing units (PU's) interconnected in a toroidal two-dimensional nearest-neighbor mesh. It is a homogeneous, nonclustered array of PU's.

QCDPAX is a MIMD (Multiple-Instruction Multiple-Data) machine. The MIMD architecture has a variety of advantages over SIMD (Single-Instruction Multiple-Data) architecture:

1. Algorithms are flexible in an MIMD machine. For example, hyperplane in-complete LU decompositioning [4], which is performed in a wave-front fashion, cannot be implemented on SIMD machines.
2. The machine clock need not be synchronized among the PU's in MIMD machines and therefore the clock skew presents no problem.

Each PU has a specially developed high-speed floating point operation system. This is common to all the projects of a machine dedicated for lattice QCD. What is characteristic of our project is the adoption of the chip L64133, produced by LSI Logic company, as the floating point processing unit. This chip is a single stage processor or scalar processor, unlike the Weitek's chip which operates in a pipeline mode. We also developed a controller of this chip by gate array technology. These points will be described later in some detail.

3.2 Hardware

3.2.1 System Configuration

The system of QCDPAX (see Fig. 3.1) consists of the PU array, a host-computer, the Sun-3/260, a color graphic display, and the interface between the host and the PU array (HPI).

A PU shares a two-port RAM with each of its four nearest-neighbors, which we call communication memory (CM). It also shares a two-port RAM(ferry) with the host through the HPI. A common bus connects all PU's and the HPI. The memory of each PU is mapped on the address space of the host-computer. The HPI serves to select which PU's are mapped to the address space of the host-computer.

The computational results from each PU are outputted to the host through the two-port RAM and the common bus. The HPI is connected to the graphic display with a video processor to display the result on line.

3.2.2 Processing Unit (PU)

Each PU (see Fig. 3.2) is an independent one-board microcomputer. As the CPU, Motorola's microprocessor MC68020 with clock cycle 40 ns is used. The local memory where the program is stored is 4 MByte DRAM with 100 ns access time. A communication memory is a 32-bit × 2K words two-port RAM. The synchronization register (SYNC) is a 6-bit register to take the synchronization of all PU's.

3.2.3 Floating Point Operation System

As mentioned earlier, we utilize the chip L64133 as the floating point processing unit (FPU). It comprises an arithmetic logic unit and a multiplier, concurrently workable. This feature is suitable for a complex calculation. The peak performance of one board is about 30 MFLOPS.

The floating point processing unit controller (FPUC) is prepared with the LSI Logic's compacted gate array with 20,000 gates. It makes possible the direct memory access between the data memory and the FPU. The FPUC works as the interface between the CPU and the FPU, the sequencer for the fundamental arithmetic calculation, and the address generator for vector operations.

The floating point operation system consists of FPU, FPUC, a look-up table (LUT) PROM, a writable control storage (WCS) and data memory which is 2 MByte memory of 35 ns CMOS static RAM.

The LUT is two 8-bit × 512 words PROMs which contain the initial data for the Newton-Raphson calculations of the inverse and the square root. The WCS is 32-bit × 2K words high-speed (25 ns) BiCMOX static memory to store the procedure for the calculation of fundamental arithmetic vector operations, and the other calculations necessary for lattice QCD such as SU(3) matrix multiplication.

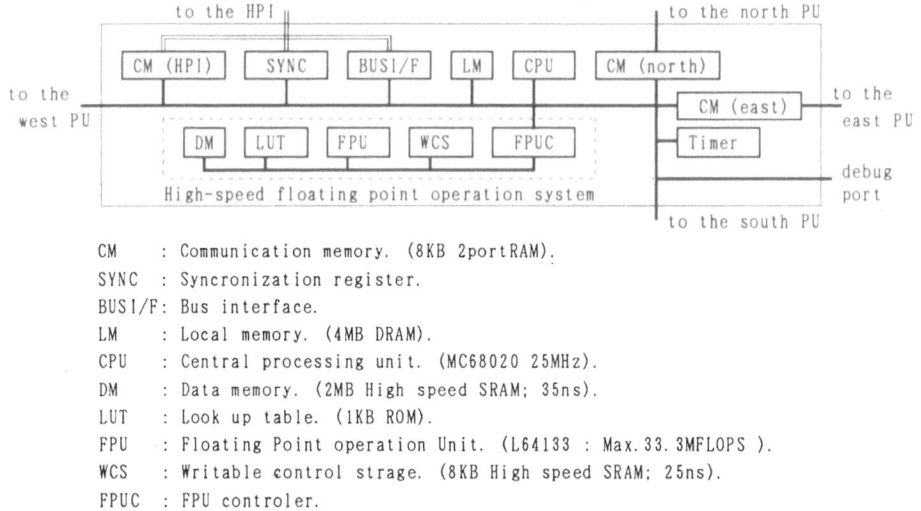

CM   : Communication memory. (8KB 2portRAM).
SYNC   : Syncronization register.
BUSI/F : Bus interface.
LM   : Local memory. (4MB DRAM).
CPU   : Central processing unit. (MC68020 25MHz).
DM   : Data memory. (2MB High speed SRAM; 35ns).
LUT   : Look up table. (1KB ROM).
FPU   : Floating Point operation Unit. (L64133 : Max.33.3MFLOPS).
WCS   : Writable control strage. (8KB High speed SRAM; 25ns).
FPUC   : FPU controler.

Fig. 3.2. Configuration of a single processing unit

3.2.4 Installation

One PU is installed on a six-layer print board of 367 mm × 400 mm (Fig. 3.3).
Sixteen PU's which are connected in a 4 × 4 array are installed in a box, which we
call a module (Fig. 3.4). One module also includes a power unit and a repeater of
the common bus. Up to 6 modules can be installed in a cabinet (Fig. 3.5). QCDPAX
is composed of six cabinets which form a hexagon (Fig. 3.6).

Fig. 3.3. Processing unit board

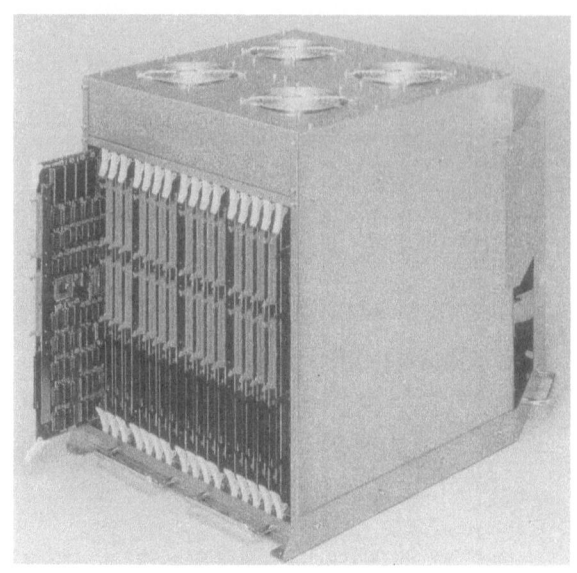

Fig. 3.4. Processing module with 4 × 4 PUs

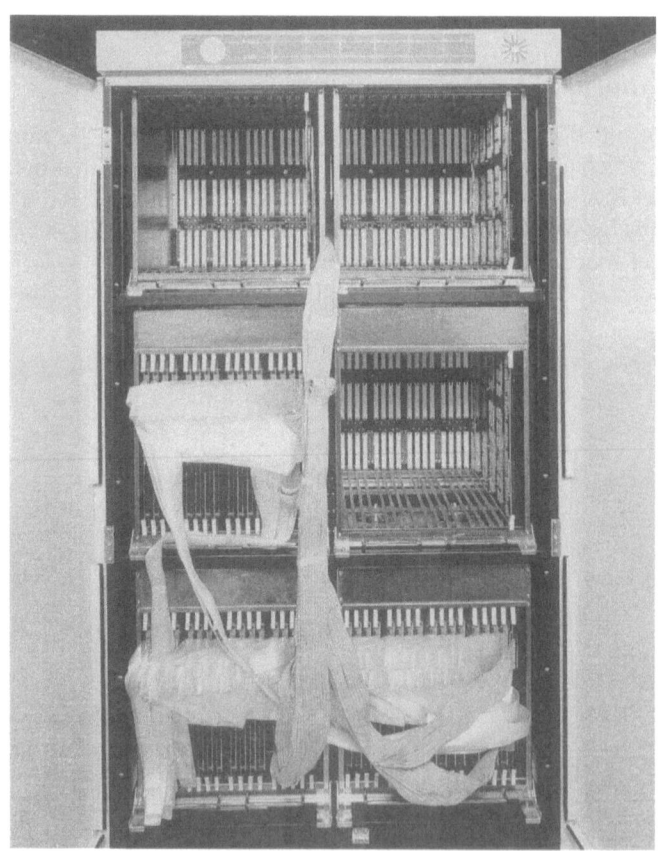

Fig. 3.5. Cabinet with three modules installed

Fig. 3.6. QCDPAX: six cabinets form a hexagon

3.3 Software

3.3.1 Development of Programs

The user of the QCDPAX should prepare two programs: one for the host computer, the other for the PU's. The program for the host computer is written in the language C. The PU program is written by a newly developed language, psc (parallel scientific C).

The psc program is compiled to an assembly language, qfa (quick floating assembler), which is specially designed for our PU. The user can optimize the code at the qfa level. The qfa program is assembled to the usual assembler and then to the machine code for MC68020. The host program loads the machine code into the PU array before starting the parallel task.

In order to set variables to the appropriate memory, variables are declared with their domain name and type. The domain names (fast, slow, east, west, north, south, and ferry) correspond to the specific memories (DRAM, SRAM, CM, and ferry), respectively.

3.3.2 psc

The psc is a C-like language for a nodal program in a PU. The vector processing is described by vfor-do statement. An example is given here:

```
vfor(i=0; i<n; i+=1) {
    a[i]=a[i−1]*a[i+1]+b[i−1]*b[i+1];
    p[i]=q[i−1]+r[i+1];
} do {
    for(j=0; j<m; j+=1)
        1_ferry[j]=1[j];
}
```

In this psc program, the block after "vfor" is executed by the FPU and the block after "do" is executed by the CPU. The float or complex arrays a, b, p, and r are located in the SRAM area. It should be noted that such recurrence iteration in vector calculation is supported. The do block describes a data transfer from the DRAM area to the ferry. These two blocks are executed in parallel. In the vfor-do statement, either the FPU or the CPU waits until the other finishes the operation.

3.3.3 qfa

The psc program is compiled to a qfa program. Here is an example: the vector psc program

vfor(i=0; i<100; i+=1) x[i]=y[i]+z[i]; do;

is compiled to

```
tr00: _z>c;
tr01: _y>b;
tr02: a>_x;
tr03: 99>e;
ir61:   1;
ir59: −1;
@lab0:
tr01, ir61;   ;
tr00, ir61;   ;
tr03, ir59 & a=b+c;   ;
tr02, ir61; ja @lab0
er: #0 & fpc: @lab0 & start;
v-wait;
```

Here "b" and "c" are the input registers in FPU, and "a" is the register for the result of addition in the FPU. Variables are expressed by the name of arrays in the psc source program with a preceding "_".

3.3.4 Two Ways of Data Transfer

There are two ways to transfer data from one PU (PU$_1$) to a nearest-neighbor PU (PU$_2$). One is an MIMD communication between the adjacent PU's by setting the flag in the communication memory (CM). First, PU$_1$ writes the data in CM and sets the flat in CM. The PU$_2$ waits until the flag is set and reads the data when the flag is set.

The other way is to take the global synchronization among all processors; this is SIMD-like MIMD. The procedure of the synchronization is the following: First, each PU writes a code to the SYNC and stops. As mentioned earlier, the SYNC has 6 bits and therefore the code can be chosen from 1 to 64. In the second step, if the HPI detects the coincidence of the contents of all SYNC's, it lets all the PU's resume the operation.

3.3.5 Library for Lattice QCD Calculations

In principle, we can write a lattice QCD program using only the tools which have been already described. However, the floating point operation should be highly optimized. Unfortunately, our compiler is not good enough to highly optimize the code. Therefore, we have to tune the qfa program by hand. Or, a more efficient way is to prepare a library for the fundamental calculations in lattice QCD. That is, we write the microcodes in the qfa language for the fundamental calculations, and then use them by a function call.

For example, let us consider the vector calculation of multiplication of SU(3) matrices: $C = A \times B$. Here A, B, and C are SU(3) matrices. We can call the function $U \times U$ by the following form:

$U \times U(\&C[m3][0][0], n3,$
    $\&A[m1][0][0], n1, \&B[m2][0][0], n2, n);$

where n1, n2, and n3 are the increments of the vector calculation, and the last n is the length of the loop. The $U \times U$ is composed of 184 steps of microcodes.

We have developed a lot of similar functions. Therefore, we can write a lattice QCD program using these functions. Now the coding is as easy as the usual coding. To date, we have completed a 3-subgroup pseudo-heat bath program for the quenched QCD simulation, as well as a minimal conjugate residual program for solving the quark propagator of the Wilson fermion with ILU preconditioning.

3.4 Present Status

The final goal is the machine composed of 480 PU's which has the peak speed 14 GFLOPS. At present we have installed 240 PU's. The debugging of PU's has been completed.

The quenched MC program is running. The link update time for the 3-subgroup pseudo-heat bath method with 8 hits is about 2.9 μs/link. The multiplication of the Wilson quark operator takes 0.75 μs/site. These numbers are the values measured on the 240 QCDPAX.

The members of the QCDPAX project are T. Hoshino, S. Ichii, Y. Iwasaki, K. Kanaya, T. Kawai, Y. Oyanagi, T. Shirakawa, and T. Yoshie.

Acknowledgments. This project is supported by the Grand-in-Aid for Specially Promoted Research of the Ministry of Education, Science, and Culture of the Japanese Government (No. 62060001). It is a pleasure to acknowledge the strong support and encouragement by Professor K. Nishijima, Kyoto University and Professor A. Arima, University of Tokyo. The author is grateful to the staff of Anritsu Corporation for their help in computer system development.

References

1. Iwasaki Y, Hoshino T, Shirakawa T, Oyanagi Y, Kawai T (1988) Comput Phys Commun 49: 449
2. Hoshino T (1989) *Computer, high-speed parallel processing and scientific computing.* Addison-Wesley, New York
3. Shirakawa T, Hoshino T, Oyanagi Y, Iwasaki Y, Yoshie T, Kanaya K, Ichii S, Kawai T (1989) Proceedings of supercomputing '89, Reno, USA, 13–17 Nov 1989
4. Oyanagi Y (1986) Comput Phys Commun 42: 333

4 Computer Applications to Materials Science and Engineering

MASAO DOYAMA[1]

Abstract. Engineering materials are very complicated. It is not easy to treat practical materials rigorously. The simplest materials are pure elements. Single crystals are not very common; the usual materials are polycrystalline and multiphase. Some materials are amorphous. In this chapter, an atomic and molecular approach has been taken from first principles. Concerning metals, the cohesive energies, elastic constants, and electronic structures of pure crystalline metals and of intermetallic compounds have been calculated. Random alloys present difficulties for such calculations. Using interatomic potentials, molecular dynamics have been applied to calculate the dynamic behavior of materials. Examples of calculations are presented. Kinetic equations among defects have been solved. The atomic configurations and stability of interstitial atoms and the atomic configurations of dislocation cores are shown. Using molecular dynamics, the rapid quenching of liquid, the tensile deformation of amorphous and crystalline iron, the shear plastic deformation of copper small crystals, and lattice vibrations are shown.

4.1 Introduction

Materials which are utilized by the human race have an engineering aspect. The properties of materials are determined not only by the components or compositions but also by the microscopic and macroscopic arrangement of atoms and molecules. Crystalline materials usually consist of polycrystals and are rarely single crystals. Silicon wafers or jewels are typical examples of single crystals. The crystallographic directions of grains in polycrystals are usually random, but sometimes grains are not randomly oriented. Silicon steels for transformers are made so the 100 directions are almost aligned in the rolling direction. Practical engineering materials often have more than one phase.

Recently computers have been rapidly developed. The computing speed has been greatly increasing, as has the capacity of memory. Computers are used not only

[1] Department of Materials Engineering, Nishi Tokyo Science University, Uenohara, Yamanashi, Japan

for computation but also for simulations, databases, and artificial intelligence. Mechanical and plastic properties of structural bodies have been calculated, as have the fluid-mechanical properties of ships and airplanes; simulations are used, and huge wind tunnels or water tanks are only used as the last resort. Computers are also used for the design of electronic circuits.

4.2 Materials Science

Human civilization has developed along with materials. The stone age, the bronze age, and the iron age are represented by the most dominantly used materials in that age. In the twentieth century, plastics, silicon, and fine ceramics are being widely used, but none of these materials predominate over all other materials. We may say that we are in the age of diversity.

Modern metallurgy started with metallography by Tamman (1861–1938). Up to 1930, the contribution of chemistry to refining metallurgy was large. Since 1930, however, along with the development of quantum mechanics, the contribution of solid state physics has been significant. Frederik Seitz systematized solid state physics in his famous book *Modern Theory of Solids* [1]. After World War II, studies of crystalline defects contributed greatly to research and development of materials. In the late 1950s not many revolutionary advances were made in metallurgy, and there was a trend toward stagnation. Metallurgy had to cast off its old skin and become transformed into materials science, absorbing the knowledge of physics, chemistry, chemical engineering, mechanical engineering, and electrical engineering, with the new tool of solid state physics. Materials science encompassed metals, semiconductors, ceramics, polymers, and biomaterials.

Almost all the departments of metallurgy in the United States changed their names to Department of Materials Science and Engineering, with minor variations. In Japan, the movement to materials science followed that in the USA, but no departments of metallurgy changed to departments of materials science at that time. The Japanese metallurgical industry was expanding very rapidly at that time, and the number of departments of metallurgy was doubled to meet the demand for graduates by industry.

In recent years, the Japanese metallurgical industry has been changing; the iron and steel industry has started new materials sections, and the nonferrous industry has started electronic materials sections to use their byproducts. Departments of metallurgy in Japan are changing to departments of materials. In Japan, there is a field of material science which emphasizes substances rather than materials. Recently, a field called material engineering was named, in order to attract applicants to universities.

The technology prediction [2] made in 1987 by the Science and Technology Agency of Japan selected the areas for emphasis in materials as (1) analysis and control at the atomic and molecular levels, (2) the design and synthesis of materials by computer science, and (3) the development of soft devices.

Recently, some designs of materials have been performed using computers.

4.3 *Ab Initio* Calculations

Let us survey materials, starting from the simplest: an element. Of the elements, 83
out of 103 are metals. Metals usually have crystalline forms. In metals, the valence
electrons are not tightly bound to an ion but rather, move freely around in a crystal
as conduction electrons. Per cubic centimeter, there are of the order of 10^{24} to 10^{25}
electrons and 10^{22} atomic nuclei. The Coulomb interactions occur between electron
and electron, ion and ion, and ion and electron. Treating these interactions is one
of the typical many-body problems which are difficult to solve. Of course, 10^{24}
electrons and 10^{22} atomic nuclei cannot be rigorously treated in a computer, even
in a supercomputer. Each atom is identical, so that the unit region (a polygon) for
one atomic nucleus is defined as the Wigner-Seitz cell. Near the nucleus, the electric
field for an electron to see is treated as a muffin-tin (MT) potential. Outside the core,
electrons are often treated as plane waves, spherical waves, etc. Moreover, Bloch's
theorem can be used. Bloch's theorem states that the wave function of a conduction
electron can be expanded into the product of plane waves and the function whose
period is the same as the crystal period.

$$\phi_k(r) = e^{ik \cdot l} u_k(r)$$

$$u_k(r + l) = u_k(r)$$

where l is a lattice translation vector, k is wave number vector, and r is a position
vector. Using Wigner-Seitz cells and Bloch's theorem, the number of particles to be
treated can be reduced to the order of several tens or hundreds. When the Wigner-
Seitz cell (Fig. 4.1), the charge of the nucleus (atomic number), and the number of
electrons (usually equal to the atomic number) are given, the relation between wave

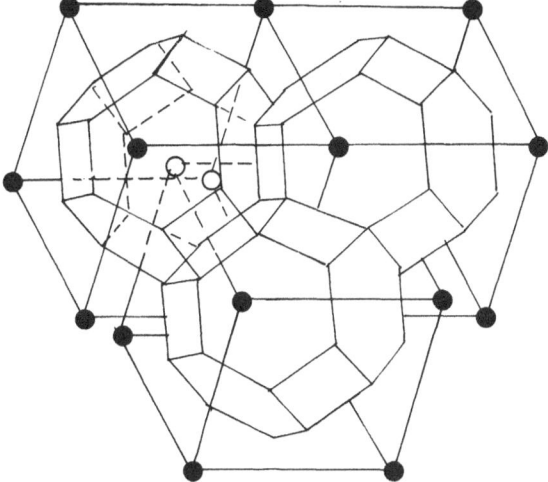

Fig. 4.1. Wigner-Seitz cell in a tcc lattice

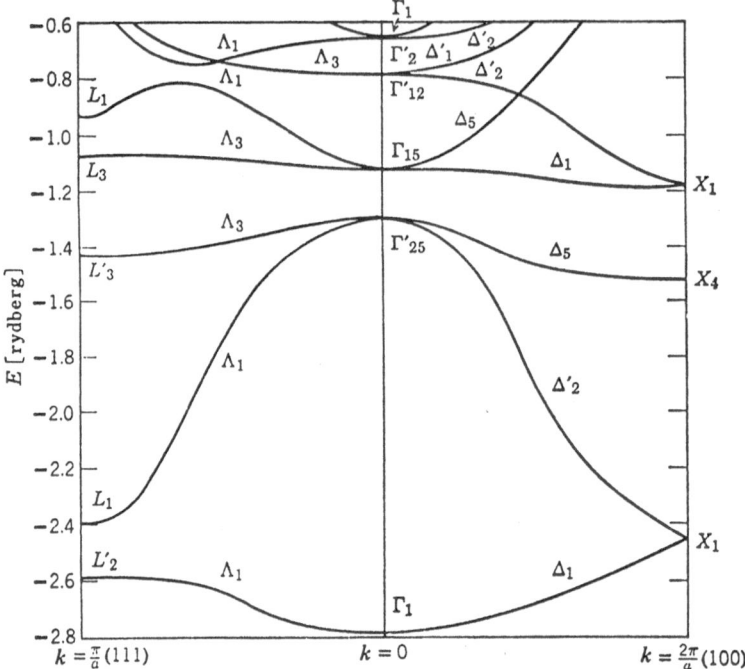

Fig. 4.2. The relation between the kinetic energy of an electron ε and wave number k in silicon. (From Kleinman and Phillips [96])

number k and energy ε (Fig. 4.2), i.e., the band structures, can be calculated for pure metals. Intermetallic compounds can be similarly treated. Calculations for pure elements have been performed, including cohesive energies, elastic constants, lattice constants, Fermi surfaces, and Fermi energies, etc. The APW (Augumented Plane Wave) method proposed by Slater [3], the KKR method proposed by Korringer and Kohn and Rostoker [4, 5], and density functional formalism [6] have been often used. In the APW and KKR methods, a muffin-tin potential which has a spherical symmetry near nuclei is taken. In the APW method, the potential outside the muffin-tin potential is taken to be constant and the wave function is expanded into many plane waves. In the KKR method, outside the muffin-tin, the wave function is expanded by spherical waves. The matrix elements of the ground state of the Hamiltonian equation depend on the eigenvalue, and this is not a standard eigenvalue problem. Linear band theory removes the energy dependence on the ground state wave functions. The behavior of the wave function in the muffin-tin sphere can be expressed in a practical energy region as a linear combination of two wave functions. Further development of the APW method has resulted in the Linear Augmented Plane Wave (LAPW) method [7], and from the KKR method has evolved the Linear Muffin-Tin Orbital (LMTO) Method [7, 8]. The band structure for copper has been calculated by the LAPW [9]. Those for Pt_3Sn [10], MgHg [11], MgTl [11], Cu_2Sb [12], $PdTe_2$ [13], $AuCu_3$ [14], AgMg [15], AuMg [15], Al_2Cu

[16], NiSi [17], etc. have been calculated by the LMTO method. The OPW (Orthogonal Plane Wave) method [18] has changed to the pseudopotential method. The linear combination of the two wave functions is enveloped with the wave functions in the muffin-tin. In the LMTO method, spherical waves are used and in the LAPW plane waves are used. The LAPW method has to treat larger-dimension matrices compared with those for APW, so that supercomputers are well suited to the LAPW method. For low atomic density solids such as silicon and germanium, the FLAPW (Full-potential Linear Augmented Plane Wave) method [19–21] is used. This method is extended from the APW method introducing deviation from spherical symmetry in the MT sphere and variation outside the MT sphere. Using this method, a superlattice such as GaAs-AlAs [10], and transition metallic impurities in silicon, BN, and solid surfaces have been calculated. Super-computers are also suited to such calculation. In the NCPP (Norm-Conserving Pseudo Potential) method [22–25], inner shell electrons are not treated straight-forwardly, but the valence electrons are in relief. The ASW (Augumented Spherical Wave) method [26] and the Linear Rigorous Cellular (LRC) method, resembling the LMTO method, have also been developed.

4.4 Alloys and Materials

For the materials mentioned in Sect. 4.3, periodic boundary conditions can be used. For most engineering materials, however, the periodic boundary conditions cannot be used. In usual materials, different kind of atoms randomly occupy the lattice. The calculation is not very simple. Most materials, such as partially ordered alloys, random alloys, amorphous metals with alloys, and liquid metals with alloys, are not periodic. Random alloys have been treated by the Coherent Potential Approxi-mation method [27]. These materials are treated as a single phase. Real materials usually have multiplephases. There are two kinds of boundaries for two phases. One is a coherent boundary, for which the atomic arrangement and structure in both phases are really the same with certain strains. The other is an incoherent boundary, for which the atomic arrangements in both phases are not matched. Mis-matched dislocations are often found at incoherent boundaries. Usually, materials also consist of polycrystals. The crystallographic directions of grains are usually at random. Not many calculations and simulations of the physical properties of polycrystals have been performed. For metallic materials, the compositions of elements are of course important; moreover, the atomic arrangements, phases, crystal structures, size of grains, and the distribution of crystal orientations, etc. are also important. Practical materials are complicated, and many atoms have to be considered.

4.5 Atomic Static Mechanics

An atom in condensed matter interacts with the surrounding atoms. The atom is pushed by the resultant force exerted by the surrounding atoms until equilibrium is achieved. It is not easy for the atom to find a real equilibrium, but it often finds

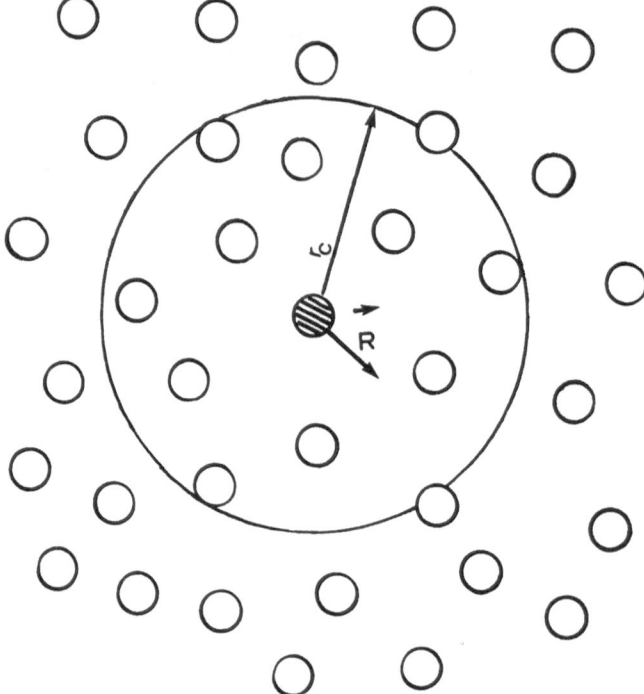

Fig. 4.3. An atom in condensed matter is assumed to interact with atoms within a radius r_c. F, force

metastable configurations. This is a static problem and the temporal evolution is not taken into account. A thermally activated process also cannot be considered. The molecular dynamics is better in this sense.

The resultant force from surrounding atoms within a radius r_c (trancation distance) is calculated (Fig. 4.3). It is important to know how to calculate the interaction between atoms. The simplest is a two-body interaction which only depends upon the distance between atoms. The force direction is on the line connecting the two atoms. Three-body interactions have been also discussed. The interaction can be calculated from first principles, but this depends on the atomic arrangement surrounding the atom. Each time a huge calculation is necessary. Even in pure elements, the determination of the interaction potential is not easy. The interaction between different species is much more difficult.

4.6 Molecular Dynamics

The calculation of a resultant force exerted on an atom is the same as that in static mechanics. From the resultant force, the accelerations, velocities, and positions of all atoms in the system at every time are calculated by solving Newton's equation.

The differential equations are reduced to difference equations. From the accelerations, velocities, and positions of all atoms in the system at time t, these values at $t + \Delta t$ can be calculated.

The first work on molecular dynamics was performed by Vineyard's group [28, 29] to show how atoms in a small crystal are displaced as a function of time after a momentum is given to an atom in the crystal. They showed that the atom given a momentum pushes the next atoms, and each displaced atom pushes the next atom, leaving a vacancy at the original position of the atom given the momentum.

Gibson et al. [30] calculated the threshold energy in the direction of $\langle 100 \rangle$, $\langle 110 \rangle$, and $\langle 111 \rangle$ in copper and they obtained the lowest energy in $\langle 100 \rangle$, then $\langle 100 \rangle$, and the highest in $\langle 111 \rangle$. Ergynsoy et al. [31, 32] imposed a momentum on an atom in a small iron crystal and the motions of all atoms in the system have been calculated as a function of time. Figure 4.4 clearly shows the channeling. The velocity auto-correlation function and the vibrational spectrum as dynamic properties, and the diffusion coefficient and viscosity as transport properties, were calculated. Radiation damage to KCl has also been calculated [33].

As the vibrational frequencies of atoms in solids are of the order of 10^{13}, the time step should be order of 10^{-15} s. The total time is of the order of 10^{-9} s even if 1 million steps are taken. Semidynamic approaches to treating this cascade have been performed [34–36].

This method has been applied to the motion of atoms in molten rare gas [37] and metals, alkaline halides [38], and silica glass [38] using a periodic boundary condition, and statistical properties such as the pair distribution function, the

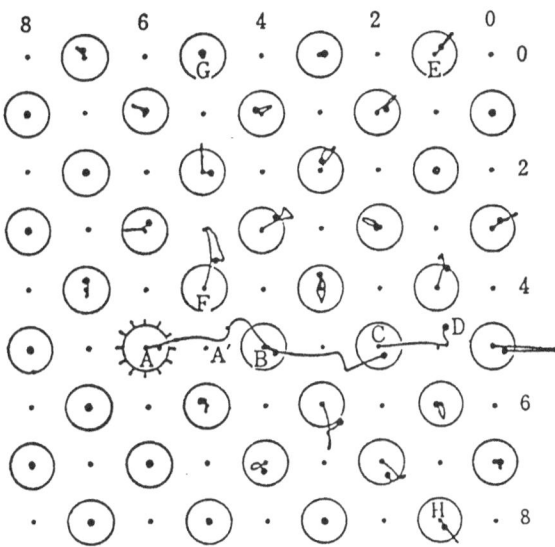

Fig. 4.4. Computed trajectories in a radiation damage cascade in copper. The plane is $\langle 100 \rangle$. 40 eV was given to atom A 15° from $\langle 010 \rangle$. The *large circles* were the original positions. The *larger black circles* are the final positions after time $99 \times 3.27 \times 10^{-15}$ s. A-F, individual atoms

diffusion of atoms, structure factor, the equations of state, thermodynamic properties, thermal expansion coefficient, enthalpy, constant volume heat capacity, constant pressure heat, etc., were obtained. The atomic configurations in amorphous metals have been calculated [39–41]. The statistics of Voronoi polyhedra have been studied [42]. ZrF_4-BaF_2 glass has been analyzed by molecular dynamics [43, 44]. Metasilicate $R_2O \cdot SiO_2$ has also been studied [45].

Ultrafine particles have been studied experimentally and theoretically. The total number of particles within ultrafine particles is not very large, so rigorous calculations are possible, but the calculations of dynamic properties require extensive computation.

4.7 Monte Carlo Method

Using a random number table, numerical calculations are performed. In the first case, the interatomic interactions have probability elements. In the second case, this method is used to create a canonical distribution.

4.8 Interaction Potential

The interaction potential between atoms can be calculated from first principles but phenomenological potentials are often used:

Born-Mayer potential [46]:
Electron core-core repulsion is often given by the Born-Mayer potential:

$$\phi(r_{ij}) = A \exp\{-\alpha(r_{ij} - r_0)\}$$

Morse potential [47]:

$$\phi(r_{ij}) = D[\exp\{-2\alpha(r_{ij} - r_0)\} - 2\exp\{-\alpha(r_{ij} - r_0)\}]$$

Girifalco and Weizer [48] determined the constants rom the lattice parameter, elastic constant, and sublimation energy [Fig. 4.5]. This is good for uniform expansion or contraction. When the distance between atoms i and j becomes $2^{-1/3} = 1.26$ times, this potential would be valid if the density of conduction electrons became one-half of the original density. Actually, when the distance between the atoms becomes 1.26 times the original, the electron density does not become one-half of the original density. The present author proposed to use the formation energy of a vacancy instead of the sublimation energy [49]

Lenard-Jones potential:
This potential represents the interaction between rare gas atoms. The power 6 is due to the attractive force coming from the electric dipole and electric dipole interaction which is induced instantaneously.

$$\phi(r_{ij}) = -\varepsilon/(n - 6)[n(r_0/r_{ij})^6 - 6(r_0/r_{ij})^n]   \qquad n > 6$$

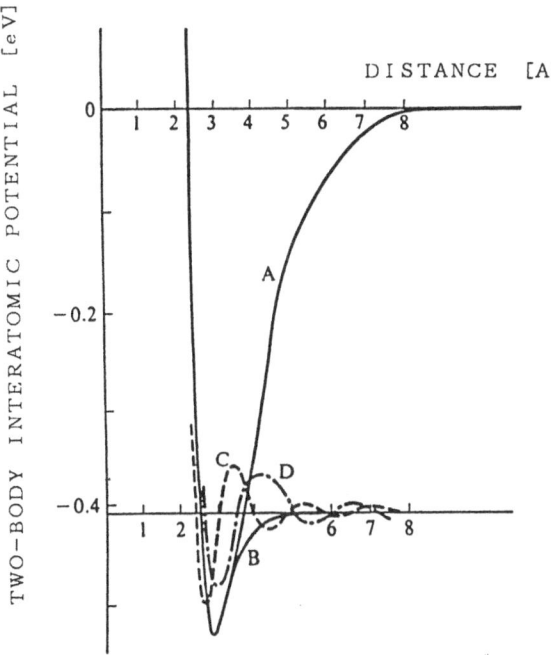

Fig. 4.5. Two-body atomic interaction potential in Al. Curve *A* was determined by using the sublimation energy; *B* by using the formation energy of a vacancy; *C* by pseudopotential (by Harrison); and *D* was experimentally determined from liquid aluminum

Buckingham potential:
In this potential, the attractive term between rare gas atoms is due to the attraction between the electric dipoles, and the repulsive term is the core electron repulsion which is exponential and represented by the Born-Mayer potential.

$$\phi(r_{ij}) = A\exp\{-\alpha(r_{ij} - r_0)\} - \varepsilon(r_0/r_{ij})^6$$

Ionic potential [50, 51]:
The interaction between ions is given by:

$$\phi(r_{ij}) = Z_iZ_je^2/r + A_{ij}b\exp\{(\sigma_i^0 + \sigma_j^0 - r)/\rho\} - C_{ij}/r^6 - d_{ij}/r^8$$

Other potentials:
Polynomials are used to represent the interactions [52].

A major question is, Can we apply the interaction potential which is determined from a perfect crystal to imperfect crystals? Interaction potentials have been discussed [53–55]. The embedded-atom method [56, 57] derived from local density-functional theory has been applied to impurities, surfaces, and other crystalline defects. In a disordered lattice, electrons are redistributed. How can we take into account this effect? When the positions of atoms are given, the wave functions of electrons (electron density at each point) which give the lowest energy of the system are calculated by introducing a virtual time, atoms are moved toward the force, and the wave functions of electrons are recalculated. This is an *ab initio* molecular dynamics method [58, 59]. This method will be widely used in the future, but so far, not many application have been published.

Atomic structures, phonon spectra, and electronic properties in amorphous silicon have been calculated [60] by this method. The atomic structure of Ge(100) [61, 62] and the twist boundary of $\Sigma = 5(100)$ [63] have been calculated.

4.9 Other Applications of Computers to Materials Science and Engineering

The phase diagrams of the electronic and statistical-mechanical theory of *sp*-bonded alloys have been calculated [64].

When the σ phase appears in nickel base refractory alloys, the alloy becomes brittle. Therefore, PHACOMP (PHAse COMPutation) [65] was developed for the predication of σ phase formation. Harada et al. [66] developed an alloy design program based on experiments and theory. Esaki et al. [67] used the cluster theory to develop nickel-based refractory alloys and titanium alloys.

The calculations of lattice constants and forbidden bands in binary mixed crystals of semiconductors such as $Al_xGa_{1-x}As$ [68] have been calculated. Self- consistent calculations of heterojunctions [69] and other many calculations have been performed. Calculations on quantum devices, devices, process simulations, process design of ultra large scale integrated circuits, and carrier transport have been also performed.

The properties of organic compounds depend on the properties of their constituent molecules. The properties of many bases are known.

Computer applications extent to ceramics, glasses, polymers, organic materials, drugs, proteins, biomaterials, chemical reaction paths, transport processes, chemical kinetics, organic reaction mechanisms, luminous reactions, quantum devices, devices and process simulations, refining, purification, solidification, crystal growth, sintering, synthesis design, etc.

4.10 Examples of Computer Applications to Materials Science

There have been a vast number of computer applications to materials science. In this paper the studies related to the author's work are shown.

4.10.1 Kinetic Equations

Figure 4.6 shows the formation of vacancy-impurity pairs during quenching [70]. Even during fast quench, vacancies can move rapidly at high temperatures. The

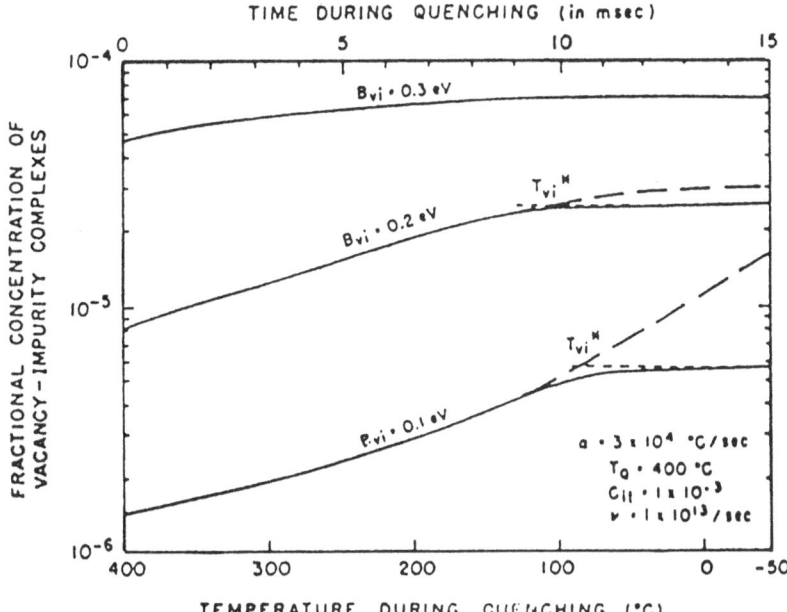

Fig. 4.6. Formation of vacancy-impurity pairs during quenching in Al-0.1 atomic percent impurity quenched from 400°C with a quenching speed of 30,000 °C/s. (α) T_Q is the quenching temperature, C_{it} is the total impurity concentration, v is the atomic vibration frequency next to a vacancy, B_{vi} is the binding-energy between an impurity atom and a vacancy and T_{vi}^M is the critical temperature, above which a thermal equilibrium between a vacancy and impurity atoms is hold

combination of vacancy-impurity pairs and break-up of the pairs is in equilibrium, but at lower temperatures the motion of vacancies becomes slow and the reaction between vacancies and impurities is frozen. The kinetic equations to be solved in this case are:

$$dc_v/dt = \alpha_1 c_{vi} - \beta_1 c_v c_i$$

$$dc_{vi}/dt = -dc_i/dt = -\alpha_1 c_{vi} + \beta_1 c_v c_i$$

ignoring the anneal of vacancies to sinks. here c_v, c_{vi}, and c_i are the fractional concentrations of single vacancies, vacancy-impurity atom pairs, and impurity atoms (atoms without a vacancy in the nearest neighbors), respectively. This method has been applied to the kinetics of formation of vacancy clusters, interstitial clusters, formation of voids, etc.

4.10.2 Static Mechanics

Figure 4.7 shows the possible atomic configurations of interstitial atoms. It was found by computer calculation [49, 71] that only the split $\langle 100 \rangle$ interstitial is stable

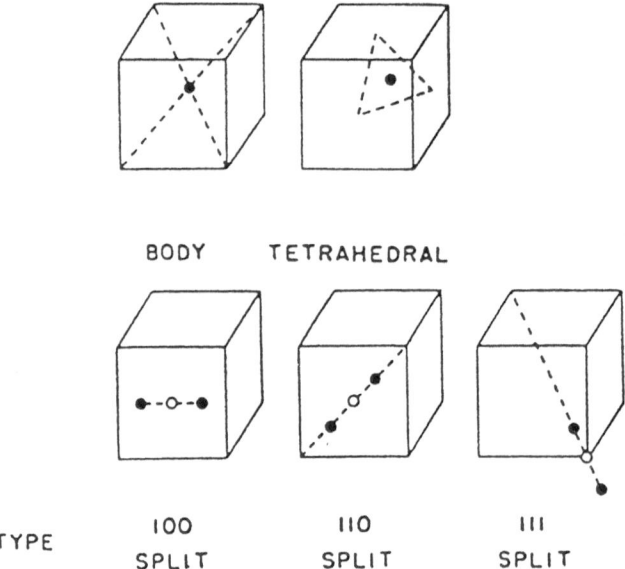

Fig. 4.7. Atomic configurations of interstitials in fcc lattice

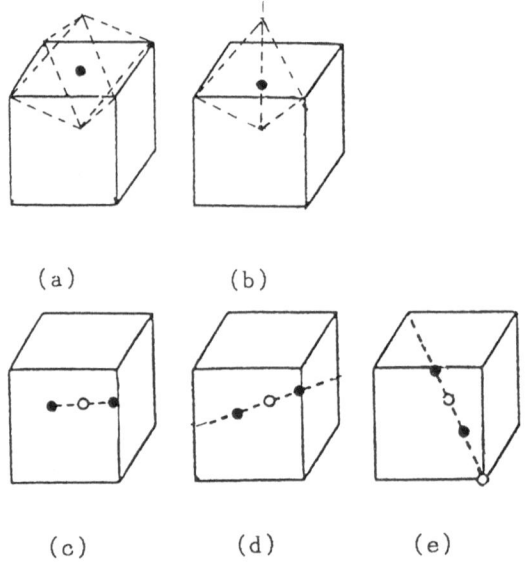

Fig. 4.8a–e. Atomic configurations of interstitials in bcc lattice. **a** Octahedral, **b** tetrahedral,
c ⟨100⟩split, **d** ⟨110⟩split, **e** ⟨111⟩split interstitial

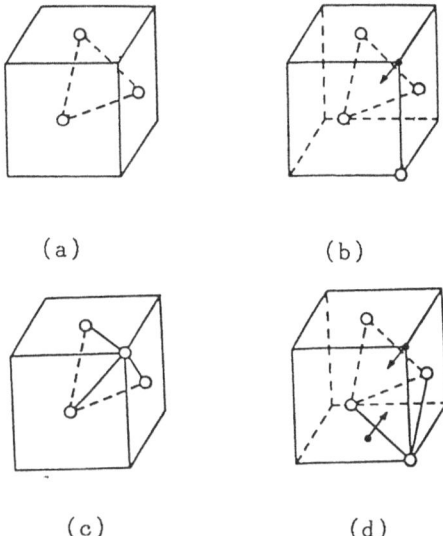

(a)   (b)

(c)   (d)

Fig. 4.9a–d. Configurations of trivacancy. **a** Three vacancies are compact: 60° trivacancy. **b** One atom above three vacancies relaxed: 3/4 vacancies are at the apexes of a tetragon. **c** Most stable quadrivacancy **d** Two atoms above and below a rhombic quadrivacancy relaxed forming an elementary stacking fault

and all others are unstable and transform to a split ⟨100⟩ interstitial without a thermal activation energy. In a body-centered cubic lattice, split ⟨110⟩ interstitial is the only stable configuration (Fig. 4.8) [72]. For the motion of interstitials in fcc and bcc lattices, the interstitials do not move straight but change in the split directions after the jump [71, 72].

It has also been shown that if four vacancies coagulate on a ⟨111⟩ plane in the nearest neighbor positions (Fig. 4.9), it may collapse, but if they form a tetragonal void, it does not collapse.

4.10.3 Dislocations

Figure 4.10 [73] shows the atomic arrangement near the center of an edge dislocation in a face-centered cubic lattice, copper. Burgers vector is $\frac{1}{2}\langle 110\rangle a$ (a = lattice constant). Figure 4.11 [73] is the projection to ⟨111⟩. It was believed that the core was melted or hollow when this calculation was performed. It was also shown by computer calculations that the complete dislocations (edge and screw) in an fcc lattice split into two partial dislocations connected with a stacking fault without activation energy. According to the first-order elastic theory, the strain energy within the radius r is given by

$$E = A\log r + B = A\log(r/r_0)$$

However, constants B or r_0 cannot be determined by the first-order elastic theory. By atomic calculations, B or r_0 can be determined (Fig. 4.12). r_0 was determined to be

PLANE OF SYMMETRY

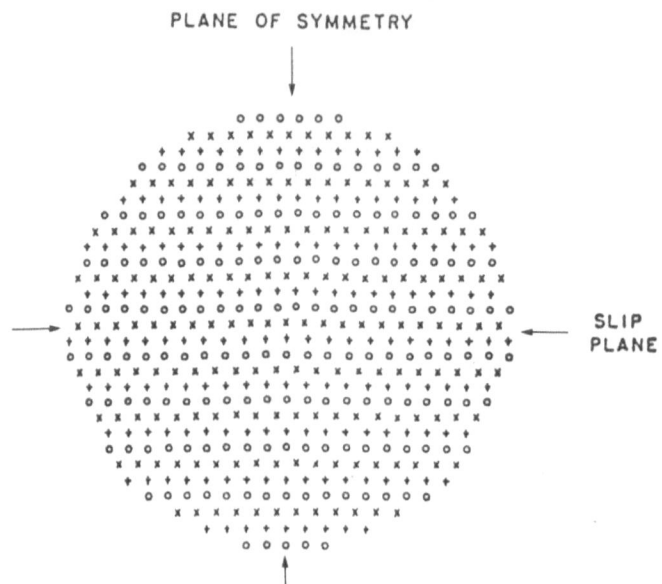

SLIP
PLANE

COMPLETE EDGE DISLOCATION

Fig. 4.10. Atomic configuration of an edge dislocation in copper projected on $\langle 112 \rangle$

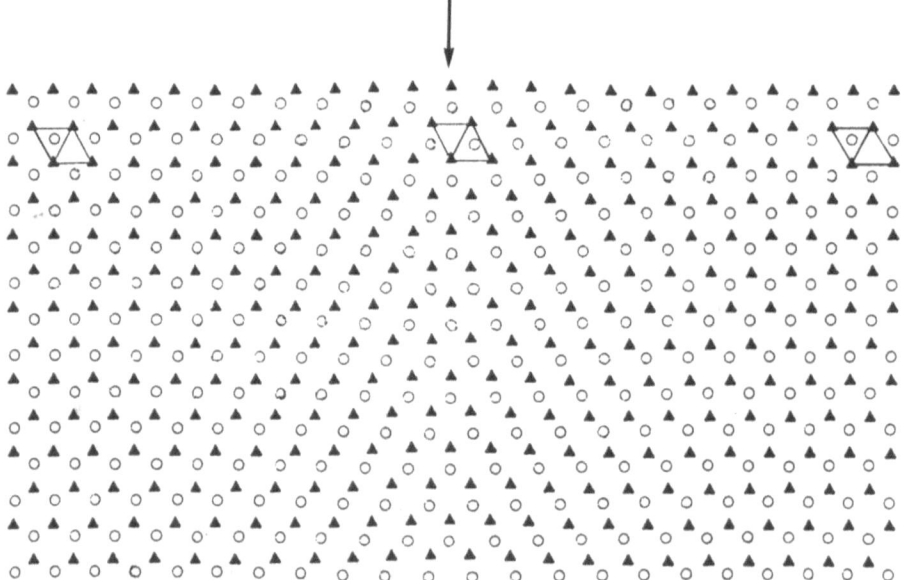

Fig. 4.11. Position of atoms in two $\langle 111 \rangle$ planes, one above (*triangles*) and one below (*circles*) the slip plane of the dissociated edge dislocation. The partial dislocations and the region of stacking fault which separates them can easily be distinguished by observing the figure from either side at a low angle

94

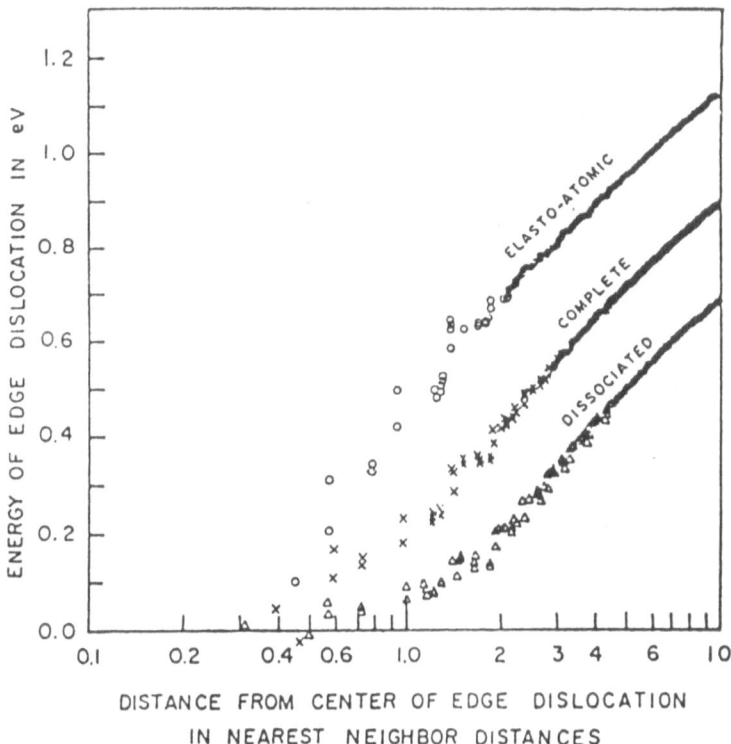

Fig. 4.12. Energy of edge dislocation within a given radius as a function of that radius as measured from the center of an edge dislocation. The three cases, elasto-atomic, complete, and dissociated are shown. The energy given in the figure is for a length $d_0/[2(3)^{0.5}]$

1.3 Å and 1.0 Å [74] for complete edge dislocation and complete screw dislocation, respectively, in copper.

J.J. Gilman [75] criticized our calculations in *Comments on Solid State Physics*, saying that unreallistic "two-body potentials" cannot be used and "the man (Doyama) and the machine are well advised to seek other employment." After one quarter of a century, it has been shown that his criticism was not soundly based; many calculations have been performed and much new information has been obtained. The present author was definitely discouraged from continuing the work for a while. These calculations have been applied to dislocations in a body-centered lattice by Vitek et al. [76, 77], and have shown that $\frac{a}{2}\langle 111 \rangle$ screw dislocations split on three equivalent planes and that, because of this, the yield stress in iron is high. Yamaguchi et al. [78, 79] applied the calculations to intermetallic compounds. Masuda [80] calculated the core structures of $\frac{a}{2}\langle 111 \rangle$ screw dislocation in α-iron under stress using the electron theory. The core structure of dislocations in silicon has been calculated using Keating potential [81, 82]. The kink and jogs were calculated

[83]. The electronic states and the structure of the core have been calculated self-consistently [84]. The core structure of a dislocation in an ionic solid has been calculated by Kurosawa [85].

4.10.4 Molecular Dynamics

4.10.4.1 Rapid quenching. The atomic configurations in amorphous metals have been calculated. The Voronoi polyhedra have been statistically studied. Quenching of liquid metals can be simulated by taking away the kinetic energy of atoms. It should be remembered that the total time elapsed is, at most, of the order of 10^{-9} s, so that the quenching speed is much faster than the experimental quenching speed. Figure 4.13 shows the radial distribution function when the temperature is lowered [86]. The second peak of the "frozen" radial distribution function has a shoulder and this is typical for amorphous metals.

4.10.4.2 Tensile deformation. A small amorphous iron specimen (Fig. 4.14) was pulled by the method of molecular dynamics [87]. The relation between energy and nominal elongation is plotted in Fig. 4.15. In some regions of elongation strain the

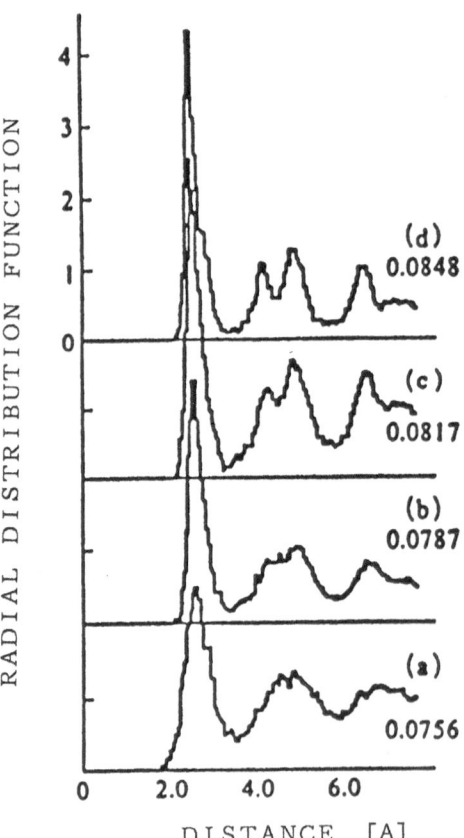

Fig. 4.13. Two-body distribution function. Quenched from liquid **(a)** (n = 0.0756), **(b)** (n = 0.0787), **(c)** (n = 0.0817), **(d)** (n = 0.0848). n is the atomic density = number of atoms/A³. A, average atomic displacement

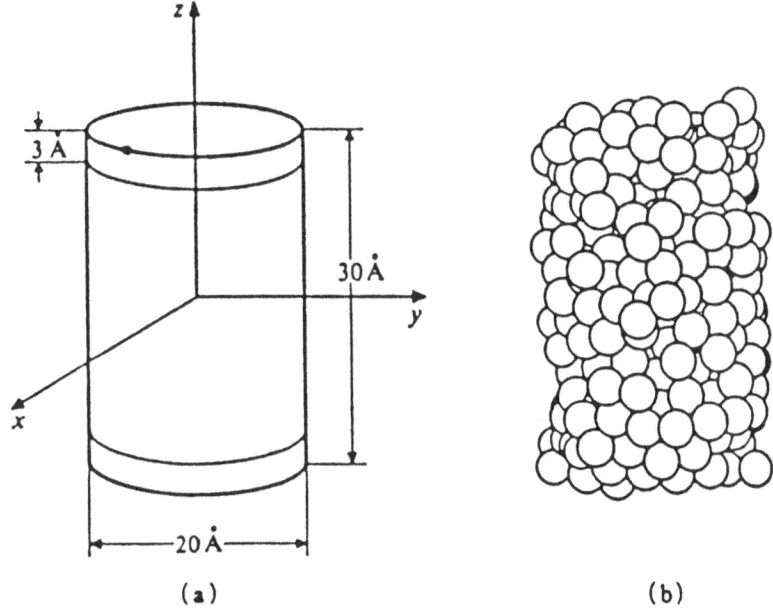

Fig. 4.14a,b. Tensile specimen of amorphous iron. **a** Dimension, **b** atomic arrangement

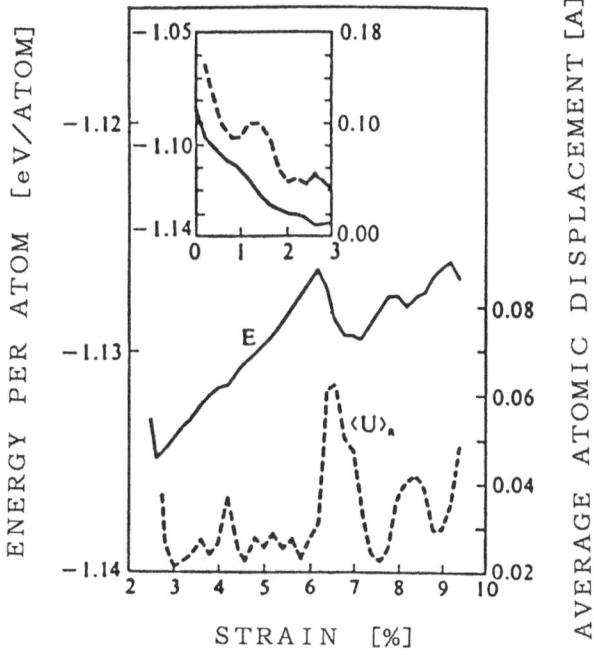

Fig. 4.15. Nominal elongation and average energy per atom, E, and the average atomic displacement $\langle u \rangle_n$

energy-elongation relation is linear, whereas in some regions the energy is relaxed suddenly. In the linear part, the displacement of atoms is as expected from the elastic theory (Fig. 4.16). In the relaxed region, the displacements of atoms above and below a plane about 45° to the stretching direction are roughly opposite, and a slip is observed (Fig. 4.17).

Crystals of iron whiskers with a small crack (Fig. 4.18) are pulled in a super-computer using the method of molecular dynamics. Figure 4.19a–f shows the projections to $\langle 112 \rangle$ [88]. A hexagonal structure was observed only under a tensile stress. The whisker was completely broken into two pieces (Fig. 4.19f). The stress-strain curve is plotted in Fig. 4.20.

4.10.4.3 Shear plastic deformation. To see the motion of dislocation more clearly, a small crystalline piece of copper was deformed in a supercomputer [89]. A displacement was imposed in the upper half plane of a rectnagular parallelepiped of a small copper crystal (Fig. 4.21a–f). Partial edge dislocation was introduced first, with a stacking fault following. Then, the other partial dislocation was created at he surface, with a lower stress because it was pulled by the stacking fault. The pair of the split dislocations moved toward the other surface and the plastic

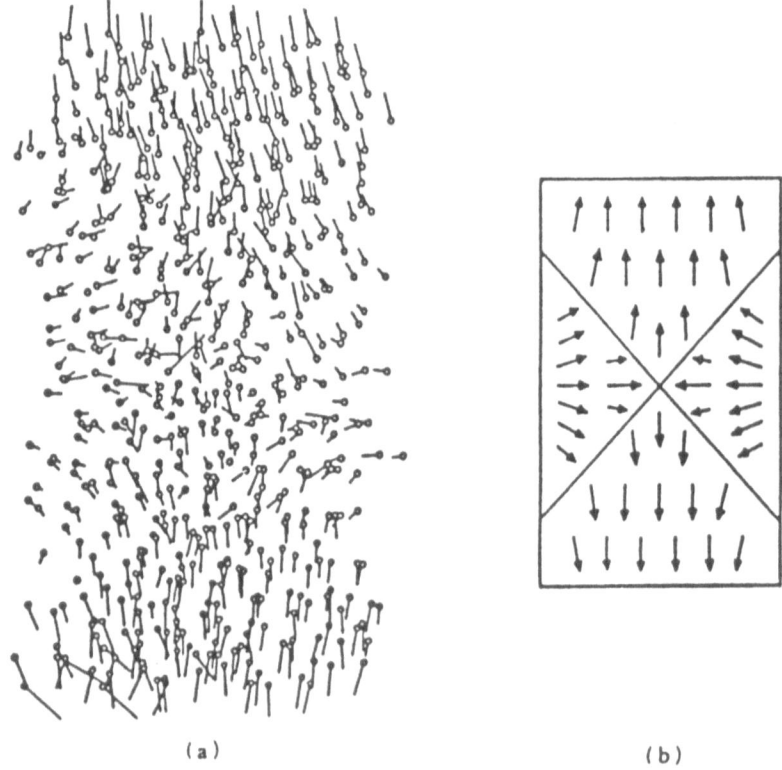

(a)   (b)

Fig. 4.16. **a** The displacements of atoms in the elastic region (nominal elongation 2.6% → 6.2%) are projected **b** on (y, z)

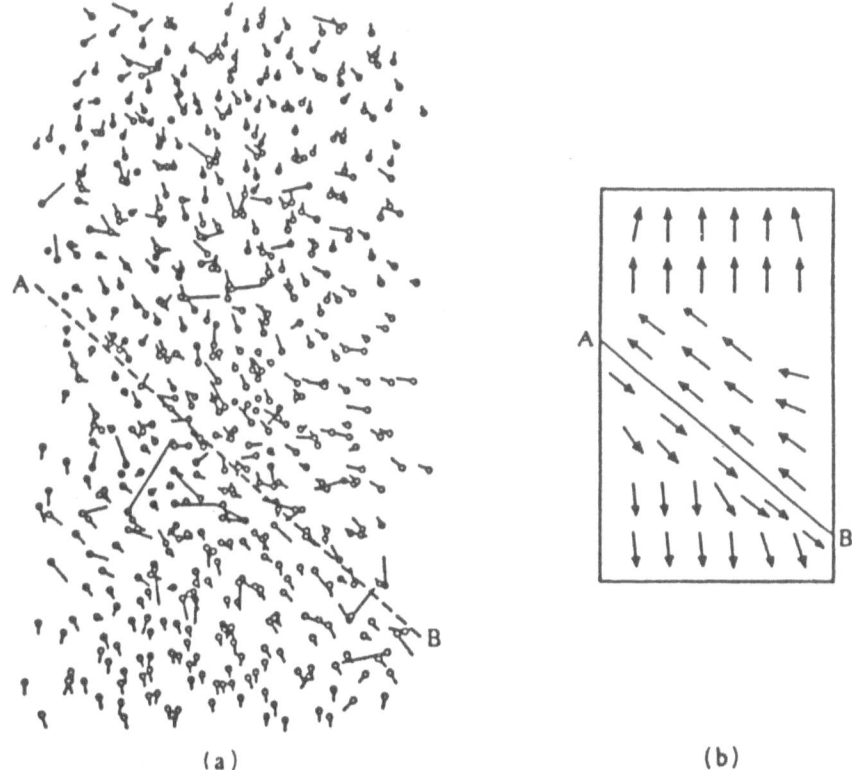

(a)

(b)

Fig. 4.17. **a** The displacements during plastic deformation (nominal elongation 6.2% → 7.5%) are plotted **b** on (y, z)

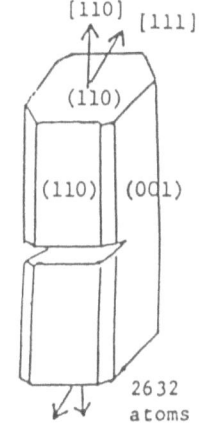

Fig. 4.18. Specimen A for tensile deformation (with a crack). The specimen contains 2632 atoms

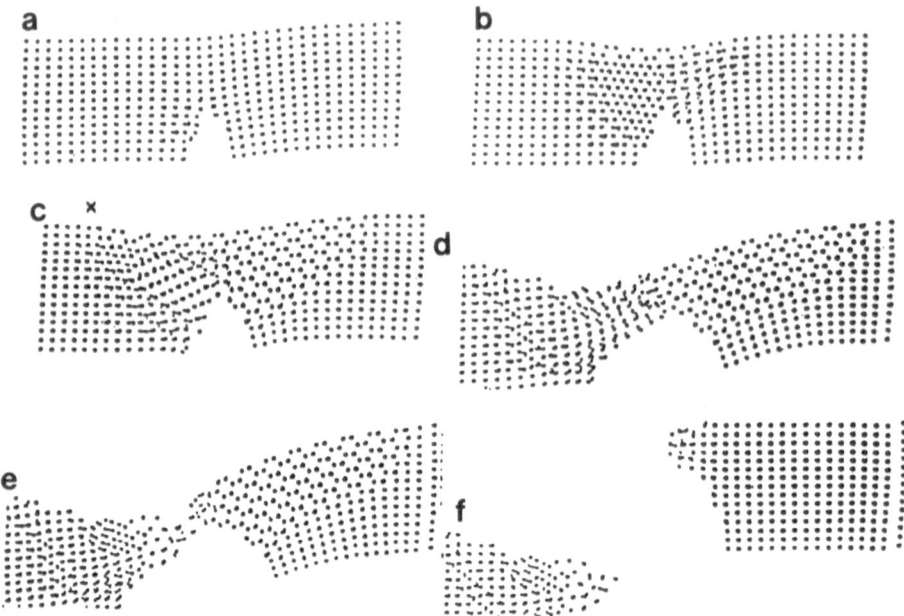

Fig. 4.19. **a** Tensile specimen A. Nominal elongation 6.4%. **b** Tensile specimen A. Nominal elongation 6.8%. **c** Tensile specimen A: twins are observed at *. **d** Tensile specimen A: necking is observed. **e** Tensile specimen A: just before fracture, **f** Tensile specimen A: just after fracture

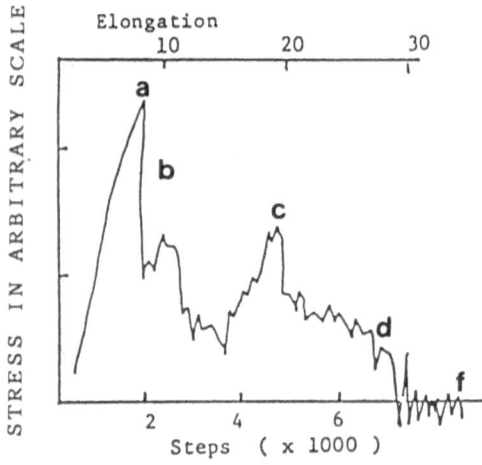

Fig. 4.20. Stress-strain curve for Specimen A pulled in $\langle 11 \rangle$ direction. The numbers represent figures of atomic configuration. a–f correspond to Fig. 4.19a–f

defomation of one atomic plane was completed. The stress needed to introduce an initial partial dislocation in a crystal is higher than that to introduce a second partial dislocation. The second edge dislocation was created with a lower stress than that for the first dislocation. The stress to introduce a dislocation is lower in a crystal with a crack than in one without a crack (Fig. 4.22).

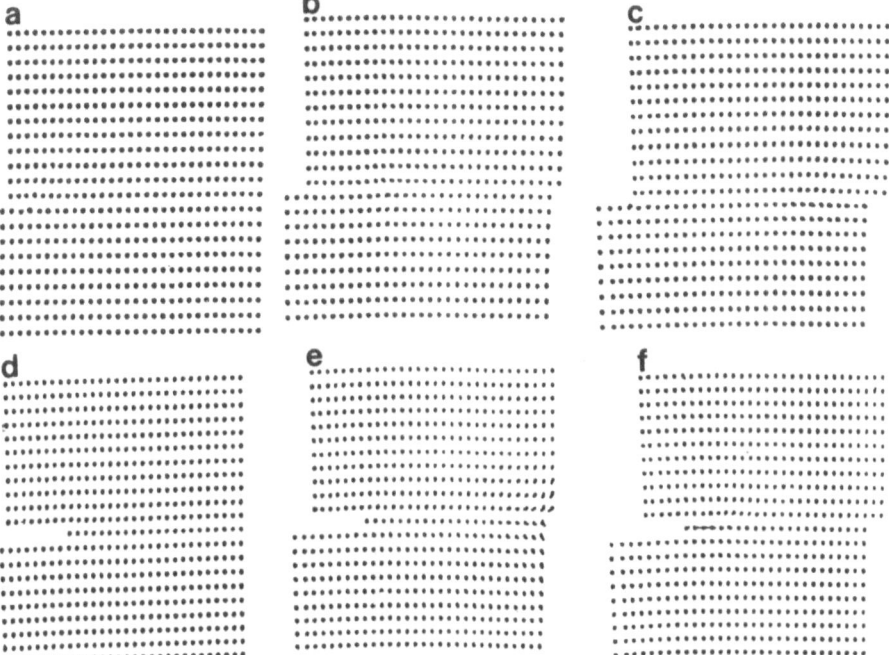

Fig. 4.21a–f. Small crystal of copper (3-dimensional), **a–c** without a crack. One surface of the *upper half* of the crystal was subjected to a displacement of 0.4 d (**a**), 1.2 d (**b**), or 2 d (**c**). **d–f** Copper crystal containing a small crack, subjected to a displacement of 0.4 d (**d**), 1.2 d (**e**), or 2 d (**f**)

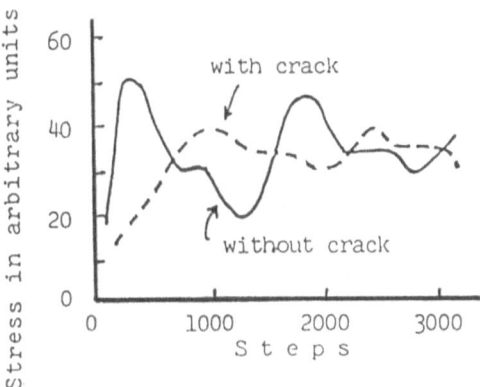

Fig. 4.22. Stress-strain curve for the small copper crystal shown in Fig. 4.22. The largest stress was required when the first partial dislocation was introduced. The stress necessary to introduce the second partial dislocation pulled by a stacking fault was lower than that of the first one. The stress to introduce a second edge dislocation was lower than that for the first one. The stress to introduce a dislocation to a specimen with a crack was always lower than that for one without a crack

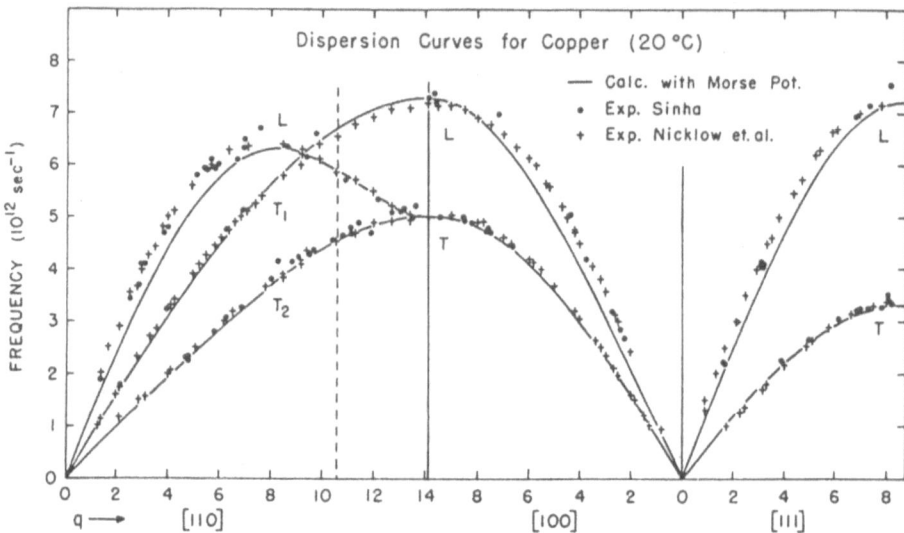

Fig. 4.23. Phonon dispersion curve in pure copper at 20°C calculated using a Morse potential (*solid line*). Experimental data obtained by Sinha [97] (●) and Nicklow et al. [98] (+) are plotted for comparison. q is in units of $2\pi/10a$, where a is the lattice constant. I, transverse wave; L, longitudinal wave

4.10.4.4 Lattice vibrations. Figure 4.23 is the phonon dispersion relation in pure copper using a Morse potential [90]. The calculated values are well matched to the experimental values. Figure 4.24 shows the relation between the phonon frequency and the phonon density of states for the nearest-neighbor atoms and the 2nd, 3rd, and 4th nearest-neighbor atoms of a vacancy in copper [91]. The nearest neighbor of a vacancy has high density at lower vibational frequencies. Figure 4.25 depicts the atomic structure and the relation between the phonon frequency and the phonon density of states at a grain boundary in iron. Figure 4.26 shows the atomic structure and the relation between the frequencies and density of states at the grain boundary with an impurity in iron [92–94].

4.10.4.5 Interaction between defects. The interactions between defects are important, particularly the interaction between vacancies and defects. Vacancies play an important role in the diffusion of atoms in crystals. The interactions between vacancy-vacancy, vacancy-impurity, and impurity-impurity have been calculated by the use of pseudopotential [95].

4.11 Conclusions

The foregoing examples are on atomic scale. To treat a macroscopic problem, a finite element method is often used. In the linear finite element method, the displacement is proportional to stress. In the nonlinear finite element method, the displace-

Fig. 4.24. **a** The relation between the phonon frequency and local density of states for the nearest neighbor, (*nn*), next-nearest neighbor, the 3rd, and the 4th neighbor of a vacancy in copper. **b** Densities of states of phonon for copper

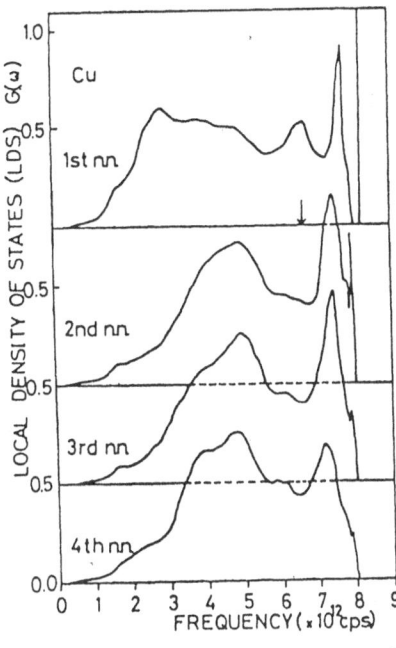

a

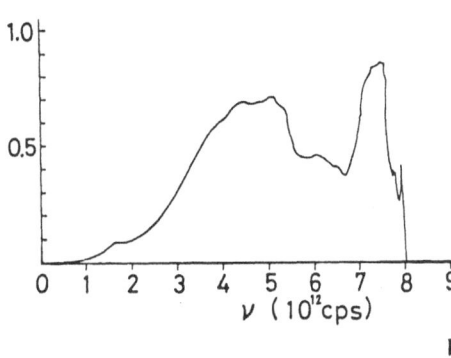

b

ment and stress relationship is given. In some cases, as the deformation proceeds the net size of finite elements is changed in the region where the displacement is large. It is, however, assumed that the stress-strain relation holds. As the element becomes smaller, to the order of grain size, this relation should be changed.

The speed of computers is becoming faster and faster, the memory capacity is becoming larger and larger, and the capacity of computers is being improved. However, since there are many problems which cannot be calculated straightforwardly, "grafting bamboo onto a tree" is sometimes necessary. Originality to handle these problems is important. If we place too much emphasis on the calculations from first principles, complicated problems such as those involving materials cannot be calculated.

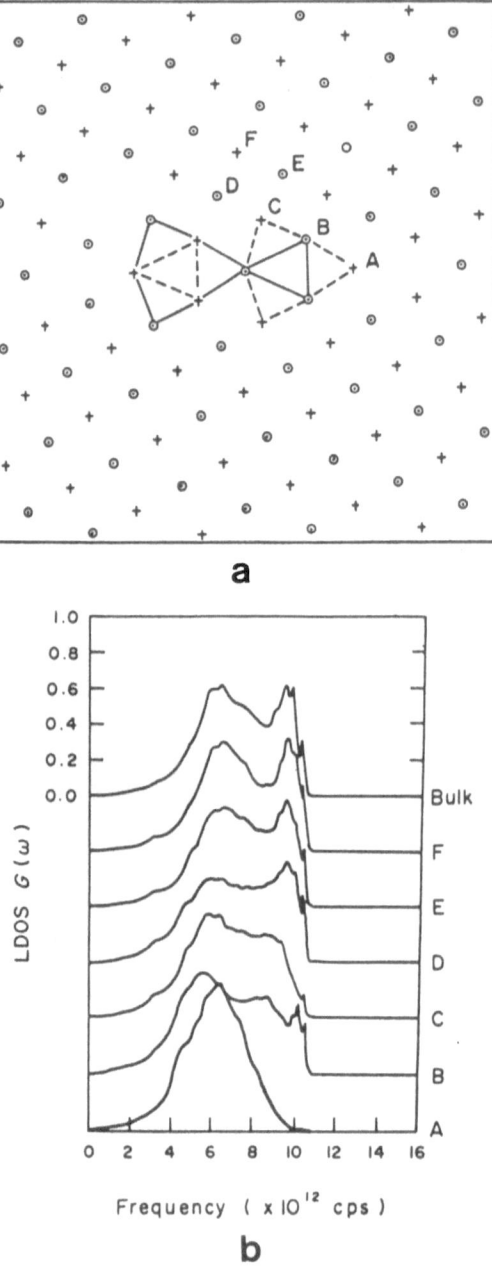

a

b

Fig. 4.25. **a** Atomic configuration and **b** the relation between phonon frequency and the local density of states LDOS near $\Sigma = 5$ grain boundary in α – Fe. $A-F$, individual atoms $\odot$ and $+$ are the projection of atoms to a (100) plane; $+$, atomic plane above or below $\odot$ plane

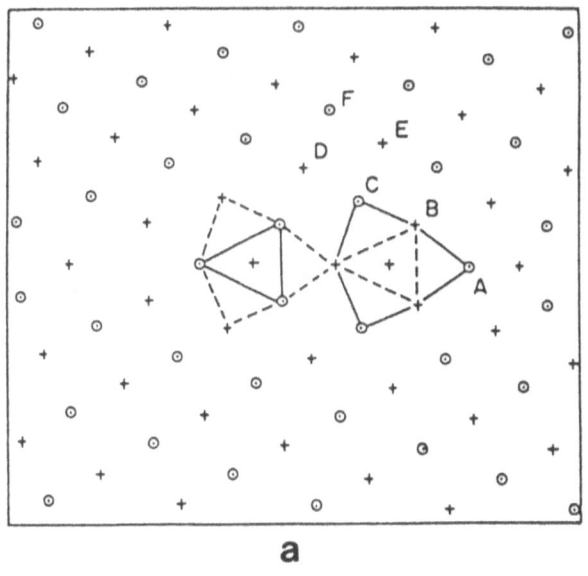

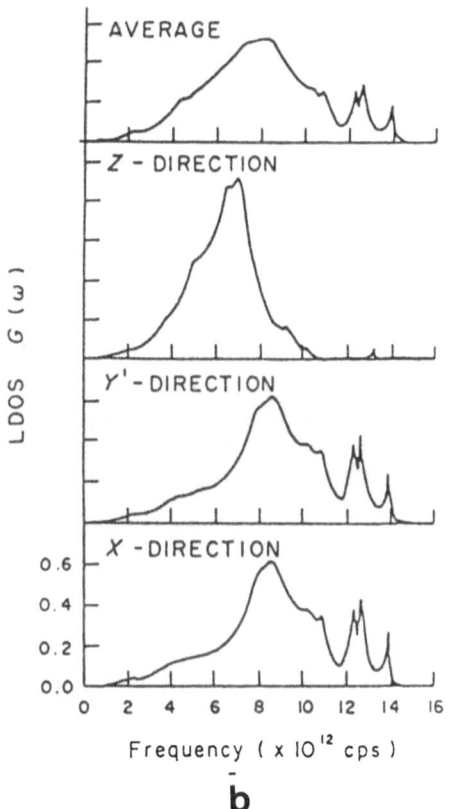

Fig. 4.26. **a** Atomic configuration and **b** the relation between phonon frequency and the local density of states LDOS near $\Sigma = 5$ grain boundary in $\alpha - $ Fe with a phosphorous impurity. $A-F$, individual atoms

References

1. Seitz F (1940) Modern theory of solids. McGraw-Hill, New York
2. Future Technology Institute (1987) Technology prediction in Japan. Science and Technology Agency, Tokyo
3. Slater JC (1937) Phys Rev 51: 846
4. Korringer J (1947) Physica 13: 392
5. Kohn W, Rostoker N (1954) Phys Rev 94: 1111
6. Hohenberg P, Kohn W (1964) Phys Rev 136: B864
7. Anderson OK (1975) Phys Rev B12: 3060
8. Skriver HL (1984) The LMTO method. Springer-Verlag, Berlin
9. Koelling DD, Arbman G (1975) J Phys F5: 2041
10. Skriver HL (1976) Phys Rev B14: 5187
11. Skriver HL (1977) Phys Rev B15: 1894
12. Jan J-P, Skriver HL (1977) Phys F7: 957
13. Jan J-P, Skriver HL (1977) J Phys F7 1719
14. Skriver HL, Lengkeek HP (1979) Phys Rev B19: 900
15. Dunsworth AE, Jan J-P, Skriver HL (1978) J Phys F8: 1427
16. Dunsworth AE, Jan J-P, Skriver HL (1979) J Phys F9: 1077
17. Boulet RM, Dunsworth AE, Jan J-P, Skriver HL (1980) J Phys F10: 2197
18. Herring C (1940) Phys Rev 57: 1169
19. Wimmer E, Krakauer H, Weinert M, Freeman AJ (1981) Phys Rev B24: 864
20. Weinert M, Wimmer E, Freeman AJ (1982) Phys Rev B26: 4571
21. Wimmer E, Freeman J (1983) Phys Rev B28: 3074
22. Bachelet GB, HaMann DR, Sculuter M (1982) Phys Rev B26, 4199
23. Yin MT, Cohen ML (1982) Phys Rev B26: 5668
24. Ihm J, Zunger A, Cohen ML (1979) J Phys C12: 4409
25. Ihm J, Zunger A, Cohen ML (1980) J Phys C13: 3095
26. Williams AR, Kubler J, Gelatt CD Jr (1979) Jr Phys Rev B19: 6094
27. Soven P (1967) Phys Rev 156: 819
28. Vineyard GH (1961) Discussions Faraday Soc 31: 7
29. Vineyard GH (1963) J Phys Soc Japan 18 (Suppl. III) 144
30. Gibson JB, Goland AN, Milgram M, Vineyard GH (1960) Phys Rev 120: 1229
31. Ergynsoy C, Vineyard GH, Englert A (1964) Phys Rev 133: A595
32. Ergynsoy C, Vineyard GH, Shimizu A (1965) Phys Rev 139: A118
33. Torrens McC. Chadderton LT (1967) Phys Rev 159: 671
34. Yoshida M (1961) J Phys Soc Jap 16: 44
35. Beeler JR Jr, Besco DG (1963) J Appl Phys 34: 2873
36. Beeler JR Jr (1966) Phys Rev 150: 470
37. Rahman A (1966) Phys Rev 45: 2585
38. Kawamura K, Okada I (1977) (in Japanese) Nippon Kinzokugakkai Kaiho 16: 834; Okaga I (1984) ibid. 23: 600
39. Finney JL (1970) Proc R Soc Lond A319: 479
40. Yamamoto R, Haga K Shibuta H, Doyama M (1978) J Phys F8: L179
41. Tanaka M (1986) J Phys Soc Jap 55: 3108; ibid. 55, 3428
42. Yamamoto R, Mihara T, Doyama M (1978) Phys Stat Sol (A) 50: 165
43. Yasui I, Inoue H (1985) J Non-Cryst Solids 71: 39
44. Inoue H, Hasegawa H, Yasui I (1985) Phys Chem Glasses 26: 74
45. Doyama M, Yamamoto R (eds) (1987) Calculational Materials Science (in Japanese). Kaibundo, Tokyo
46. Born M, Mayer E (1932) Z Phys 75: 1

47. Morse PM (1929) Phys Rev 34: 57
48. Girifalco LA, Weizer VG (1959) Phys Rev 114: 687
49. Doyama M, Cotterill RMJ (1967) In: Hasiguti RR (ed) Lattice defects and their inter-actions. Gordon and Breach, New York, p 79
50. Fumi FG, Tosi MP (1964) J Phys Chem Solids 25: 31
51. Tosi MP, Fumi FG (1964) J Phys Chem Solids 25: 45
52. Johnson RA, Wilson WD (1972) In: Gehlen PC, Beeler JR, Jaffee RI (eds) Interaction potentials and simulation of lattice defects. Plenum, New York, p 301
53. Gehlen PC, Beeler JR Jr, Jaffee RI (eds) (1972) Interaction potentials and simulation of lattice defects. Plenum, New York
54. Torrens IM (1972) Interatomic potentials. Academic, New York
55. Lee JK (ed) (1981) Interatomic potentials and crystalline defects. Metallurgical Society of AIME, New York
56. Daw MS, Baskes MI (1983) Phys Rev Lett 50: 1285
57. Daw MS, Baskes MI (1984) Phys Rev B29: 6443–6453
58. Car R, Parrinello M (1985) Phys Rev Lett 55: 2471
59. Payne MC, Joanno JD, Allan DC, Teter MP, Vanderbilt DH (1986) Phys Rev Lett 56: 2656
60. Car R, Parrinello M (1988) Phys Rev Lett 60: 204–207
61. Needels M, Payne MC, Joannopoulos JD (1987) Phys Rev Lett 58: 1765–1768
62. Needels M, Payne MC, Joannopoulos JD (1988) Phys Rev B: 5543–5546
63. Payne MC, Bristowe PD, Joannopoulos JD (1987) Phys Rev Lett 58: 1348–1364
64. Hafner J (1987) From Hamiltonians to phase diagrams. Springer-Verlag, Berlin
65. Boesch WJ, Slaney JS (1964) Metal Progress 86: 109
66. Harada H, Ohno K, Yamagata T, Yokokawa T, Yamazaki M (1988) In: Reichman S, Duhl DN, Maurer G, Antolovich S, Lund C (eds) Superalloys. The Metallurgical Society
67. Esaki H, Morinaga M, Yukawa N, Adachi H (1986) Philos Mag A53: 709
68. Chen AB, Sher A (1981) Phys Rev B23: 5645
69. Pikett WE, Louie SG, Cohen ML (1987) Phys Rev B17: 815
70. Doyama M (1966) Phys Rev 148: 681–694
71. Johnson RA, Brown E (1962) Phys Rev 127: 446
72. Johnson RA, Dienes GJ, Damask AC (1964) Acta Met 12: 1215
73. Cotterill RMJ, Doyama M (1966) Phys Rev 145: 465–478
74. Doyama M, Cotterill RMJ (1966) Phys Rev 150: 448–455
75. Gilman JJ (1969–1970) Comments on Solid State Physics 2: 37–39
76. Vitek V (1976) Proc Soc Lond 352A: 109
77. Vitek V, Perrin RC, Bowen DK (1970) Philos Mag 21: 1049
78. Yamaguchi M, Vitek V, Pope DP (1981) Philos Mag 43A: 1027; ibid. 43A, 1265
79. Yamaguchi M, Paidar V, Pope D, Vitek V (1982) Philos Mag 45A, 867; ibid. 45A, 882
80. Masuda K (1981) Philos Mag 43B: 1
81. Heggie M, Jones R (1983) Microscopy of semiconducting materials. Inst Phys Conf Ser 67: 45
82. Marklund S (1984, 1985) Solid State Commun 50: 185 (1984); 54, 555 (1985)
83. Masuda KJ, Kojima K, Hoshino T (1983) Jap J Appl Phys 22: 1240
84. Veth H, Teichler H (1984) Philos Mag 49B: 371
85. Kurosawa T (1964) J Phys Soc Jap 19: 2096
86. Yamamoto R, Mihara T, Taira K, Doyama M (1979) Phys Lett 70A: 41
87. Yamamoto R, Matsuoka H, Doyama M (1979) Physica Status Solid (A)51: 163
88. Doyama M, Yamamoto R (1985) In: Suzuki H, Ninomiya T, Sumino K, Takeuchi S (eds) Dislocation in solids. University of Tokyo Press, p 85
89. Doyama M, Yamamoto R (1989) Materials Science Forum 37: 77

90. de Wett FW, Cotterill RMJ, Doyama M, (1966) Phys Lett 23: 309
91. Yamamoto R, Haga K, Mihara T, Doyama M, (1978) Phys F8: L179
92. Hashimoto M, Ishida Y, Yamamoto R, Doyama M (1984) Acta Met 32: 1
93. Hashimoto M, Ishida Y, Wakayama S, Yamamoto R, Doyama M (1984) Acta Met 32: 13
94. Wakayama S, Hashimoto M, Ishida Y, Yamamoto, Doyama M (1984) Acta Met 32: 21
95. Takai O, Yamamoto R, Doyama M, Hisamatsu Y (1974) Phys Rev B10: 3113
96. Kleinman L, Phillips JC, (1960) Phys Rev 117: 460
97. Sinha SK (1966) 143: 422
98. Nicklow RM, Gilat G, Smith Hg, Raubenheimer LJ, Wilkinson MK, Bull AM (1966) Phys Soc 11: 263

5 Language and Input-Output for Large-Scale Parallel Computing[1]

HIROSHI KASHIWAGI[2]

Abstract. Programs for scientific and engineering calculations are swelling beyond the program productivity of academic researchers. One of the main reasons is that the burden of the control of data transfer between the main memory and external memories is left with programmers. A sample program, which would be written in just several tens of lines if it could be performed with the main memory, expands by as much as fifty times when plural kinds of memories must be used. This paper gives a proposition to overcome this problem by introducing a new high-level language supported by an input/output architecture. The new language is a modified version of PARAGRAM, which is a program language for parallel processing.

5.1 Introduction

In 1988, the author published a paper [2] titled "The Potential for Parallel Processing in Molecular Science Calculations." In that paper was reviewed the current status of large-scale molecular orbital calculations around the world, after which were set forth some guidelines for the next generation of parallel computers. Programs for molecular orbital calculations are swelling from lengths of tens of thousands of lines to hundreds of thousands of lines, bringing them beyond the reach of single researchers and thereby becoming an impediment to original research. This problem is particularly prominent in molecular orbital calculations, but is by no means limited to this field. It is something which afflicts all calculations in which large amounts of data must be handled.

The speeds available from electronic computers are rising steeply, and floating point operations are now being realized at speeds of $10^{10} - 10^{11}$ per second. Silicon-based main memories are also progressing rapidly, but they still only have a capacity of 10^7–10^8 words, which means they are 2–3 digits short of enough space to store the data put out by the CPU in one second. The main memory is a

---

[1] Based on [1]
[2] Faculty of Computer Science and Systems Engineering, Kyushu Institute of Technology, Kawazu, Iizuka, 820 Japan

working space for a large and indeterminate number of jobs, and not a space for long-term data storage. That is why magnetic disks or other large-capacity non-volatile external memories are needed. The access speeds for these memory media are, however, far slower than for the main memory, which has caused a bottleneck to appear in arithmetical processing. The extended memory, a kind of silicon medium, is provided in order to make up for this, but no radical improvements have been made in architecture and operating systems, so memory configurations become plural, and the burden of their control is left with the user. As will be shown later with actual examples, this situation causes programs, which would be written in just tens of lines if they could be performed with the main memory, to expand by as much as fifty times when plural kinds of memories must be used. It is therefore necessary to develop new methods by which the user could be relieved from the excess burden of controlling data access to and from external memories, and by which the throughput of the entire job would be improved.

5.2 Example: Linear Transformation of a Supermatrix

Let us look at the linear transformation of a supermatrix, i.e., four-dimensional matrix $S(p, q, r, s)$. This transformation can be written in a single line of mathematical notation; "C" indicates the transformation matrix:

$$W(i, j, k, l) = \sum_{p,q,r,s=1}^{N} S(p, q, r, s)C(p, i)C(q, j)C(r, k)C(s, l)) \tag{1}$$

If programmed as is, the number of operations becomes N^8. In order to reduce the number of operations, the process will be divided up into four steps:

Step 1
$$T(i, q, r, s) = \sum_{p=1}^{N} S(p, q, r, s)C(p, i) \tag{2a}$$

Step 2
$$U(i, j, r, s) = \sum_{q=1}^{N} T(i, q, r, s)C(q, j) \tag{2b}$$

Step 3
$$V(i, j, k, s) = \sum_{r=1}^{N} U(i, j, r, s)C(r, k) \tag{2c}$$

Step 4
$$W(i, j, k, l) = \sum_{s=1}^{N} V(i, j, k, s)C(s, l) \tag{2d}$$

When performed in this manner, the number of operations becomes $4N^5$. A FORTRAN-like code of the transformation is listed here. It is assumed that the elements of transformations matrix C and supermatrix S are already in the memory.

```
SUBROUTINE HENKAN (N,C,S,T)
DIMENSION C(N,N),S(N,N,N,N),T(N,N,N,N)
/*Step 1*/
   DO 10 i=1,N
   DO 10 q=1,N
   DO 10 r=1,N
   DO 10 s=1,N
```

```
      T(i, q, r, s)=0
      DO 11 p=1,N
11 T(i,q,r,s)=T(i,q,r,s)+S(p,q,r,s)*C(p,i)
10 CONTINUE
/*Step 2*/
      DO 20 i=1,N
      DO 20 j=1,N
      DO 20 r=1,N
      DO 20 s=1,N
      S(i, j, r, s)=0
      DO 21 q= 1, N
21 S(i, j, r, s)=S(i,j,r,s) + T(i,q,r,s)*C(q,j)
20 CONTINUE
/*Step 3*/
      DO 30 i=1,N
      DO 30 j=1,N
      DO 30 k=1,N
      DO 30 s=1,M
      T(i,j,k,s)=0
      DO 31 r=1,N
31 T(i,j,k,s)=T(i,j,k,s)+S(i,j,r,s)*C(r,k)
30 CONTINUE
/*Step 4*/
      DO 40 i=1,N
      DO 40 j=1,N
      DO 40 k=1,N
      DO 40 l=1,N
      S(i,j,k,l)= 0
      DO 41 q=1,N
41 S(i,j,k,l)=S(i,j,k,l)+T(i,j,k,s)*C(s, l)
40 CONTINUE
      STOP
      END
```

Written in this form, the program takes thirty-six lines. The number of operations involved could be reduced somewhat if the writing was changed, but there would be no substantial differences. This style was adopted because it is easier to understand. If N is small and S and T are stored in the main memory, there are no problems at all with this program. The problems we are dealing with, however, involve N's of between 100 and 1000, which means that S and T swell to 10^8-10^{12} words, more than the main memory can handle. At 10^{12} words (1 teraword), the program cannot run even with magnetic disks, and involves a large load on the CPU. It is therefore necessary to conserve operations by taking advantage of the sparseness of the supermatrix.

The question then arises of how big such a program would be in actuality. First, we will store supermatrix S on the disk in the following form:

WRITE(DISK) M, (IS(K), K = 1, 4*M), (S(K), K = 1,M)

M is the number of nonzero elements in the record. In IS are contained $p, q, r,$ and s, and in S are contained the element values. The order of the elements is generally random. This form is almost the same as the sparse structure in PARAGRAM [3], a language for parallel processing. The traditional algorithms for the transformation described above can be partitioned into the following three steps for execution:

1. The elements inside a record are sorted for a common r, s, and then these are stored in another data set.
2. Only those with a common r, s are read, and steps 1 and 2 of the transformation are performed. In other words, $S(i,j,r,s)$ is obtained and the elements inside a record are put together so that they have a common i, j and then are put out to disk.
3. Once all of (2) is performed, all $S(i,j,r,s)$ with a common i, j are read, and steps 3 and 4 of the transformation are performed.

When this is done on a supercomputer, the program must be optimized for vectorization. As a result, the JASON2 [4] program we coded has a transformation program of 1800 lines. The sorting in (1) takes 700 lines, the transformation in (2) and (3) takes 1000 lines, and the control section takes the remaining 100 lines. The program thus swelled to fifty-times the size of the 36 lines required by a program using only the main memory.

All programs in which the entire data is in an external memory and a part of it is moved to the main memory for processing will probably require a similarly large amount of programming effort. Molecular orbital calculations involve several different kinds of steps, but most of them are similar to this program in the data treatment, which is why large programs like those in Table 5.1 have come about. When a program reaches 50,000 lines, it requires about 10 person-years to complete, putting it beyond the reach of any single university laboratory unless it is extremely well provided for, or has a very "gung-ho" team. If all one's time is spent writing programs, there is none left over for creative thought or for writing papers, which then threatens one's position in the scholarly community. This means that one is forced to choose between creating one's own program, or using someone else's program with loss of originality. In order for creative research to be performed in the field of computer science, therefore, it is necessary to reduce the amount of labor involved in writing programs. A way must be found to bring the 1800 lines down to something a bit closer to 36.

Table 5.1. Sizes of *ab initio* molecular orbital calculation programs (language is generally FORTRAN)

Program	Size (10,000 lines)	HF	MCSCF	CI	Country of development
JAMOL4	7	o			Japan
JASON2	5		o		Japan
MICA3	3			o	Japan
GSCF3	3	o		o	Japan
MOLYX	5	o		o	Japan
GAUSS8X	15	o		o	USA
GAMESS	7	o	o	o	USA
MELD	6	o		o	USA

HF, Hartree-Fock; MCSCF, multi-configuration self-consistent fields; CI, configuration-interaction

5.3 Expanding the Functions of PARAGRAM

PARAGRAM [3] is a high-level language for parallel processing that was developed by a group at the Hitachi Central Laboratories under the Japanese Ministry of International Trade and Industry's supercomputer development project. It is used to describe problems in numerical simulation, and is not only highly descriptive, but also extremely efficient in the execution of programs, especially in parallel computing environments. Definition functions for sparse matrixes are included in the PARAGRAM array declaration, so it was decided to use this as a base from which to expand the language's functions. The expansion required is a function to extract partial dimensional arrays from a multidimensional array. Since this operation has the significance of a selective extraction, we have named it "sget." Its opposite, the creation of a multidimensional array from partial dimensional arrays, we have called "sput." When described using PARAGRAM, sget, and sput, the transformation formulas (Eq. 2) for the supermatrix are coded like this:

```
proc    HENKAN(N:i,C:i,S:u,IS4:u,#IS4:u);
scal    N     value(param),
        #IS4 value(param),
        EPS   value(1.OE-8);
cntl    p,q,r,s,i,j,k,l;
iarray  IU1 size([1:N].[1:1]).
        IS4 size([1:#IS4].[1:4]),
        IT4 size([1:#IS4].[1:4]);
array   (U) size(N)
        structure SPARSE(iarray(IU1),eps(EPS)),
        (C,V) size(N,N)
        structure DENSE,
        (S) size(N,N,N,N)
        structure SPARSE(iarray(IS4),eps(EPS)),
        (T) size(N,N,N,N)
        structure SPARSE(iarray(IT4),eps(EPS)):
proc;
/*step 1*/
    pcalc for r in [1,N];
    pcalc for s in [1,N];
      iter for q in [1,N];
        sget from S(*,q,r,s) to U(*);
        iter for i in [1,N];
          V(i,q)=0;
          iter for p in [1,N];
            V(i,q)=V(i,q)+U(p)*C(p,i);
          end iter;
        end iter;
      end iter;
/*step 2*/
    iter for i in [1,N];
      iter for j in [1,N];
        U(j)=0;
```

```
        iter for q in [1,N];
            U(j)=U(j)+V(i,q)*C(q,j);
        end iter;
    end iter;
    sput from U(*) to T(i,*,r,s);
end iter;
end pcalc;
end pcalc;
/*step 3*/
    pcalc for i in [1,N];
    pcalc for j in [1,N];
        iter for s in [1,N];
            sget from T(i,j,*,s) to U(*);
            iter for k in [1,N];
            V(k,s)=0;
            iter for r in [1,N];
                V(k,s)=V(k,s)+U(r)*C(r,k);
            end iter;
            end iter;
        end iter;
/*step 4*/
        iter for k in [1,N];
        iter for l in [1,N];
            U(l)=0;
            iter for s in [1,N];
                U(l)=U(l)+V(k,s)*C(s,l);
            end iter;
        end iter;
        sput from U(*) to S(i,j,k,*);
        end iter;
    end pcalc;
    end pcalc;
    end proc;
    end;
```

This program contains 52 lines (the number of semicolons). We shall now give a brief overview of PARAGRAM's specifications [3]. The first "proc" sentence indicates that this is a subprogram. An "i" after the argument colon indicates that the argument is input data, while a "u" indicates that it is input and output data. The "scal" and "cntl" lines declare the scalar and control variables respectively. The "array" line is the array declaration. If the structure is DENSE, the array is the same as in FORTRAN, but if it is SPARSE, only the nonzero elements given in the index array which follows are lined-up in the index array order. The index array is declared using "iarray." This relationship is shown in Fig. 5.1. The "pcalc for r in [1,N];" and "end pcalc;" are instructions to the parallel processor to perform parallel calculations for control variable "r." On the other hand, the "iter for q in [1,N];" and "end iter;" pair are the same as a DO loop in FORTRAN.

The specifications for "sget" and "sput" were chosen by the author as follows:

sget from S(*,q,r,s) to U(*);

This sentence means, "Get elements of a partial array with fixed q, r, and s from the total array S and put them into U."

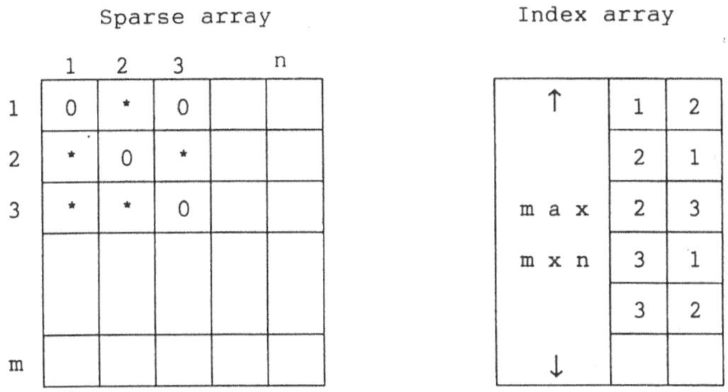

Sparse array   Index array

	1	2	3		n
1	0	*	0		
2	*	0	*		
3	*	*	0		
m					

↑	1	2
	2	1
m a x	2	3
m x n	3	1
	3	2
↓		

Fig. 5.1. Index array for the sparse array. The "nonzero index array" is an integer array having a size determined by multiplying the maximum number of nonzero elements by the number of dimensions. The index of nonzero elements is contained as shown. In this case, the sparse array is two-dimensional. *max*, maximum, new dimension of the index array is $m \times n$ (m, n; see left panel)

The reason that the program was divided up into steps 1 and 2, and steps 3 and 4 is to follow the traditional algorithms for the case where four-dimensional arrays S and T do not enter the main memory. If, in steps 1 and 2, n and s are fixed, the steps are equivalent to linear transformation of a two-dimensional matrix, which could be accomplished in the main memory. However, it is impossible to put the entire $T(i,j,r,s)$ in the main memory, so the parts of T must be output one-by-one to an external memory. (It may be better to state explicitly in the language specifications that S and T are files.)

As is the case with the calculation environments when traditional algorithms are used, it is assumed that the calculation environment for this language has a dual memory, and efficiency under these conditions is taken into account. The two-dimensional array V can be put in the main memory, but in this environment the four-dimensional S and T are in the external memory. We shall now look at how "sget" and "sput" are actualized.

5.4 Memory Layers and Actualization of "sget" and "sput"

The addition of "sget" and "sput" to PARAGRAM presents no problem as the language specification but we must now look at the conditions by which the commands are to be efficiently executed on the computer. Current computers are insufficient for the efficient execution of "sget" and "sput." We will therefore proceed to design a model system, which will be coming out in the near future. First, let us set the amount of data to be handled. If N is 1000, then the total number of elements of S is 10^{12}. If nonzero elements are assumed to be 1% of the total, that gives 10^{10} words. In other words, it is necessary to be able to handle 100 GB of data at high speeds. On a 10 GFLOPS CPU, 10^{10} operations can be processed in one second, so the problem is the input/output speeds to and from the main and external memories.

Magnetic disks provide nonvolatile memories able to store data for long periods of time. However, with transfer speeds of only several MB/s, the disks that are currently available are out of the running. A transfer speed as close as possible to 100 GB/s is needed here. The closest thing to that at the current time is the extended memory made from silicon. This offers speeds of 2 GB/s in its present status, and if speeds could be boosted 5-fold, 100 GB of data could be accessed in 10 seconds. This memory is volatile, so it will be necessary to back it up with a large nonvolatile memory. This, then, gives a three-layered configuration, consisting of a main memory, extended memory, and magnetic disk. A transfer speed of 10 GB/s would be expected between the expansion memory and magnetic disk as well. If 100 KB of data is contained on each track and the disk rotates at a speed of 1 revolution per 10 ms, a transfer time of 10 MB/s would be obtained for each track. If each cylinder contains 30 tracks, and disk drive units are improved so that parallel input and output can be accomplished from many heads, and if this parallel input and output is simultaneously performed from 32 volumes, a total of 10 GB/s could be attainable, which more or less meets the requirements. Instead of disks, this may be possible with rewritable, high-speed optical disks and other new media that are expected to come out in the near future.

Assuming the memory layering described above, the following three methods are envisioned for the actualization of "sget" and "spout." The third is the most desirable:

1. *Virtual Memory Method*
The arrays described with PARAGRAM are all in a unitary memory, and processed by the operating system using the virtual memory method. This method, however, contains a large amount of waste and is thought to be poor in terms of efficiency.

2. *CPU Selector Method*
As in record-unit access methods, the entire blocks for an array are put into a buffer on the main memory, and only the elements of a certain partial array are extracted therefrom ("sget"). For "sput," data are stored piece by piece in the buffer, and are output once the buffer is full. In order to accomplish this, however, it must be possible to transfer data between the extended and main memories at sufficiently high speeds. There is also a lot of load on the CPU.

3. *Disk Cache Method*
The extended memory will be considered a kind of disk cache, and "sget" and "sput" performed on it. The extended memory should be equipped with data selectors. This method features the lowest load in terms of both input/output and the CPU.

5.5 Computer Systems for Scientific and Engineering Calculations

We will now look at the field in which the linear transformation of a supermatrix that we have been using as our example would actually appear. In molecular orbital calculations, this kind of operation is required when molecular orbitals are used as the base of subsequent calculations. As can be seen from the Appendix, this step is indispensable if one wants to execute the Configuration-Interaction (CI) or Multi-Configuration Self-Consistent Fields (MCSCF) calculations in order to find a more precise wave function after molecular orbitals are obtained by the Hartree-Fock (HF) method. In standard molecular orbital methods, a molecular orbital is expressed as a linear combination of atomic orbitals. In Fig. 5.2 can be seen computer graphic representations of atomic orbitals named as "s," "p," and "d." Molecular orbitals are obtained by aligning the orbitals of a number of atoms, as can be seen in Fig. 5.3. The supermatrix elements that appear in the molecular orbital calculation express the amount of the repulsion interaction between an electron in an area where two orbitals overlap and another electron in an area where other two orbitals overlap. The linear transformation is used to calculate the electron repulsion in a molecular orbital base, and is indispensable when trying to find more precise wave functions in a molecular orbital base.

   This transformation is the critical step to limit the size of the whole calculation in terms of CPU time, input/output time, and memory use. It is one of the reasons

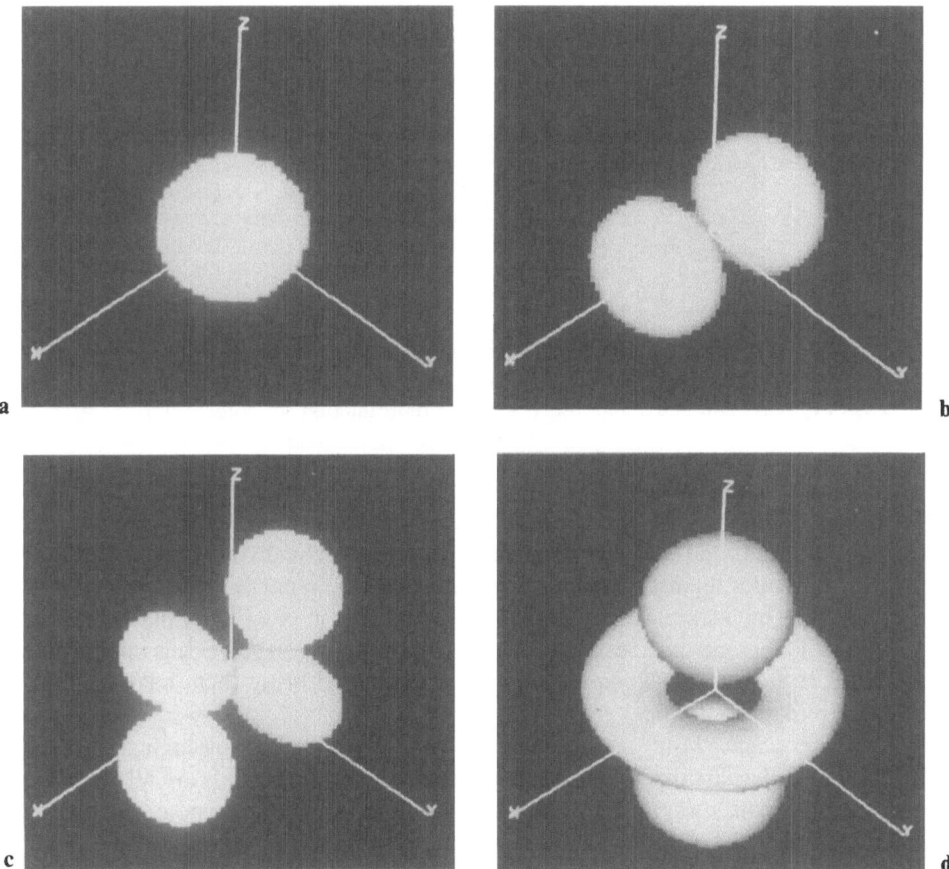

Fig. 5.2a–d. Various atomic orbits. **a** $2s$; **b** $2px$; **c** $3dxz$; **d** $3dz^2$

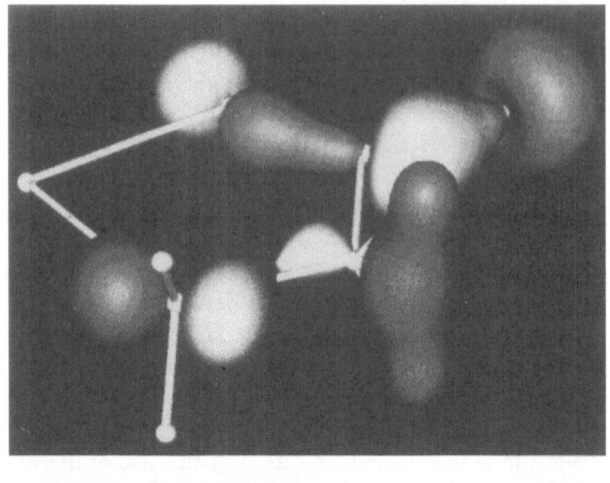

Fig. 5.3a,b. Examples of molecular orbitals. **a** A molecular orbital of a copper-glycine complex. **b** A molecular orbital of an iron-porphyrin-ammonia-oxygen complex, which is a model of the active site of hemoglobin. (For color reproduction see color insert)

why so much labor is involved when the object of calculations is to be widened. There are already some ten or twenty papers published on algorithms for this transformation. If one is a researcher performing theoretical studies on molecules, it is the molecules themselves that one is interested in. What is more, all his labor is being spent on a simple formula that can be written in one line of mathematical notation and requires no special mathematical techniques to solve. It is imperative, therefore, to free scientists from such menial labor and bring them back to more essential research activities.

Computer science holds out amazing potential to fields like molecular science. In the case of molecular science, living organisms, liquids, and solids are all made up of aoms and molecules, and we know that computations have the potentiality to elucidate much about the mechanisms by which their structures and movements change. It is therefore obvious that molecular science calculations will soon be introduced to all industries that deal with living organisms or materials. Generally speaking, scientific and engineering calculations involve large amounts of data, and will probably, therefore, run into more or less than the same kinds of data-processing problems as mentioned in this paper. We are now seeing computers, which have for the most part been developed as office machines, being turned to fully-fledged machines for scientific and technical calculations, and it is hoped that high-level languages back up by layered memory controls will be appearing for these machines in the near future.

References

1. Kashiwagi H (1989) Report on general tests in 1988. Association for Research into High-Speed Computer System Technology for Scientific and Technical Calculations. Supercomputer Workshop, Report 7, (Computer Center of Institute for Molecular Science, p 119
2. Kashiwagi H (1988) Report on general tests in 1987. Association for Research into High-Speed Computer System Technology for Scientific and Technical Calculations. Supercomputer Workshop, Report 6, Computer Center of Institute for Molecular Science, p 108
3. Yamamoto F, Umetani M, Yamamoto M (1988) Papers of the Electronic Information Telecommunications Society J71D (8): 1407
4. Yamamoto S, Nagashima U, Aoyama T, Kashiwagi H (1988) J Comput Chem 9: 627

Appendix: Molecular Orbital Method
(From reference [2])

The molecular orbital method is powerful for describing the electron behavior in molecules. It is one way of solving the Schrödinger equation, which is the basic equation in quantum mechanics. We will begin by introducing the LCAO SCF MO (Linear-Combination-of-Atomic-Orbitals Self-Consistent-Field Molecular-Orbital) method, which is the most standard.

The Schrödinger equation and the Hamiltonian H for electrons are shown:

$$H\Psi = E\Psi \tag{A1}$$

$$H = \sum_{1} \left\{ -\frac{1}{2} \nabla^2(i) - \sum_a \frac{Z_a}{r_{ia}} \right\} + \sum_{i<j} \frac{1}{r_{ij}} \tag{A2}$$

In this case "i" and "j" represent electrons, while "a" represents the atomic nucleus. The first term in the large braces is the energy of motion, the second the attraction by nuclei. The last term is the energy of repulsion between electrons. The wave function Ψ for the closed-shell state in which all α-spin and β-spin electrons form pairs can be expressed in the form of a determinant as seen in Eq. A3. Other states which are called as open-shell electronic states are expressed using one or more linearly-combined determinants.

$$\Psi = \frac{1}{\sqrt{n!}} \begin{vmatrix} \phi_1(1)\alpha(1) & \phi_1(1)\beta(1) & \cdots & \phi_{n12}(1)\beta(1) \\ \phi_1(2)\alpha(2) & \phi_1(2)\beta(2) & \cdots & \phi_{n12}(2)\beta(2) \\ \cdots\cdots\cdots\cdots\cdots\cdots\cdots\cdots\cdots\cdots\cdots\cdots \\ \phi_1(n)\alpha(n) & \phi_1(n)\beta(n) & \cdots & \phi_{n12}(n)\beta(n) \end{vmatrix}, \tag{A3}$$

where $\alpha(i)$ and $\beta(i)$ are the upwards and downwards spin functions, respectively. The particular determinant above shows a state in which one upward and one downward spinning electron occupy all molecular orbitals from ϕ_1 to $\phi_{n/2}$. The entire system fulfills the Pauli Principle. The molecular orbital ϕ_i is described by a linear combination of atomic orbitals χ_p as shown in the formula in Eq. A4 and the optimal coefficients C_{pi} are sought;

$$\phi_i = \sum_p x_p C_{pi} \tag{A4}$$

$$x_p = \sum_k b_{kp}(x - x_a)^{1p}(y - y_a)^{mp}(z - z_a)^{np} \times \exp(-a_k|r - r_a|^2) = \sum_k \Psi_k b_{kp} \tag{A5}$$

Most programs use a linear combination of Gaussian functions ψ_k for the atomic orbital. Led by the variation principle, the Fock formula (Eq. A6), to obtain the coefficient matrix C of the molecular orbital, takes the following form:

$$FC = SC_\varepsilon \tag{A6}$$

$$S_{pq} = \int x_p^*(1) x_q(1) \, dv_1 \tag{A7}$$

$$F_{pq} = h_{pq} + \sum_{rs} \left(\sum_{i=1}^{n/2} C_n C_{si} \right) \{2(pq|rs) - (pr|qs)\} \tag{A8}$$

$$h_{pq} = \int x_p^*(1) \left\{ -\frac{1}{2} \nabla^2(i) - \sum_a \frac{Z_a}{r_{ia}} \right\} x_q(1) \, dv_1 \tag{A9}$$

$$(pq|rs) = \int x_p^*(1) x_q(1) x_p^*(2) x_2(2) \frac{1}{r_{12}} \, dv_{12} \tag{A10}$$

The Fock formula is used to find the energy ε and coefficient matrix C of the molecular orbital. As can be seen from Eq. A8, the left side of the Fock formula contains C. This requires one to start from a given C and look for the solution by iterative calculations. Between 10 and 100 iterations are necessary to find a wave function.

One-electron integrals h_{pq} (Eq. A9) and two-electron integrals $(pq \mid rs)$ (Eq. A10) are needed to solve Eq. A8. These are calculated beforehand from the atomic orbitals. The number of h_{pq} is about $N^2/2$ when N is the number of atomic orbitals. For $(pq|rs)$ the number is $N^4/8$. Therefore, if N equals 100, the number is 10^7 for $(pq|rs)$, while if N equals 1000, the number becomes a gigantic 10^{11}. In actual calculations, a lot of techniques are used to reduce the number of the integrals $(pq|rs)$. Nevertheless, the calculations of $(pq|rs)$ and the memory to store them, as well as the calculations for Eq. 8, determine the limits of the LCAO SCF MO calculation [4]. At the present time, the maximum value for N is 1560. This record-making calculation is explained in Sect. 3.2 of reference [2].

The SCF method focuses on a single electron and looks for an orbital of the electron which moves in an average field created by other electrons (Hartree-Fock Field). Because of this the precision of the wave functions and the physical quantities calculated with the method are not always high. The perturbation method, the cluster expansion method, and the configuration interaction (CI) method are used to go eyond the SCF method. Among them we will limit our explanations here to an overview of the last one. The wave function for a many-electron system Φ_μ is expressed as a linear combination of the functions in Eq. A3:

$$\phi_\mu = \sum_1 \Psi_1 A_{IU} \tag{A11}$$

The solution becomes the eigenvalue problem of the following matrix H:

$$HA = EA \tag{A12}$$

$$H_{IJ} = \sum_i \sum_j h_{ij} d_{ij,IJ} + \sum_i \sum_j \sum_k \sum_l (ij|kl) \cdot D_{ijkl,IJ} \tag{A13}$$

$$h_{ij} = \sum_p \sum_q h_{pq} C_{pi} C_{qj} \tag{A14}$$

$$(ij|kl) = \sum_p \sum_q \sum_r \sum_s (pq|rs) C_{pi} C_{qj} C_{rk} C_{sl} \tag{A15}$$

At the present time, the maximum number of dimensions for the matrix shown in Eq. A12 is 20 million [2]. The evaluation and diagonalization of the Hamiltonian matrix shown in Eq. A13 becomes the rate-determining step for the process. The $d_{ij,IJ}$ and $D_{ijkl,IJ}$ are known as the first and second order density matrices respectively, and are determined by the combination of basic functions I and J. In most cases, however, they are zero, so the problem is not as difficult as would seem.

Generally, the eigenvalue problem is solved by the Davidson method, which is an expansion of the Lanczos method. The h_{ij} and $(ij|kl)$ are the molecular integrals on a molecular orbital base, and are calculated by the linear transformation of atomic orbital base integrals, as can be seen in Eqs. A14 and A15. The transformation in Eq. A15 involves going from data of N^4 to data of N^4, and the number of operations depends on N^5. This makes it one of the most difficult of all calculations in the molecular orbital method.

In addition to CI, the MCSCF (Multi-Configuration SCF) method has also been developed as a way to go beyond the Hartree-Fock approximation. The method is a combination of both the SCF and the CI techniques. The wave function is found as in Eq. A11, and repeats are made until the CI calculations and optimization of molecular orbitals converge. Since the comparatively short linear combination Eq. A11 is obtained by using optimal molecular orbitals, it is easy to understand the physical meaning of the solution. However, higher speeds are required for each of these steps because calculations in Eqs. A12–A15 are repeated over and over again. The author's team has recently developed an MCSCF program called JASON2 [4] and used it to perform calculations for ån iron-porphyrin complex with 236 electrons. This is, at the present time, the largest MCSCF calculation to have been performed.

As was mentioned in Sect. 1 of reference [2], it is essential that potential energy surfaces be sought if chemical reactions are to be predicted. However, even disregarding translations and rotations, the degree of freedom in a polyatomic system is (number of atoms) $\times$ 3 $-$ 6, so that when the number of atoms becomes very large it becomes extremely difficult to find the entire surface. Still, if only the bottoms, saddles, and the paths that join them are known, it is possible to understand the molecular structure and reaction paths. All that needs to be done is to calculate the slope of the surface. In the SCF method, the energy gradient is given by the following formula:

$$\frac{\partial E}{\partial x} = \sum_{p,q} D_{pq} \frac{\partial}{\partial x} h_{pq} + \frac{1}{2} \sum_{p,q,r,s} D_{pq} D_{rs} \frac{\partial}{\partial x} \{2(pq|rs) - (pr|qs)\} + \sum_{pq} W_{pq} \frac{\partial}{\partial x} S_{pq}$$

(A16)

$$D_{pq} = \sum_{i=1}^{occ} 2 C_{pi} C_{qi}$$

(A17)

$$W_{pq} = \sum_{i=1}^{occ} \varepsilon_i C_{pi} C_{qi}$$

(A18)

In this case ∂x expresses the partial differential of the spatial coordinates. For example, when looking for a bottom, the SCF calculation is performed for an appropriate molecular structure, the molecular structure corrected a bit in the direction of the gradient vector, and the calculation repeated. The bottoms are the places where $\frac{\partial E}{\partial x}$ equals zero. $\frac{\partial}{\partial x}(pq|rs)$ is calculated in the same way as $(pq|rs)$, but since there are more variations, the calculations take several-times more time than for $(pq|rs)$. The speed of the energy gradient method is determined by the calculation time for the integrals.

We have looked at the differential formula for the SCF energy. Energy gradients could also be calculated for MCSCF and CI, though they become a bit more complex. In addition, if the second-order differentials are sought, the area around the bottoms and saddle points can be elucidated quite well and proper oscillations can also be analyzed. Calculations for the second-order differentials, however, require several more times the labor of the first-order differential calculations.

Participants' Contributions

6 Supercomputing of Incompressible Fluid Flow

Toshio Kobayashi[1]

Abstract. For years, many papers have been given in flow field analysis arguing for the wider applicability of the numerical simulation method. Many problems are still unsolved, however, including optimum calculational methods and conditions for the numerical scheme of the algorithm, turbulence models, grid density, boundary conditions, etc. This is partly due to the complex contours of the flow field and also because flow separation or a large wake complicates matters, preventing the simple transfer of technology from aeronautical and astronautical fields. Turbulent separating flows are encountered in many engineering applications and play important roles. The advent of powerful digital computers and the development of hypotheses pertaining to turbulence modeling are bringing about a dramatic improvement in our ability to calculate flow phenomena of engineering relevance. Such a predictive capability for turbulent separating flow is, however, conspicuously lacking. Turbulent separating flows occupy a unique position within the general group of flows. The intense streamline curvature present in separating flows produces a strong anisotropy in the normal stresses, and dramatic changes in the shear-stress field. In spite of this, however, most available turbulent models are based on the Boussinesq-viscosity assumption, which cannot capture the interaction between separation and the turbulence stress field. At this moment, it is necessary to develop calculation methods including the turbulence models.

6.1 Introduction

The analysis and control of a fluid flow have a big impact upon various fields of science and technology. Especially, the numerical analysis will make such a large contribution to their development that it can break through the limits of experimental research, and a lot of information offered by it will stimulate the expansion

---

[1] Institute of Industrial Science, University of Tokyo, 22-1 Roppongi-7, Minato-ku, Tokyo, 116 Japan

of the theory of fluid flow, which is opening the new field of computational fluid dynamics (CFD).

CFD enables us to estimate quantitatively the unsteady and/or local structures of turbulent flow which were difficult to observe in previous experiments, because, in CFD, the conditions of the flow field can be easily controlled: for example, initial and boundary conditions, time and spatial scale of measurement, or physical properties of fluid. Also, flows which are difficult to reproduce in the laboratory can also be investigated, such as flows in nuclear fusion or high-vacuum vessels, high-temperature or high-velocity flows, or flows under exactly symmetrical or periodical conditions. In other words, CFD expands widely and deeply the range of investigation possible, by way of "experiments" on computer to explore unknown fields in fluid dynamics.

However, there are a lot of problems to solve in order that CFD can be applied as a useful tool to future engineering. They are, simply speaking, reliability and efficiency. We have been researching these issues step by step, and so we think that CFD is developing toward application to engineering.

The basic equations governing a fluid flow are the Navier-Stokes equation (involving Reynolds' stress equation), the continuity equation, and the energy equation. The numerical analysis of a fluid flow is able to evaluate velocity and pressure through these governing equations. The influences of physical variables, except velocity and pressure, are added to the equation of motion in terms of external forces. However, it should be considered that the density and viscosity are each expressed by the function of its physical variable. In this sense, we should note the analysis of incompressible thermal fluid flow, which includes thermal transport and incompressible turbulent flow, by using a turbulence model.

The fluid flow appearing in the various fields of industry and engineering is actually turbulent flow of incompressible fluids. I have chosen this fluid flow for the main theme of this article. As far as incompressible fluid flows are concerned, we do not consider discontinuous variation of the physical variable of a fluid flow in either space or time. I exclude the sonic wave, shock wave, abrupt chemical reaction, and temperature variation in this article. This means that the continuity equation is mathematically described in the time-independent form. In this case, there is the characteristic that the variations of velocity and pressure are instantly transported to the far field. This characteristic makes a big difference to the analysis of compressible fluids in the numerical simulation. Though such discontinuities as a solid surface or a free surface exist in the analysis of an incompressible fluid, these are mainly treated in terms of the boundary conditions.

The points that a scientist and/or an engineer should consider in the analysis of a fluid flow are as follows [1–3]:

(1) predicting the characteristics of a fluid flow, the problem of how we choose a proper model in a basic equation; (2) the problems of the stability of a numerical calculation and of artificial diffusion, which are deeply related; (3) the speed of a matrix calculation and algorithm in the numerical calculation; (4) the setting of the boundary conditions; and (5) the choice and generation of the numerical grid. Now, let me introduce some important points about each of these.

6.2 Modeling of Fluid Flow

An analysis of a fluid flow is equivalent to the modeling of the phenomena of the fluid flow by using a certain characteristic length and time scale. This characteristic length is generally equal to the space or time interval. In order to describe the phenomena correctly, it is necessary to divide more finely time and space intervals, so as not to neglect or miss the phenomena. However, it is very difficult to obtain such high resolution in current computers. For example, let us consider the direct simulation of turbulence. We need numbers of grid points in proportion to the $\frac{9}{4}$ power of the Reynolds number in order to divide the space domain to the extent that one characteristic length scale of turbulence – that is Kolmogorov microscale – can be completely described [4]. If we consider the characteristic time related to the energy dissipation of turbulence, we also need the numbers of the time-step in proportion to the $\frac{1}{2}$ power of the Reynolds number. The number of points of the space grid in the present calculation of maximum order using the highest-level supercomputer is about 6,000,000 meshes, and the calculation time is a few days, but this is not enough in relation to the number of points needed. The number of points of the space grid is usually about 100,000 meshes, and the calculation time is a few hours, for an engineering use. In present and future CFD, there exists a limit to the solution capability in the hardware. We must provide a prescription to reduce this limitation for the efficient use of CFD.

Various models of turbulence have been provided from the experimental or theoretical results in the analysis of turbulence. For example, in the most practical (k-ε) model of turbulence, the time mean properties of turbulence are modeled for the reduction of this limitation. As we divide the space more and more finely, we expect that the value will approach the true one in this model – that is, we expect asymptotic behavior. In the turbulence calculation of the large eddy simulation (LES) model, which is modeled as the basis of the space mean properties, we divide a flow field into a large-scale and a small-scale field, and impose the turbulence model on the latter in order to reduce the limitation on the number of points of the space grid. The idea of this model is that the space scale needed for the analysis is within the capability of the model itself, and the values approach the true ones gradually when dividing time-intervals finely [5, 6].

There is one more limitation in the time scale – that is, the unstable behavior of a numerical calculation over time. In the choice of the difference scheme, if we choose a big time interval relative to the space one, the solution diverges because of the increase of any small error which occurs in time, due to the increasing time interval in the calculation procedures. It should be noted that this instability is basically different from the one occurring in true physical phenomena [7].

In the analysis of fluid flow, we must first determine which model to use for solving the phenomena of the fluid flow. The development pattern of the analysis technology for the internal flow of the turbomachinery is shown in Fig. 6.1. The subsidiary analysis technology and experimental methods are fed back into the process, as shown toward the right of Fig. 6.1. The quasi-three-dimensional analysis has been widely used in practical problems such as performance predictions. This high-level

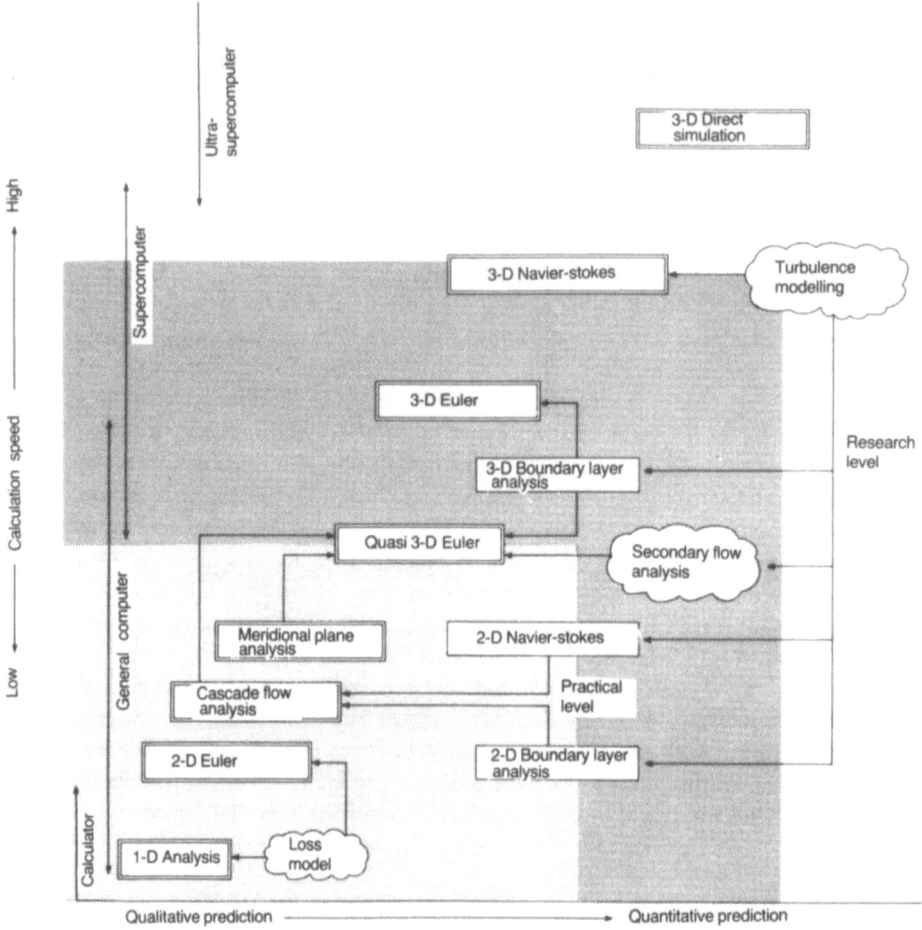

Fig. 6.1. Development of analysis technology for an internal flow in turbomachinery. *1-D, 2-D, 3-D*, one-, two-, and three-dimensional. (From [18] with permission)

analysis technology is being used for the understanding of transient phenomena, evaluation of the applicability for non-design points, etc [8].

Because the space and time scales in the analysis of fluid flow are finite, even though their resolutions can be increased, cases where the physical phenomena cannot be naturally described exist. Under these circumstances, we should describe the phenomena using a mathematical model based on the law of physics. In this case, though it is absolutely necessary to discuss the accuracy of a model containing a numerical calculation, there are some difficult problems. In order to solve these problems, after we isolate some important factors from the physical law governing the phenomena of an objective fluid flow, we can start by choosing the negligible parameters. This contributes not only to the reduction of the computer load, but also the simplification of the model. If we use an analysis code which has been modeled for any phenomena as possible as considered, it would seem that the computation would result in the correct solution. However, there is the possibility that an inference made in such a model, could destroy the calculation due to the numerical errors in the terribly complicated equations. Though a defect of the model may be clear in a case where calculation is destroyed, a more serious discrepancy is very difficult to evaluate and/or diagnose in the computational results given by a model in which the code is complicated.

While these limitations must be considered, the present demands for numerical analysis are for advanced and complex analysis. For example, if we define a small volume around a fixed point of space, and introduce a model describing the physical phenomena inside this volume, then this approach may be used in the analysis of a chemical reaction; the fluid flow accompanied by combustion and phase change; the fluid flow of the thin film formation in the semiconductor industry; or the establishment of an artificial boundary condition by considering the surface reaction in small volumes). The understanding of the microphysics of a small volume in the engineering sense, and the modeling based on it, seem to be the key factors for fluid analysis to be applied widely in engineering and industry. This means that we introduce two new scales into the numerical analysis: the space and time scales in the modeling of a small volume.

6.3 Stability of Numerical Calculation and Artificial Diffusion

Because the space and time scales are the necessary conditions in the numerical analysis, these have a big influence on the accuracy of the analysis results. The discretization method and the accuracy of the discretization scheme also effect the approximation accuracy of solution. The stability of the numerical analysis, and the artificial diffusion in particular, will be a problem in relation to the truncation error of a scheme. Because the artificial diffusion has behavior identical with that of actual diffusion, there is the possibility of change in important parameters, such as the Reynolds number. Though it is reasonable to use the central difference scheme not involved in the artificial diffusion, it is widely known that this scheme is unstable in a high Reynolds number. In order to solve this problem, the upwind scheme of odd order about the convective term is frequently used. Figure 6.2 shows the stream patterns generated by various difference schemes for the convective term for laminar viscous flow in a two-dimensional square cavity. We find that a few schemes cause false solutions in the case of a high Reynolds number flow [9].

The oscillation of solution, caused by the high-order truncation error of the odd order upwind scheme of the convective term, is not fully understood. Because discontinuous change does not appear in the case of analysis of incompressible fluid flow, it seems that this instability has not been discussed as intensively as in the case of a compressible fluid. However, the solution of the Reynolds stress transport model that does not have the second-order diffusion term explicitly, and the LES that emphasize not mean velocity but the statistical quantities of high order, depend on the characteristics of the scheme of the convective term. Though the effects on the solution caused by the artificial diffusion term become small when the space

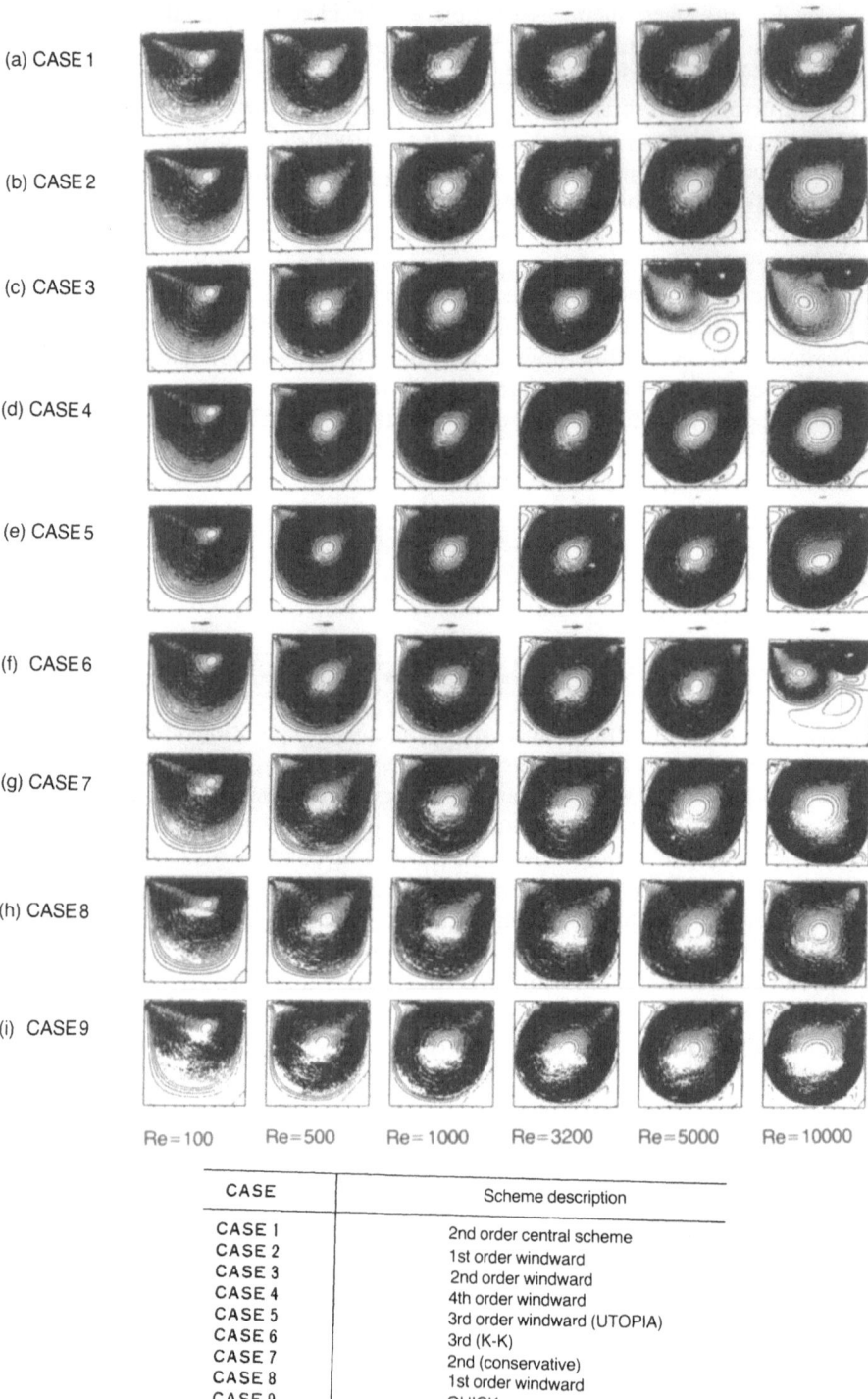

(a) CASE 1

(b) CASE 2

(c) CASE 3

(d) CASE 4

(e) CASE 5

(f) CASE 6

(g) CASE 7

(h) CASE 8

(i) CASE 9

Re = 100   Re = 500   Re = 1000   Re = 3200   Re = 5000   Re = 10000

CASE	Scheme description
CASE 1	2nd order central scheme
CASE 2	1st order windward
CASE 3	2nd order windward
CASE 4	4th order windward
CASE 5	3rd order windward (UTOPIA)
CASE 6	3rd (K-K)
CASE 7	2nd (conservative)
CASE 8	1st order windward
CASE 9	QUICK

grid is made finely, they always exist. Attempts to model smaller scale flows than a grid, when involving artificial diffusion, should be treated with caution in an analysis of high-order accuracy incorporating the accumulated know-how concerning the behavior of the diffusion term. In particular, the use of the second-order diffusion term, which has the same effect as the physical diffusion, should be avoided as much as possible.

6.4 Algorithm and Matrix Calculation

In the analysis of fluid flow, there are cases when steady-state values are necessary and cases when unsteady values are necessary. The latter makes use of the method of time-marching. The choice of the scheme of time difference is an important factor in the time-marching method. The proper time-difference scheme varies according both to the time scale of the phenomena discussed and to the limitation of time increment chosen for the numerical stability. If the time interval necessitated by the physical phenomena satisfies the numerical stability, as in many cases of LES calculation, the explicit method of solution will be used, because there is no reason to use an implicit method taking up more computation time.

In practical analysis, the number of cases needing only steady values may be large. In a turbulent flow, it is easy to think of steady values in the case of using a turbulence model of the time mean type. We have two methods to obtain steady values. One is to obtain the stable state by using a time-marching method extended over a long time period. The other is to obtain steady values directly. The latter is equivalent to the steady method of solution as an extension of the implicit method of solution, and, as represented by the SIMPLE method, has produced many accomplishments. If we attempt to analyze a flow field in which there are frequent fluctuations, such as in the case of the Karman vortex, by using a steady-state method of solution based on the turbulence model of time mean type as Fig. 6.3 shows, there is the possibility of obtaining a flow field not originating the periodic change. It is reasonable to use the time-marching method in this case. Ideally, the two methods should be used case-by-case.

Because the incompressible fluid is subjected to the continuity equation, and the change of velocity and pressure will be transported to the whole domain instantly, an implicit method of solution should be introduced, at least, into a part of the

◁ *Fig. 6.2.* Schemes showing the effects of a convective term having influence on 2-dimensional square cavity flow patterns. The analysis of flow in a cavity has been frequently used to check the analysis method. As an example, the clockwise flow pattern that occurs in a cavity with an upper moving belt is analyzed and depicted using streamlines. The *ordinate* and *abscissa* represent respectively a discretization method and the Reynolds number (R_e; an important flow parameter). Even though the same column shows the results of the same flow condition, they show the different results occurring due to the different discretization methods. Generally, in the case of a high velocity and a big cavity, the errors of numerical analysis become high. The results for high Reynolds numbers in this example highlight the differences resulting from different discretization methods. (From [18] with permission)

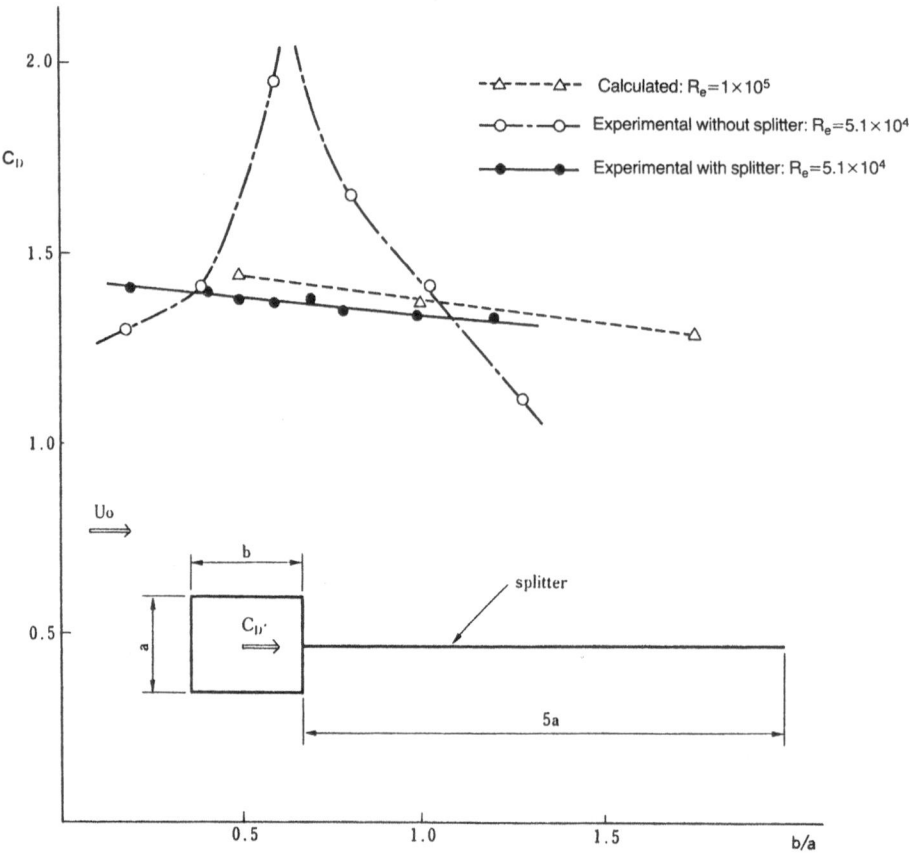

Fig. 6.3. Drag coefficients of a square cylinder by steady analysis with the k-ε model. A body that is placed in a flow with a velocity U_0 is subjected to force. In the case of a square cylinder, the experimental results(o) of various aspect ratios (b/a) are quite different from the predictions($\triangle$) from steady-state calculation [the *abscissa* and *ordinate* represent respectively aspect ratio and drag coefficient C_D (dimensional number representing the force obtained in the stream-wise direction)]. This is the reason why the periodic eddies observed in an experiment are not calculated. If a splitter is installed, the periodic eddies disappear and the experimental results($\bullet$) are in good agreement with the corresponding calculation. Concerning the flow generating the periodic fluctuation, the time-mean value can not be correctly obtained from the steady-state calculation. R_e, Reynolds number. From Bearman et al. [17]

algorithm in order to satisfy a problem. Matrix calculation is essential in the analysis of the incompressible fluid, and it has a great influence on the computational efficiency. Though the direct and the iteration methods are both used in matrix calculation, the latter has been overwhelmingly used for extensive calculations. Because the interactions of the equations for velocity components and pressure (and other physical variables) are weak in comparison those encountered in the analysis of a compressible fluid, we can use the decoupled method. So, in the finite difference method (FDM) and finite volume method (FVM), we shall treat the structural band matrix, which is nearly symmetric, as conforming to the space distribution of one of the physical variables. The point-by-point method (SOR) and the line-by-line method (ADI, TDMA) are widely known for their methods of solution. More effective methods such as preconditioned conjugate gradient method (CG) and strong implicit method (SI) have already been proposed [10]. Though the point-by-point and line-by-line methods are widely used because of their simplicity of formulation, if it is possible to use the reliable "library," there is no reason to avoid using the more efficient methods. Because the finite element method (FEM) has a coefficient matrix of the asymmetric, irregular type, and the band width becomes wide when using a unstructural grid, the application of the iteration method will be complicated. Improvements of the scheme on the concentration of mass, the various preconditionings, and the introduction of the CG method have been devised [11].

For large-scale analyses, the technology of parallel computation is essential now. Its function is incorporated not only in the supercomputer, but also in general computers and engineering workstations (EWS). Though there is considerable parallelism technology, it has gradually been absorbed into the compiler function, and there is a tendency for the part available to the user to decrease. It is necessary for users to understand and classify the algorithm clearly.

6.5 Boundary Condition and Analysis Grid

It is reasonable that the change of a physical variable is continuous, in the analysis of an incompressible fluid flow. So, the restriction of the boundary condition will be loose in comparing it to the analysis of a compressible fluid. However, it should be considered whether the turbulence model is described correctly in the solid boundary of the turbulence field. The finite volume method and finite element method for evaluating boundary flux are superior to the finite difference method in this respect. Even though the slip (Neumann) and no-slip (Dirichlet) conditions for velocity are basic as the boundary conditions occurring in the solid boundary, the power law of $1/n$ (general Neumann condition = fixed gradient) and the law of the logarithm (a simultaneous equation of a fixed gradient or a constraint condition) have been used as the boundary conditions for turbulence analysis. Moreover, for pressure, because the pressure gradient in the normal direction of the surface of a body can be negligible in a boundary layer, the simple Neumann condition (non-gradient) is effective.

The computational domain and its outlet condition often become the topic of discussion. For example, in the case of fluid flow taking up an unlimited region (such as a jet issuing into free space) or the case of fluid flow around a body, analyses have been accomplished by using the setting of a large domain or a correction method in the experiments, though it is necessary to consider the influences of the size of the computational domain and the outlet boundary condition. In the field of structure analysis, a combined use of the boundary element method (BEM) has been studied for these problems, and has been valuable for discussing fluid flow analysis. The free surface has the difficulty of the introduction of Lagrangian analysis in addition to the problem of the solid boundary. Though methods including the Lagrangian coordinate (ALE) method, the marker tracer (original MAC) method, and the VOF method (extending the marker trace method) have been proposed as a countermeasure, the cases studied are not sufficient.

The most important problems in the analysis grid depend on the merits and demerits inherent in the structural and unstructural grids. This evaluation will be continually changed according to developments of numerical methods and computer engineering. Though it is difficult to conclude at present, roughly speaking, advances in numerical methods will depend on improvements in the BFC grid generation method and the domain split method. An example of the application of a BFC grid is shown in Fig. 6.4 [12]. Figure 6.5 shows the results of analysis of laminar flow with comparatively complex geometry using the domain split method [13], and Fig. 6.6 shows an example of grid generation using a Voronoid diagram as one of the unstructural grids [14]. We have used the method to solve a differential equation (Thompson's method), an algebraic interpolation function, or the various iteration methods as a BFC grid generation method, and usually C,O,H,L type

NORMALIZED
PRESSURE

Fig. 6.4. Example of application of a BFC grid. An example of the flow analysis around a propeller of a new type, which is being developed for application in a big airplane in the near future. It is a reproducible finding that the particles within the flow disappear by rolling up into the eddies occurring at the top of the propeller. The three-dimensional analysis has been carried out using the BFC grid for a complex geometry and the turbulence model for the effects of turbulent flow. Though using an ultra-modern analysis method and supercomputer, several hours are needed for one case. (From [18] with permission)

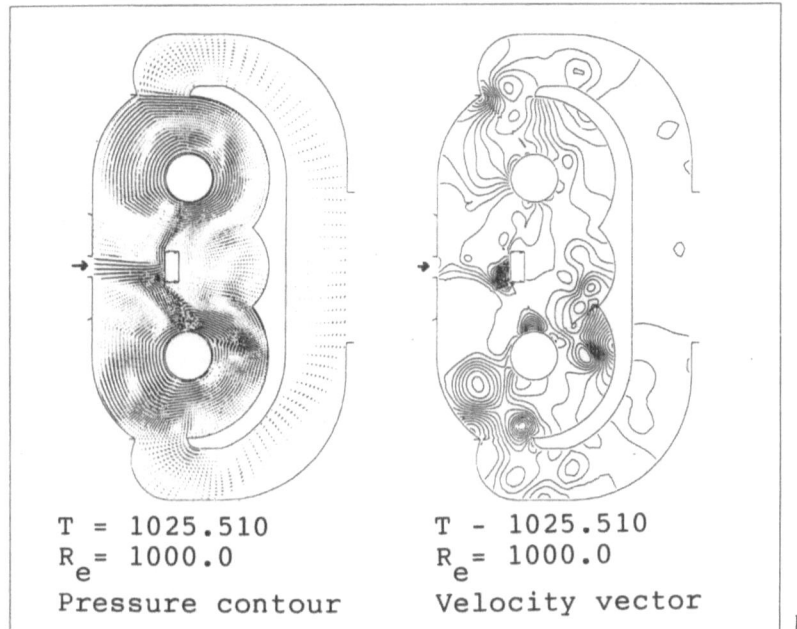

T = 1025.510
R_e = 1000.0
Pressure contour

T - 1025.510
R_e = 1000.0
Velocity vector

a   b

*Fig. 6.5*a,b. Fluid flow analysis of a vortex flowmeter. An example of the analysis of steady flow within a complex vessel. This is the equipment that measures the flow rate passing into the vessel by using the frequency of a periodic flow occurring within the vessel. The flow enters the vessel in the *left-middle* position, and collides with the obstacle. The phenomena bent periodically in the *up* and *down* directions have been analyzed. The instantaneous vector diagram flowing in the *down* direction is shown in **a**, and the equi-pressure lines in **b**. In order to deal with the complex geometry, the analysis domain is divided into several small regions, and the analysis method using the BFC grid has been applied. The calculation time is about one hour by a supercomputer. *T*, non-dimensional time; R_e, Renolds number. (From [18] with permission)

related to the solid boundary in a fluid field as a grid geometry. The conditions imposed on the BFC grid in the large-scale analysis of fluid flow are generally continuity, concentration, and orthogonality (especially at the solid boundary), but the systematic evaluation of the effects on the computational results is now the subject being focused on [15]. Besides this, the porous body model concerning the porosity of volume and surface will be applied in tackling the particular problem of the description of a free surface for the present. The grid generation of BFC will continue to be an important theme of research in the analysis grid.

6.6 Toward the Practice of Fluid Flow Analysis

I presented an outline of the modeling of a fluid flow, numerical calculation method, and analysis grid in the case of the numerical analysis of incompressible turbulence. In addition, in order to utilize effectively the extended numerical analysis of fluid

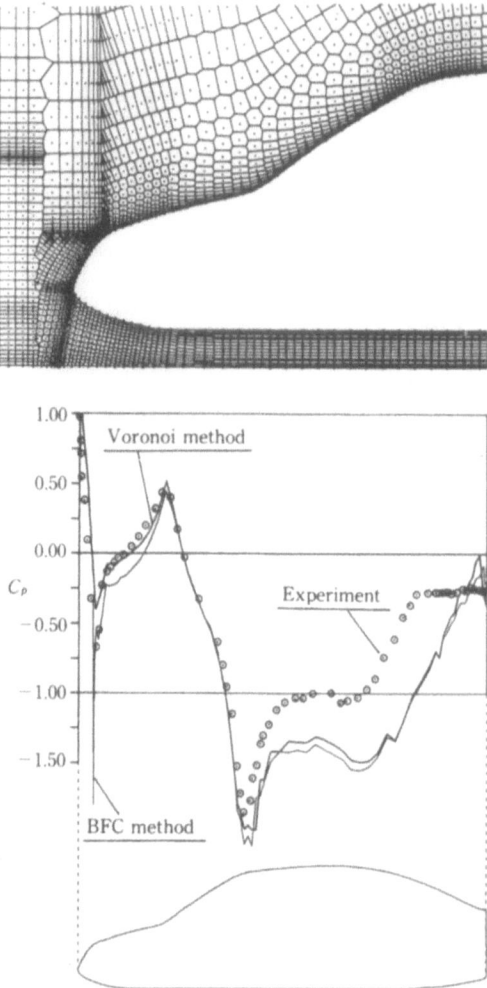

Fig. 6.6. Unstructural grid using the Voronoid splitting method. There is a method for analyzing complex geometries that places calculation points irregularly. In contrast to the placement of the calculation points using a coordinate system (structural grid), the placement of irregular calculation points is called the unstructural grid. The figure shows an example of the unstructural grid for analyzing the flow around a two-dimensional automobile. The diagram shows the splitting pattern of the calculation domain by irregular polygons, reminiscent of cells. The calculation technique used for the information processing of a map have been applied in this method. This is an example of a technique from another field is connected through a computer. C_p, pressure coefficient. (From [18] with permission)

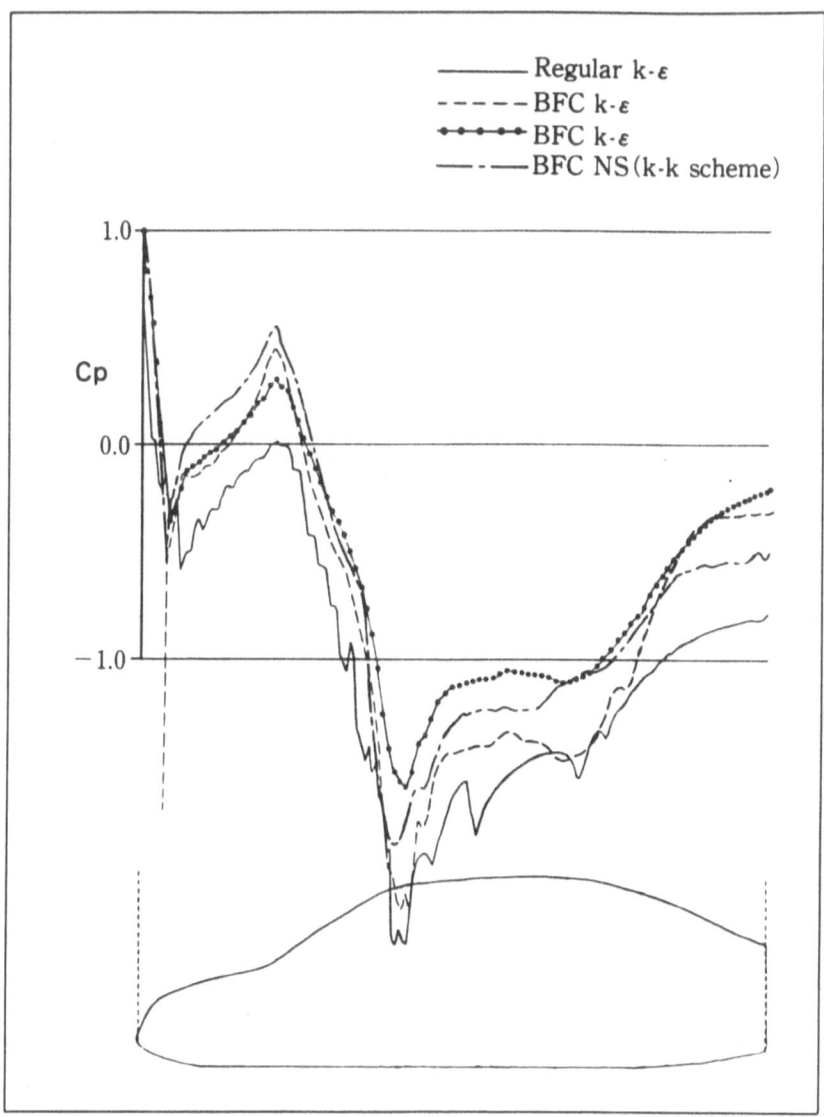

Fig. 6.7. Pressure coefficient (C_p) distribution on the upper surface of the 2-dimensional body of an automobile. The flow around the 2-dimensional body of an automobile was analyzed by the four analysis codes, and the pressure coefficient distributions of the upper surface were compared. Each code has been independently developed on the basis of different analysis methods. Though they are all high-level techniques for turbulence analysis, the results are very different. It seems that the reasons are the differences of turbulence model, grid system, discretization method, and so on. The prediction of a complex flow structure occurring in the downstream flow field of an automobile is an example of one of the difficult problems. *BFC, NS,* Napier-Stokes; *k-ε,* time-mean model. (From [18] with permission)

flow, it will require satisfactory methods of generation of calculation grids representing the flow field properly in a short time, technology for image-processing or animation that treats a great volume of computational results, and high-speed calculation using the supercomputer, and linking to data transportation and interfaces. With the combination of these technologies, a general purpose code has already been developed, and there is a trend toward the development of new codes. Though these codes have their respective characteristics, presently, individual idea is needed so as to obtain the good results of fluid flow analysis through these codes. For example, let us consider the case of turbulence around an automobile, as an example of a turbulence field existing in a region of big separation. The fluid flow around an automobile with the same geometry was calculated by four kinds of codes, and the results comparing the pressure distributions over the upper surface of the body are shown in Fig. 6.7. The differences result from the superpositions of

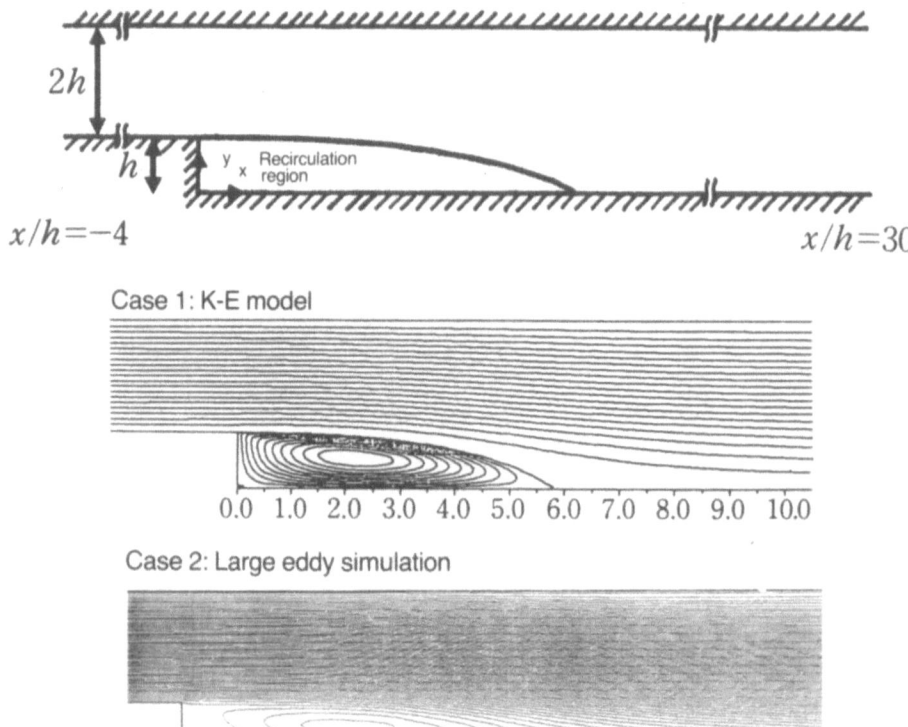

Fig. 6.8. Predicted flow patterns of a backfacing-step. The flow of a backfacing-step has been frequently taken as an example of a basic flow field exposing the differences in the turbulence models. The analysis results using the representative turbulence model based on the time-mean (k-ε) and large eddy simulation (LES; based on space-mean) models have been compared here. The streamline show clockwise recirculation behind the backfacing-step. These two analysis methods produce different lengths for this recirculation region. So, attempts to improve the two models have been made. x, y, coordinates; h, height. (From [18] with permission)

several factors: the differences between turbulence models, analysis grid, space interval, etc. Let us compare the analysis results considering the differences between turbulence models. The analysis results of standard k-ε and LES methods have been compared [16]. Figure 6.8 shows the equi-value lines of stream function, noting the recirculation region of back step flow under the same conditions concerning the number of space grids, boundary condition of the wall, inlet and outlet conditions, and algorithm in the coupling between momentum and continuity equations. In this comparatively simple flow field, we find that the basic time mean behavior of the recirculation appears to differ with the different turbulence models used. As a matter of course, the mutual reconciliation of the results can be approached, in both cases, by the adoption of various ideas. In this case of fluid flow, verification and improvement of the code are needed through comparison with experimental data.

If the problems of reliability and efficiency in the analysis of fluid flow can be overcome, and the know-how for large-scale analysis accumulated, the numerical analysis of fluid flow will have a great impact on the wide field of science and technology. It is expected that it will make contributions to the understanding of the plasma turbulence in a nuclear fusion reactor, difficult to reproduce experimentally, and it will be important for studying the microphysics of high-temperature combustion phenomena and similar areas not presently amenable to study.

References

1. Daiguji H (1989) Numerical analysis I. In: The 647th text of course. JSME
2. Kobayashi T (1989) Numerical analysis II. In: The 647th text of course. The Japan Society of Mechanical Engineers
3. Patankar SV (1980) Numerical heat transfer and fluid flow. McGraw-Hill, New York
4. Tani I (1980) Improvement in fluid mechanics: turbulence. Maruzen, Tokyo
5. Horiuti K (1985) Large Eddy simulation of turbulent cannel flow by one equation modeling. J Phys Soc Jap 54: 2855
6. Morinishi Y, Kobayashi T (1989) A study on wall boundary condition in LES. Trans Jap Soc Mech Eng 55: 615
7. Roache PJ (1976) Computational fluid dynamics. Hermora
8. Inoue M (1989) Trend in research and development of analysis methods on the internal flows of the fluid machinery, Proceedings of the 66th The Japan Society of Mechanical Engineers spring annual meeting
9. The Japan Society of Mechanical Engineers (1988) Report on the first CFD workshop, 1988
10. Togawa H (1971) Numerical method on matrix. Ohm, Tokyo
11. Natori M, Nodera T (1987) Supercomputer and large scale numerical calculation, bit-supplement. Kyoritsu Shuppan, Tokyo
12. Matsuo Y (1989) Numerical analysis of a high-speed turbo-prop flow. PhD dissertation, University of Tokyo
13. Kobayashi T (1989) Characteristics of Karman vortex type flowmeter. Proceedings of the 6th fluid measurement symposium The Society of Instrument and Control Engineers
14. Taniguchi N, Atakawa C, Kobayashi T (1989) Construction on a flow-simulating method with finite volume based on Voronoi diagrams. Trans Jap Soc Mech Eng 55: 1324

15. Thompson JF, Thompson JF, Warsi ZUA, Martin CW (1985) Numerical grid generation: Foundations and applications. North-Holland, New York
16. Kobayashi T, Kobayashi T, Morinishi Y, Sada K (1988) Numerical calculation of turbulent flow behind a backward-facing step. Proc 2nd CFD Symp, p 371
17. Bearman DW (1965) Investigation of the flow behind a two-dimensional model with a blunt trailing edge and fitted with splitter plates. J Fluid Mech 21-2: 241–255
18. Kobayashi T (1989) Development of Computational Fluid Dynamics and Supercomputing. Datapro Books 7: 53–64

7 Glass Transition and Stability of Glasses: Simulations and Visual Presentations by Computer Graphics

FUMIKO YONEZAWA[1]

Abstract. Computer simulations of crystallization, glass transition, and annealing for a model system composed of 864 Lennard-Jones (LJ) atoms under a periodic boundary condition, are carried out using constant-pressure molecular dynamics techniques with temperature control. An LJ liquid, when quenched slowly, crystallizes into a stack of layers with stacking faults. Each layer forms a two-dimensional close-packed structure with occasional point defects but without any dislocations. When the quench rate is high enough, an LJ liquid transforms into a disordered structure without a discontinuous change in volume. The dependence of the glass transition on the quench rate is determined by examining macroscopidally observable physical features such as thermodynamic, structural, and dynamic properties. Several microscopic structure parameters are introduced in order to analyze, at the atomic level, the structures of the glasses produced by different quench rates. When annealed, a glass carefully made with a low enough quench rate is stable against crystallization. The number of atoms in the system having local icosahedral symmetry is identified as a promising measure of characterizing the stability of a glass.

7.1 Introduction

It is thousands of years since glasses first appeared in the history of mankind and almost a century has passed since glasses were brought to the realm of science. Glassy or amorphous materials have been intensively studied for the last few decades, both from academic and application perspectives. Nevertheless, the essential nature of glassy structures is not yet fully understood. The complexity of topological disorder contained in these materials has made experimental analyses difficult.

It is the purpose of this work to clarify the characteristic features of glassy structures at the atomic level by means of computer simulations. For this purpose,

---

[1] Department of Physics, Keio University, Hiyoshi 3-14-1, Kohoku-ku, Yokohama, 223 Japan

constant-pressure molecular-dynamics (MD) simulations (with accurate temperature control) are used to study crystallization, glass formation though the glass transition, and the annealing of glasses.

A notable aspect of this work is the detailed analyses of the atomic structures in glasses by means of several microscopic structure parameters and the Voronoi tessellation [1, 2]. These types of structural analyses are possible only because complete information about atomic positions can be computed, i.e, these results can never be obtained experimentally.

In Sect. 7.2, we explain the model and method. The results of crystallization simulations are shown in Sect. 7.3 while glass formation results are presented in Sect. 7.4. The methods used for the microscopic structure analyses are discussed in Sect. 7.5, and the stabilization of glasses is examined in Sect. 7.6. A summary of this work is presented in Sect. 7.7.

7.2 Models and Methods

We study a model system composed of atoms interacting with one another via (12-6) Lennard-Jones (LJ) pair potentials characterized by length σ and minimum energy ε,

$$\phi(r) = 4\varepsilon \left(\left(\frac{\sigma}{r} \right)^{12} - \left(\frac{\sigma}{r} \right)^{6} \right).$$

For these simulations, a combination of the constant-pressure MD method proposed by Andersen [3] and the temperature-control MD method proposed by Nosé [4, 5] is used. The equations of motion are solved by a fifth-order predictor-corrector algorithm and periodic boundary conditions are assumed. We present the results for the case where the number of atoms, N, is 864.

In the discussions to follow, we choose parameters appropriate for argon, i.e, $\sigma = 3.446$ Å, $\varepsilon = 125$ K, and $m = 39.9$ g/mol. The time step for integration is taken to be 0.5×10^{-14} s. The pressure is chosen to correspond to atmospheric pressure.

The simulations were carried out using the HITAC S810/20 supercomputer at the University of Tokyo Computer Center. The CPU time for a system of 864 atoms is 0.085 per timestep.

By using computer graphics, we have produced a video film to visualize the atomic motions in amorphous structures [6, 7]. The video film to visualize atomic motions was produced using a VAX11/750 with a 20-inch color monitor. The CPU time to draw one picture was a few minutes with a subroutine package SAIL (based on SIGGRAPH CORE), and more than 50,000 pictures were taken to complete the work[2].

---

[2] The video films (as well as the 16mm movie files) are available from Mita Visual Image Co. Ltd. Please contact: Hongo 3-2-12, Bunkyo-ku, Tokyo, 113 Japan; Tel. 813-818-1013; Fax. 813-818-1016.

7.3 Crystallization

By starting from a disordered configuration of atoms at 100 K, the structural change upon cooling is also studied. When the temperature of the LJ liquid is reduced from 100 K to 60 K, the volume decreases continuously. The same volume(V)-temperature(T) curve, defined by the open squares in Fig. 7.1, is obtained between 100 K and 60 K, irrespective of the cooling rate. This indicates that the system is in an equilibrium liquid state above 60 K. When the temperature is lower than 84 K but higher than 60 K, the system is expected to be in a supercooled region, but the lack of dependence on the cooling rate confirms that the system is still in equilibrium.

The cooling rate dependence appears below 60 K. When this rate is reasonably slow, nuclei grow and the system crystallizes. A rapid cooling rate yields a glass. The strong dependence on the cooling rate below 60 K indicates the departure of the system from a supercooled liquid in thermal equilibrium.

When the cooling rate was low enough for argon (4×10^{10} K/s, for instance), the volume decreases at about 54 K as denoted by the small dots in Fig. 7.1. By analyzing the actual atomic configurations of this branch in the approximate temperature region $T < 50$ K, we confirm that the structure is a stacking of close-packed layers with occasional point defects, but that there exist no dislocations. The difference in volume between the fcc crystal (illustrated by filled circles in Fig. 7.1) and the resulting close-packed structure (illustrated by small dots) is accounted for by the density decrease due to the point defects.

The diffusion constant calculated from the mean square displacement (MSD) in this low-temperature phase guarantees that the system is nothing but a solid.

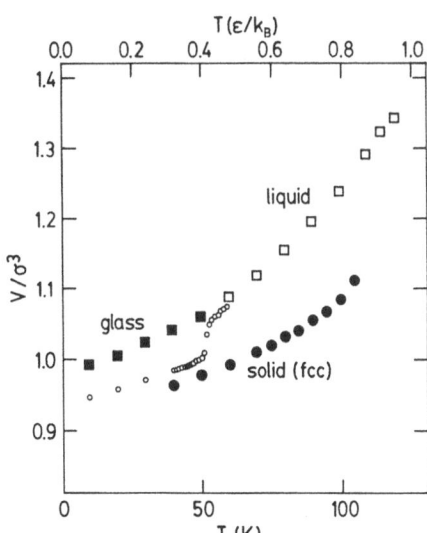

Fig. 7.1. Results of our simulations as expressed in terms of the volume (V) vs temperature (T) relation; heating (*solid circles*), melting, cooling (*open squares*), crystallization (*small dots*), and glass formation (*solid squares*)

Careful examinations of the system above and below 54 K show that the crystal-lization occurs near 54 K when the LJ liquid is cooled with a cooling rate of 4×10^{10} K/s.

The cooling rate for these simulations is defined by the ratio of the decrement of temperature to timesteps. For example, the cooling rate used is derived from 1 K/5000 timesteps = 4×10^{10} K/s. This cooling rate is actually higher, by two or three orders of magnitude, than the highest cooling rate attainable in laboratories. The results of these cooling and nucleation simulations suggest that an argon liquid would crystallize even when it is quenched with a cooling rate as high as 4×10^{10} K/s. In other words, a quench rate higher than this is required to produce an argon glass through the so-called glass transition. This is notable, since an argon glass has never been achieved in laboratories. The poor glass-forming ability of argon is attributed to the isotropic pair potential. Thus, it is interesting to identify the critical cooling rate in an LJ system that separates the crystal-forming cooling rates from the glass-forming cooling rates. According to our simulations, the critical cooling rate is between 4×10^{10} K/s and 4×10^{11} K/s.

7.4 Occurrence of the Glass Transition

In the rapid-quench simulations discussed in this section, the macroscopically observable physical properties are measured to identify the occurrence of glass transition in the system. As shown subsequently, these physical properties behave in the same way as those observed in the glass-forming processes of actual materials. It can therefore be asserted that the glass transition does take place in the system when the quench rate is high enough.

The quench rate, q, for the rapid-quench simulations is chosen as follows: $q = 2 \times 10^{13}$ K/s (decrease of 10 K over 5000 timesteps).

7.4.1 Thermodynamic Properties

The change in volume V as a function of temperature is shown by filled squares in Fig. 7.1 for a quench rate of 2×10^{13} K/s. There is no sharp change in volume, in contrast to the case of crystallization (as denoted by small dots in the same figure). It is well known from experiments that the V-T curve is continuous throughout the temperature region where the glass transition takes place. It is also well known that the V-T relation is linear in a sufficiently high temperature region (in a liquid state) as well as in a sufficiently low temperature region (in a glassy state). These features, which are regarded as characteristic of the glass-forming process, are reproduced in these simulations as seen from Fig. 7.1.

In computer simulations, the glass-transition temperature is defined by the temperature at which the extrapolations from the liquid and glassy lines intersect. The glass-transition temperature, T_g, of this system is thus determined about 50 K.

Similar behavior is obtained for the temperature dependence of other thermodynamic properties such as enthalpy, which also agrees with experimental results as well as with theoretical predictions.

7.4.2 Structural Properties

The pair distribution function $g(r)$ of a glass is similar to $g(r)$ of a liquid, in that there exist no peaks specific to crystalline structures since both a glass and a liquid have random atomic configurations. However, there are certain distinct differences between them. The $g(r)$ of glass, compared with that of a liquid, has the following features: (1) the first peak is sharper and narrower; (2) the second peak is characterized by the splitting; (3) the third and further peaks decay more slowly. All these features can be ascribed to the excluded-volume effect in the more compact configuration of atoms in a glass.

The $g(r)$s of the LJ system are shown in Fig. 7.2 for several temperatures in the rapid-quench process. It is clear that the lower the temperature, the more distinguished the splitting of the second peak. The second peak is not really split at 60 K while the splitting becomes undeniable at 40 K, thus implying that the system undergoes the glass transition between those two temperatures. This is consistent with the estimation of T_g obtained from the V-T relation. Features (1) and (3) are also clearly revealed in the simulation results shown in Fig. 7.2.

7.4.3 Dynamic Properties

The glass transition per se is a transformation from a liquid to a solid without any discontinuous change in thermodynamic properties such as volume and enthalpy. A system is conventionally regarded as a solid when the structural relaxation time therein is on the order of days. In a liquid state, the viscosity and the diffusion constant are known to obey the Arrhenius form.

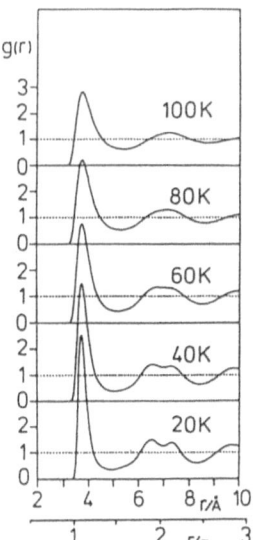

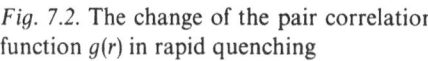

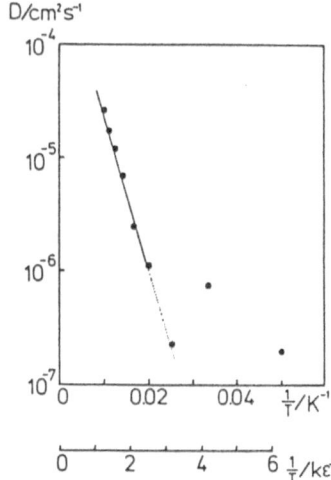

Fig. 7.2. The change of the pair correlation function $g(r)$ in rapid quenching

Fig. 7.3. The diffusion constant (D) vs $1/T$ derived from the mean-square displacement

As stated above, the diffusion constant D is calculated from the MSD of atomic positions. The logarithmic presentation of the diffusion constant D in the simulated rapid-quench process is given in Fig. 7.3 as a function of $1/T$. The curve for $T > 50$ K satisfies the Arrhenius relation, and D becomes as small as 10^{-6} cm^2/s around $T = 50$ K, suggesting that the system is certainly solidified around this temperature.

7.5 Microscopic Structure Analyses

7.5.1 Fivefold Symmetry

One of the advantages of MD simulations is that the complete information about the positions of all the atoms in the system is available. This permits microscopic analysis of the structure. By itself, the list of all atomic positions does provide great insight. It is therefore important to find methods for extracting useful information from these data. For this purpose, previous papers on MD simulations and structure analyses by the present authors have introduced microscopic structure parameters such as the distortion parameters, the Voronoi-face parameters, and the local-symmetry parameters. [1–3, 8–10].

This paper shall be concerned with parameters in the last category.

It is well known in crystallography that fivefold symmetry contradicts the trans-

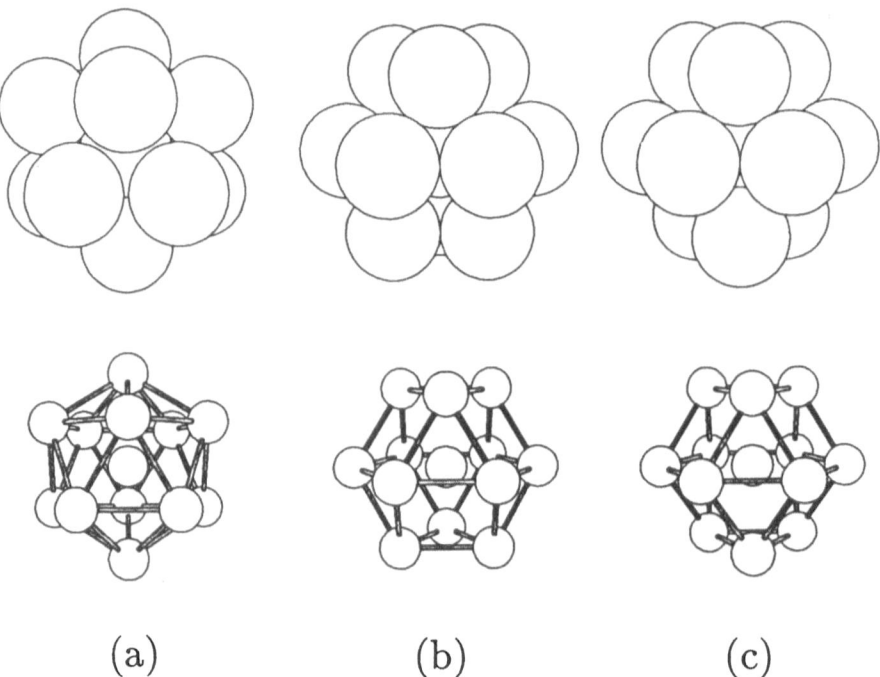

(a)   (b)   (c)

Fig. 7.4a–c. Clusters in which 12 atoms surround a central atom: **a** an icosahedral cluster; **b** an fcc cluster; and **c** an hcp cluster

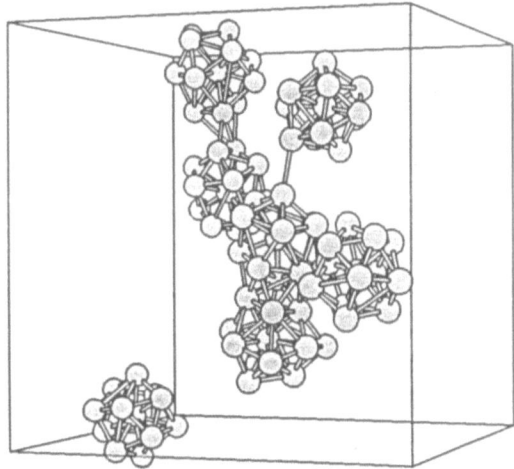

Fig. 7.5. Atoms with the local icosa-hedral symmetry. (Other atoms are not shown)

lational symmetry of a crystal. On the other hand, microclusters of LJ atoms (or even some kinds of metallic atoms) can have shapes with fivefold symmetry based on energy considerations. For instance, a cluster of 13 atoms, in which 12 atoms surround the central atom, has a lower energy when it has the icosahedral symmetry (Fig. 7.4a) than when it has either fcc or hcp symmetry (Figs. 7.4b, c). This is because the number n of the nearest-neighbor bonds is larger for an icosahedral cluster, n being 42, then for an fcc or hcp cluster, n being 36.

When a liquid is quenched rapidly, the atoms in the system do not have time to rearrange themselves into a crystalline structure, which is expected to have the minimum free energy. Instead, they try to lower the energy by adjusting at least the local configurations. Therefore, some of the atoms are expected to take local distributions that are energetically preferable for microclusters.

In the glasses simulated by the rapid-quench MD method, significant numbers of atoms with the local icosahedral or fivefold symmetry are found, as shown in Fig. 7.5. Since the fivefold symmetry is not reconcilable with the translational symmetry of a crystal, it seems reasonable to suppose that the abundance of atoms with the local fivefold symmetry could serve as a measure for the degree of amorphousness.

7.5.2 Local-symmetry Parameter

On the basis of the argument in the preceding subsection, we introduce a parameter that reflects the local symmetry around each atom. The parameter is related to the bond-orientational parameters proposed by Steinhardt et al. [11] as follows: associate a vector $r \equiv r_j - r_i$ pointing to a nearest-neighbor atom at r_j from the central atom under consideration located at r_i, a set of numbers

$$Q_{lm}(r) = Y_{lm}[\theta(r), \phi(r)], \tag{1}$$

where the $Y_{lm}[\theta(r), \phi(r)]$ are the spherical harmonics, and $\theta(r)$ and $\phi(r)$ are the polar angles of the vector measured with respect to some reference coordinate system.

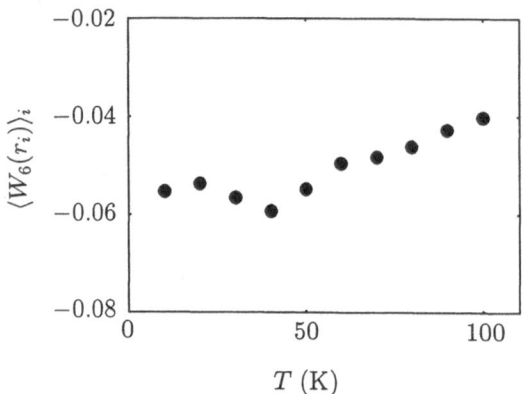

Fig. 7.6. The local-symmetry parameter ($\langle W_6(r_i)\rangle_i$) vs temperature ($T$) in a process of rapid quenching

Take the average $\langle\cdots\rangle_V$ of the above quantity over all the vectors which connect the central atom and its nearest-neighbor atoms, and calculate the rotationally invariant parameter of the third order given by

$$W_l(r_i) = \frac{\sum\limits_{\substack{m_1,m_2,m_3 \\ m_1+m_2+m_3=0}} \begin{pmatrix} l & l & l \\ m_1 & m_2 & m_3 \end{pmatrix} \langle Q_{lm_1}(r_i)\rangle_V \langle Q_{lm_2}(r_i)\rangle_V \langle Q_{lm_3}(r_i)\rangle_V}{\left(\sum\limits_{m} |\langle Q_{lm}(r_i)\rangle_V|^2\right)^{3/2}} \tag{2}$$

in which the coefficients are the Wigner $3j$ symbols. Here, the nearest neighbors are defined in terms of the Voronoi tessellation, and the suffix V of the average notation indicates "*Voronoi*." The vectors defined here are often called *bonds* for convenience.

This parameter is different from the parameters derived by Steinhardt et al. [11] in that it is defined by the average over all the vectors or bounds *around each atom*. The parameters of Steinhardt et al. are defined by the average over all the bonds *in the system*. They assert that their parameters indicate the bond-orientational order. The parameter defined in the present paper, on the other hand, has been shown to serve as a measure for the degree of the local fivefold symmetry [8–10].

The parameter $W_6(r_i)$ is particularly significant since $|W_6(r_i)| = 0.17$ for an icosahedron while $|W_6(r_i)|$ is order of 0.01 for a cluster with crystalline symmetry such as an fcc, bcc, hcp, or sc cluster. The temperature dependence of $\langle W_6(r_i)\rangle_i$ in the process of rapid quenching is shown in Fig. 7.6 where $\langle\cdots\rangle_i$ denotes the average over all atoms $\{i\}$. The results shown in Fig. 7.6 and analyzed in a series of the present authors' papers on glass transition [8–10] suggest that, in a glassy state, there exist both kinds of atoms, i.e., atoms with local icosahedral symmetry and atoms with local cubic symmetry.

7.5.3 Classification of Atoms in Amorphous Structures

In our visual analysis of the amorphous or glassy structures, atoms are classified into three categories:

1. An atom at r_i is regarded as having the icosahedral symmetry when it satisfies the following conditions:

a) The value $|W_6(r_i)|$ is such that

$$0.10 \leq |W_6(r_i)| \leq 0.17. \tag{3}$$

b) The atom has more than one nearest-neighbor atoms with the value of $|W_6(r_i)|$ in the region defined in Eq. 3.

2. An atom at r_i is regarded as having crystalline symmetry when it satisfies the following conditions:

a) The value $|W_6(r_i)|$ is such that

$$0.005 \leq |W_6(r_i)| \leq 0.02. \tag{4}$$

b) Among the bonds connecting the central atom with its nearest-neighbor atoms, there is at least one pair of bonds whose relative angle is between $170°$ and $190°$.
c) The atom has more than four nearest-neighbor atoms that fulfill conditions (a) and (b).

3. The other atoms which belong neither to category (1) nor to (2).

In an amorphous or glassy structure, atoms hardly can have any regular symmetry, but the local symmetry around each atom is rather distorted. The regions defined by the inequalities in Eqs. 3 and 4 take this situation into account.

Figure 7.5 illstrates atoms classified to be in category (1). Atoms with icosahedral symmetry are coloured blue, atoms with cubic symmetry are yellow, and the other atoms are white. The actual analysis of the atomic configurations is carried out using this classification of atoms. This is explained in detail in the next section.

7.6 Stability of Glasses

7.6.1 Annealing of Glasses Prepared with Different Quench Rates

It is well known that, since glasses or amorphous materials are metastable, their structures as well as their physical properties depend on the preparation conditions such as the quench rates. As an example, consider the quench-rate dependence of the glass-transition temperature T_g, as shown in Fig. 7.7, in which the enthalpy H vs temperature T are plotted for the following two quench rates:

A. 4×10^{11} K/s (decrease of 10 K over 100 timesteps)
B. 2×10^{13} K/s (decrease of 10 K over 5000 timesteps)

It can be seen from Fig. 7.7 that the higher the quench rate, the higher the glass-transition temperature T_g.

The quench-rate dependence of T_g is appreciable but not very large. In contrast, the quench-rate dependence of the stability of glasses is rather strong. In order to examine the stability of glasses, two kinds of the LJ glasses are annealed at 40 K (which is below T_g). The glasses are prepared with the two quench rates denoted by A and B.

To study the evolution of the atomic configurations during annealing, ther-

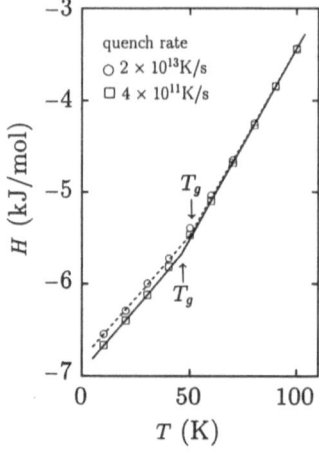

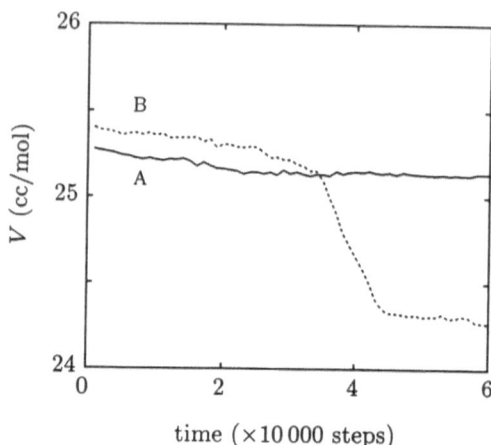

Fig. 7.7. Enthalpy (H) vs temperature (T) for two cooling processes with the quench rates of 2×10^{13} K/s and 4×10^{11} K/s

Fig. 7.8. Volume (V) vs timestep (t) on the annealing process: A, quench rate $q = 4 \times 10^{11}$ K/s; B, $q = 2 \times 10^{13}$ K/s

modynamic properties such as volume and enthalpy are measured, as well as microscopic structure parameters such as $W_6(r_i)$. In Fig. 7.8, the volumes of these glasses are expressed as functions of annealing timesteps. This indicates that the glass prepared using quench rate A remains in a glassy state even after annealing for 200,000 timesteps, while the glass prepared using quench rate B crystallizes at about 30,000 timesteps. On the basis of this result, it can be asserted that the higher the quench rate, the less stable is the glass obtained.

7.6.2 Visual Display of the Atomic Configurations

In order to investigate the stability of glasses in more detail, the evolution of these two glasses during the annealing is studied. For this purpose, all the atoms in the system are classified into the three categories defined in the preceding section. The evolution of the atomic configurations is shown in the video[2] from which the still pictures shown in Figs. 7.9 and 7.10 are taken.

From the visualization in Fig. 7.9 of the atomic configurations during the annealing of a glass prepared using quench rate A, it can be observed that the clusters of atoms having icosahedral symmetry (coloured blue in the video[2]) are rather persistent throughout the annealing process. These clusters never disappear even though their apparent sizes vary with time. Obviously, these clusters with icosahedral symmetry prevent clusters with crystalline symmetry from growing, thus impeding the crystallization of the whole system.

From the visualization in Fig. 7.10 of the atomic configurations during annealing of a glass prepared using quench rate B, it is clear that, at the beginning of the annealing, there exist many atoms with icosahedral symmetry. The number of these

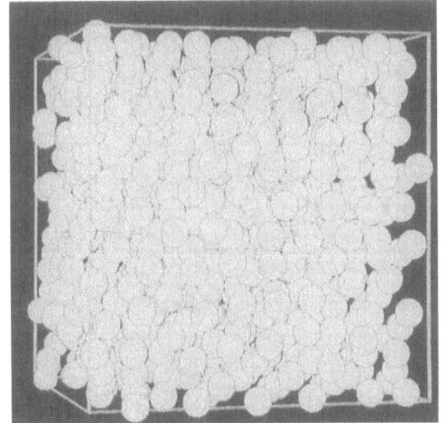

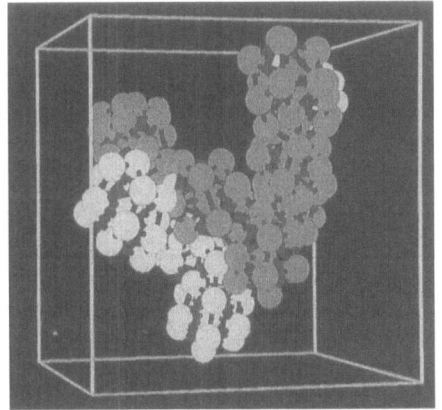

b

a

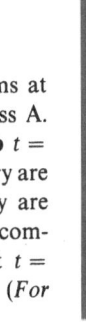

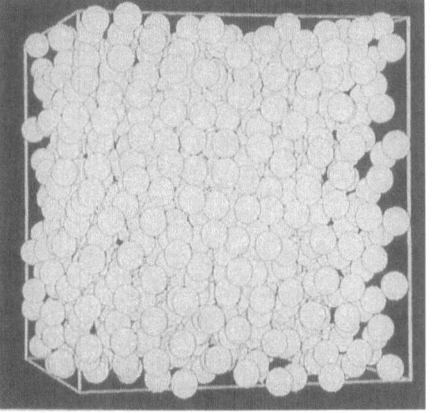

Fig. 7.9a–c. The configuration of atoms at some timesteps in the annealing process A. **a** 864 atoms at time step $t = 10,000$; **b** $t = 20,000$, atoms with icosahedral symmetry are *blue* while atoms with cubic symmetry are *white*; *blue clusters* and *white clusters* compete with each other. **c** 864 atoms at $t = 50,000$; the system is still disordered. (*For color reproduction see color insert*)

c

atoms decreases quickly as time proceeds, while the number of atoms with crystalline symmetry increases. The crystallization starts at about 30,000 timesteps.

7.6.3 Analysis of Quench-rate Dependence of Stability

The quench-rate dependence, described in Sect. 7.6.1, of the stability of glasses may be explained as follows. When the quench rate is not high enough to exclude entirely the redistribution of atoms beyond the immediate neighbor, but not low enough to allow extended redistribution towards crystallization, the obtained configuration is expected to contain clusters with the fivefold symmetry whose sizes are larger than a single icosahedron, although clusters with the crystalline symmetry are also allowed to grow in the process of quenching. Since clusters with the icosahedral symmetry of appropriate sizes are not reconcilable with the crystalline structures characterized by the translational symmetry, the existence of the icosahedral symmetry prevents crystallization from taking place and makes the glassy state stable.

When the quench rate is very high, the redistribution of atoms over a wide range is nearly impossible, and consequently the least energetic configuration is found by

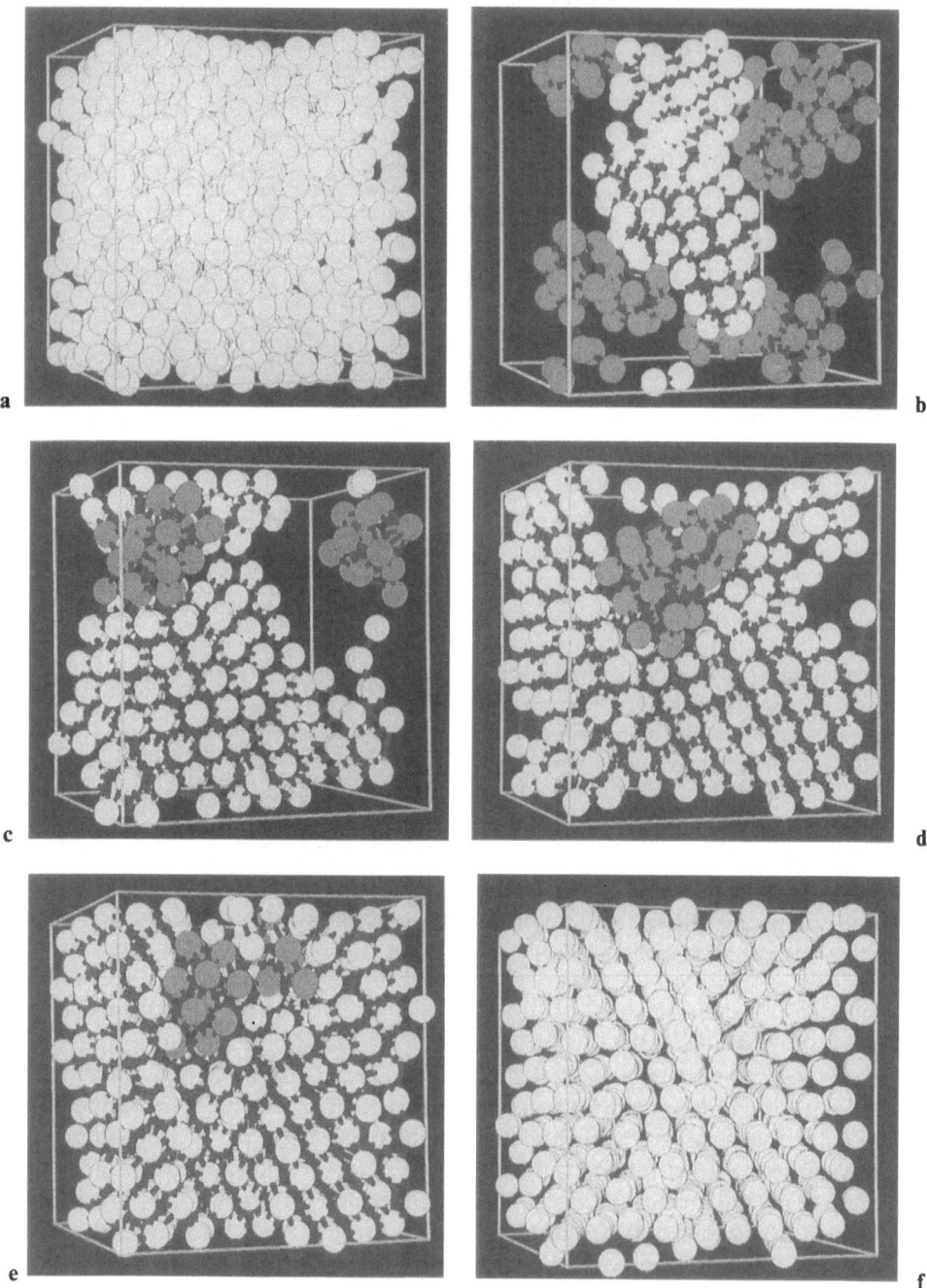

Fig. 7.10a–f. The configuration of atoms at various timesteps in the annealing process B. **a** 864 atoms at time step $t = 10,000$; **b–e** atoms with icosahedral symmetry are *blue*, while atoms with cubic symmetry are *white*. **b** $t = 29,000$, **c** $t = 39,000$, **d** $t = 42,800$, and **e** $t = 46,000$; the white cluster is growing step by step. **f** 864 atoms at $t = 50,000$; the system is almost ordered. (*For color reproduction* see color insert)

adjusting only the immediate neighbor of each atom, thus resulting in a configuration containing many icosahedra. In this situation, however, the connectivity of atoms with the icosahedral symmetry is not very firm because, as already stated, there is no strong correlation of symmetry between neighboring atoms. Accordingly, the configuration yields to crystallization rather easily.

7.7 Summary

Isothermal-isobaric MD simulations of an LJ system have been carried out to study melting on heating, crystallization on slow cooling, and glass transition on rapid cooling. These simulations were also used to analyze the microscopic structures of glasses and to examine the stability of glasses against crystallization.

Some of the results obtained were:

1. When the quench rate is small, an LJ liquid crystallizes. It transforms into a glass without any discontinuous change in volume when the quench rate is relatively high. The critical quench rate that separates the crystal-forming quench rates from the glass-forming quench rates is between 4×10^{10} K/s and 4×10^{11} K/s.
2. The occurrence of the glass transition can be monitored by using several physical properties, which are macroscopically measurable. The glass-transition temperature T_g depends on the quench rate.
3. In the microscopic structure analysis, the local-symmetry parameter $W_6(r_i)$ provides a good measure for identifying the types of the symmetry around an atom at r_i. This is specifically the case for icosahedral symmetry.
4. A video film[2] using computer graphics has been produced to show the time development of the atomic configurations during annealing. In order to show the local symmetry around each atom, atoms are classified into three categories: (1) atoms with local icosahedral symmetry, which are coloured blue in the video; (2) atoms with crystalline symmetry which are yellow; and (3) atoms that belong neither to (1) nor to (2), which are white. Some still pictures are shown in Figs. 7.9 and 7.10.
5. From the analyses of these atomic configurations, it can be concluded that when the quench rate is high enough to form a glass, then the lower the quench rate, the more stable the glass obtained against crystallization on annealing.

Acknowledgments. The main part of the present paper is based upon the work performed in collaboration with Prof. S. Nosé and Dr. S. Sakamoto. In particular, the visualization of the atomic motions in the amorphous systems and the production of the movie (and video) film are entirely due to Dr. S. Sakamoto, whose efforts are highly appreciated.

References

1. Kimura M, Yonezawa F (1983) In: Yonezawa F, Ninomiya T (eds) Topological disorder in condensed matter. Springer, Berlin
2. Yonezawa F (1990) In: Ehrenreich H, Turnbull G (eds) Solid state physics. Academic, Boston

3. Andersen HC (1980) J Chem Phys 72: 2384
4. Nosé S (1984) Mol Phys 52: 255
5. Nosé S (1984) J Chem Phys. 81: 511
6. Yonezawa F, Sakamoto S, Nosé S (to be published) Supercomputer Applications (special issue, 1990)
7. Sakamoto S (1990) PhD to thesis, Department of Physics, Keio University, Yokohama
8. Yonezawa F, Nosé S, Sakamoto S (1988) Z Phys Chem (Neue Folge) 156: 77
9. Yonezawa F, Nosé S, Sakamoto S (1987) J Non-Cryst Solids 95'96: 83
10. Yonezawa F, Nosé S, Sakamoto S (1987) J Non-Cryst Solids 97'98: 373
11. Steinhardt PS, Nelson Dr, Ronchetti M (1983) Phys Rev B28: 784

8 Craving for a Supercomputer: For the Study of Catalysis and of Geometries of HCCN

OCCHIO NOMURA[1]

Abstract. Catalysis is a field in which there is the prospect for supercomputers to play a great role. A triangular shape of HCCN was predicted by large-scale computations. This geometry is possible from a theoretical point of view, but has not been experimentally observed. The shape of this molecule has been in dispute between theorists and experimentalists, both of whom are leading scientists in their own field. The former assert that is has a carbene-type bond, while the latter, an allene-type bond. The problem is not yet settled, in spite of the new techniques developed for the molecule.

8.1 Catalysis

I am engaged in studying catalysis, and one area of particular interest is catalytic mechanisms from a theoretical point of view. There are interesting systems to be elucidated. One of them is a copper catalyst which is the only catalyst effective for the formation of methacrylamine. Why it is specific and why no substitute can be found are essential problems in catalysis. Another example is provided by a molybdenum atom which plays the central role in nitrogen fixation by nitrogenase found in azotobacter. These problems are pending until the advent of a parallel processor in the next generation of computers.

Catalytic phenomena are summarized as follows:

1. Adsorption of reactants on a catalyst surface. An adsorbed state is quasistable, a little more reactive than in a gas phase. theory of chemical bonds helps us to study the adsorption.
2. Interchange of the chemical bonds with the help of a catalyst: exchange of atoms is nothing but a reaction. The theory of reactivity provides us with information on the sites of reaction. If, on the other hand, one is interested in how fast a reaction proceeds, then one has recourse to reaction kinetics. Thus, the theory of

---

[1] Laboratory of Catalysis, RIKEN (The Institute of Physical and Chemical Research), Hirosawa 2-1, Wakoh, Saitama, 351-01 Japan

catalysis has no methodology of its own. We must make use of as many approaches as are available to us.

Chemical bonds are due to electrons, whose behavior is quantum-mechanically described. The microscopic description of a chemical reaction requires quantum mechanics as well as statistical mechanics. Thermochemical observables are derived from the microscopic quantities which depend on the modeling of a system. A metal is a good catalyst, because it has many levels available for adsorption and reaction. Metal atoms on the surface are thought effective for the catalytic activity. A fresh surface chemically prepared from a metallic powder has a higher activity than a metallic surface into which it changes as a result of a reaction to heat. Interpretation of a phenomenon would be different on which phase of the surface it is based. It is difficult, however, to test the validity of the model by computation, since a large number of metal atoms must be taken into account to explain the catalysis to an extent comparable with experiment. A single configuration approximation is not sufficient, when there is a transition element in a system, although the approximation applies well to organic molecules. A multiconfiguration approximation is required to describe the system satisfactorily. Geometry optimization is necessary when one wishes to discuss a reaction. These requirements are not fulfilled with the computers now available to us, since limited memory space is allowed for end-users. Several thousands of hours are needed to elucidate a mechanism of catalysis. The computer cost occupies a large part of a research budget. The most serious problem is software. We have few programs that satisfy our needs. No program can manage a system of metals with a reaction. We have no algorithm yet for the study of surface phenomena, among other aspects of catalysis. It would take several years for us to develop an algorithm and to make a program convenient for surface chemists. Little official support has been given to either quantum chemists or computational chemists for the development of a program that can design a catalyst. It is a general trend in Japan to beg or to buy a program, but not to invest in making a program and fostering software engineers. Ten years would be needed for us Japanese to catch up with the level of molecular engineering in the United States or Europe.

8.2 Geometry of HCCN

Setting aside the problems to be solved in the future, I will describe a large-scale calculation which has actually been done with a computer: the determination of the geometry and characterization of a chemical bond of HCCN. It required more than ten thousand hours to get a perspective view of the problem. Another ten thousand hours will be necessary to settle the problem. If we could have a supercomputer at our disposal, the problem could be solved in a shorter period.

This molecule consists only of four atoms, which are all elements of the first two rows of the periodic table (H through F), about which plenty of experience and knowledge has been piled up. Few problems are left unsolved. They are satisfactorily treated with a selfconsistent field method which was established in the early sixties. There would seem to be no problem with this molecule. A controversy has persisted, however, for more than eight years between experimentalists [1-3] and theorists [4-6]. The dispute seems to be escalating, and is becoming exciting.

In 1983 theorists discussed the chemical bond and, with calculation, confirmed their conclusion that the chemical bond is of the carbene type: a hydrogen atom and a cyano group (CN) being bonded with the central carbon atom [4]. Carbene is an important radical in organic synthesis. It is used as a reagent for an addition reaction as well as an insertion reaction. There are two kinds of carbenes, singlet and triplet, showing slight differences in some reactions. There was a heated argument about the carbene radical concerning the energy difference between singlet and triplet. Both theorists and experimentalists became involved in the controversy which prompted the development of experimental methods and devices. Theory and calculational methods also made progress. The dispute came to an end, with both experimental and theoretical results being revised.

Two years have not passed until the controversy of HCCN was clearly perceived by theorists. The microwave spectra of HCCN were analyzed by Saitoh and Hirota of the Institute for Molecular Science. They claimed that the analysis has no ambiguity in concluding that the molecule is linear in its lowest state [3]. This report was accepted by experimentalists all over the world, since their technique was thought advanced enough and reliable. The theorists, on the other hand, are also of first-class. Prof. Pople made a program package called Gaussian Series and distributed it among the computational chemists [7]. This program has a characteristic feature in determining geometries of a molecule to an extent comparable with experiment using a perturbation method. Another theorist, Prof. Schaefer, made use of a configuration interaction method (CI). He contrived a method of geometry optimization with CI automatically done by a computer. His success was applauded, since geometry optimization with CI had been thought to be impossible. He calculated the molecule again with an extended basis set and expanding the size of CI to a million configuration state functions, capitalizing on the great improvement in computers in the eight-year period [5]. Large-scale calculations became possible that could not have been imagined. Methods of computation were also improved and a number of new techniques were introduced. He reported the result in late 1987 in the top-level journal in this field, the *Journal of Chemical Physics* [5]. The theoretical conclusion was unchanged: the chemical bond of HCCN being of carbene-type.

The report stimulated the experimentalists who have stuck to linearity. Hydrogen is the key atom that determines the shape of the molecule: linear or bent. They planned an experiment with the hydrogen substituted by deuterium: DCCN. Substitution of hydrogen with deuterium gives more accurate results, since the mass of deuterium is twice that of the hydrogen. The preliminary results were reported at the meeting on Molecular Structure held in Sapporo in the summer of 1989. The experimentalists assertion was the same as before: DCCN was found to be linear and there was no indication of bending observed. Thus, the controversy between theory and experiment remained.

Another geometry has been proposed by us, while the dispute over bent and linear conformation was at a deadlock [6]. Our calculation revealed that HCCN can take a triangular form in the singlet A' state. Calculations were done with a Gaussian 82

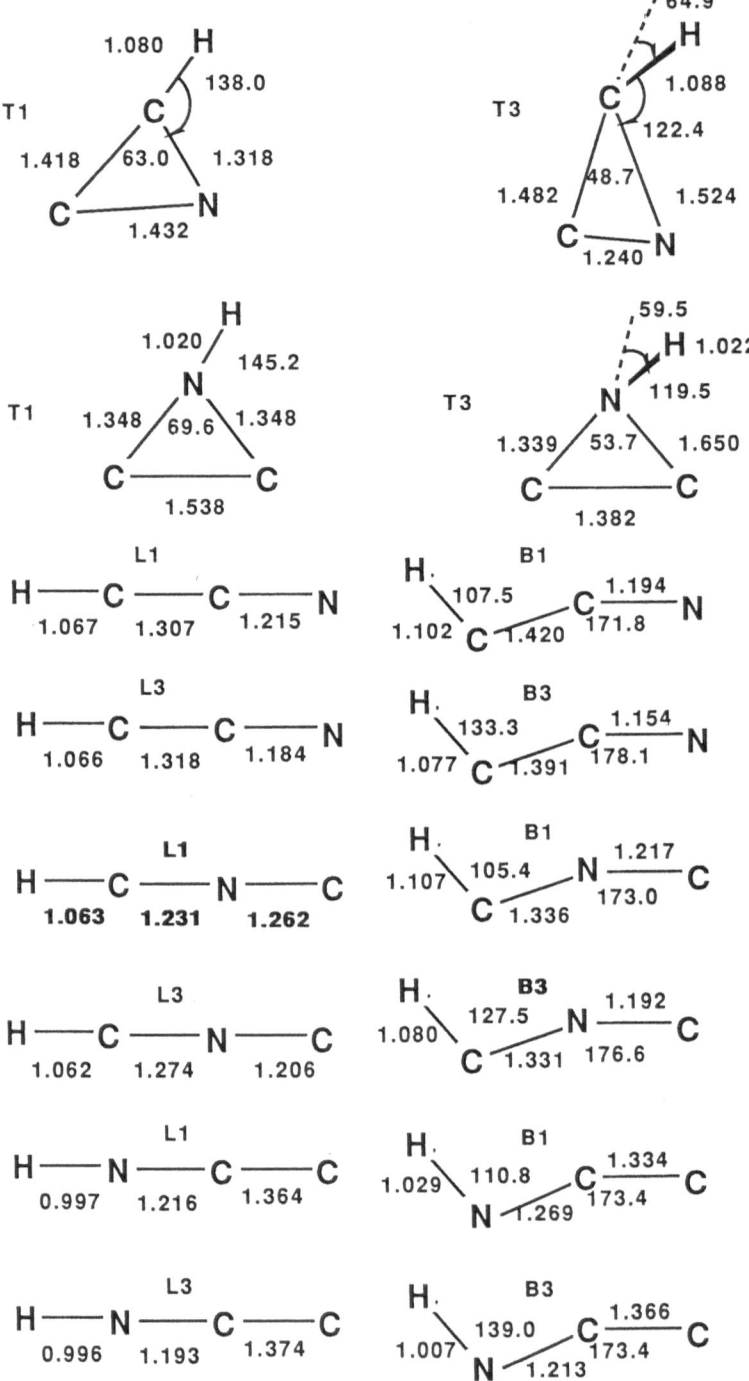

Fig. 8.1. Optimized geometries of HCCN and its isomers in singlet and triplet states. *L*, linear; *B*, bent; *T*, triangular

Table 8.1. Energies of HCCN and its isomers in singlet and triplet states

Species[a]	SCF	MPS	MP4 (SDTQ)
HCCNT1	− 130.647917363	− 131.07278431	− 131.11196717
HCCNT3	− 130.597977489	− 131.00289033	− 131.004383779
HNCCT1	− 130.590020842	− 131.01569257	− 131.05935155
HNCCT3	− 130.528802375	− 130.95137882	− 130.99432822
HCCNL1	− 130.606132610	− 131.02667089	− 131.07157093
HCCNL3	− 130.695817896	− 131.05763771	− 131.10621666
HCNCL1	− 130.565562270	− 130.98628324	− 131.03027556
HCNCL3	− 130.640999917	− 131.01968760	− 131.06487527
HNCCL1	− 130.561002487	− 130.98270207	− 131.02891157
HNCCL3	− 130.622899764	− 131.01486320	− 131.05843809
HCCNB1	− 130.639414352	− 131.06067361	− 131.10416510
HCCNB3	− 130.695867123	− 131.06440647	− 131.10989579
HCNCB1	− 130.629099345	− 131.04076971	− 131.08743989
HCNCB3	− 130.660927239	− 131.04062245	− 131.08382236
HNCCB1	− 130.59450920	− 131.01644560	− 131.06499969
HNCCB3	− 130.624879638	− 131.01677277	− 131.06133128

Species[a]	MP3	MP4 (SD)	MP4 (SDQ)
HCCNT1	− 131.08773415	− 131.08888825	− 131.09200425
HCCNT3	− 131.01883488	− 131.0208024	− 131.02667367
HNCCT1	− 131.03574812	− 131.03785249	− 131.04218103
HNCCT3	− 130.95427000	− 130.95496754	− 130.96056373
HCCNL1	− 131.04041914	− 131.04210410	− 131.05125231
HCCNL3	− 131.08344725	− 131.08598324	− 131.09417448
HCNCL1	− 131.00273005	− 131.00450089	− 131.01115369
HCNCL3	− 131.04270442	− 131.04536394	− 131.05176334
HNCCL1	− 131.00240547	− 131.00495111	− 131.01112919
HNCCL3	− 131.03679296	− 131.03826494	− 131.04407074
HCCNB1	− 131.07309106	− 131.07736273	− 131.08458348
HCCNB3	− 131.08709578	− 131.08982130	− 131.09734812
HCNCB1	− 131.05933532	− 131.06309465	− 131.06909734
HCNCB3	− 131.06137857	− 131.06422484	− 131.07007098
HNCCB1	− 131.03770531	− 131.04024351	− 131.04657491
HNCCB3	− 131.03886414	− 131.04033259	− 131.04653492

[a] The last two digits of the molecular species have the following implications: T, triangular; B, bent; L, linear; 3 triplet; l, singlet. *SCF*, self consistent field calculations; *MP2*, Møller-Plesset perturbation of the second order; *MP4 (SDTQ)*, Møller-Plesset perturbation method of the fourth order with single, double, triple, and quadruple substitution of orbitals; *MP3*, Møller-Plesset perturbation method of the third order; *MP4 (SD)*, Møller-Plesset perturbation method of the fourth order with single and quadruple substitution of orbitals. MP4 (SDQ), Møller-Plesset perturbation method of the fourth oder with single, double, and quadruple substitution of orbitals

program developed by Pople [7] and a basis set of double-zeta quality proposed by Prof. Dunning [8]. All the conceivable geometries were calculated. Geometries were optimized with the second-order perturbation method of Møller-Plesset's. The final energy was obtained with the geometry by means of a fourth-order perturbation. More than ten thousand hours were required to search minimum points of this molecule. Large-scale calculations were further needed to convince us that triangular geometry was the lowest state. The calculated results are given in Fig. 8.1 and Table 8.1. The calculation shows that the geometries of triplet open chains, i.e., bent and linear, are almost the same as given by Schaefer, together with the energy difference between linear and bent. There has been no experimental report on the triangular shape. In late 1988, a collaborator of mine tried to detect the triangular form with the help of Prof. Saitoh and Dr. Kawaguchi. No sign was observed of the existence of the triangular form. One of the reasons is that the species might have too short a lifetime to be observed by means of a microwave spectrometer owing to frequent collisions in the laboratory system. The late Dr. H. Suzuki suggested that HCCN could be found in a molecular cloud in the universe [9]. We are now preparing to observe a spectrum at the Radiation Laboratory of Nobeyama.

Acknowledgments. Our calculations are supported by The Nobeyama Radiation Laboratory, The Institute for Molecular Science, The Ring-Cyclotron Laboratory of the Institute of Physical and Chemical Research, and Century Research Center Ltd., all of which kindly offered us their facilities for computation. The present work has been accomplished with the collaboration of Prof. T. Hirano, Dr. A. Murakami, Dr. T. Saitoh, Dr. N. Nakagawa, and T. Takasaki.

References

1. Baird NC, Taylor KF (1978) J Am Chem Soc 100: 1333
2. Dendramis A, LeRoi GE (1977) J Chem Phys 66: 4334
3. Saitoh S, Endoh Y, Hirota E (1984) J Chem Phys 80: 1427
4. Kim S, Schaefer HF, Radom L, Pople JA, Binkley JS (1983) J Am Chem Soc 105: 4148
5. Rice JE, Schaefer F (1987) J Chem Phys 86: 7051
6. Hirano T, Nakagawa N, Murakami A, Nomura O (1980) Chem Phys Lett 165: 374
7. Binkley JS, Frisch MJ, de Frees DJ, Ragavachari K, Whiteside RA, Schlegel HB, Fleuter G, Pople JA (1983) Carnegie-Mellon University, Pittsburgh
8. Dunning TH, Hay PJ (1977) In: Elecronic structure theory. Plenum, New York
9. Suzuku H (1983) Astrophys J 272: 579

Panel Discussion 1

Needs and Seeds of Supercomputing

CHAIRMAN   *Dr. Masaaki Shimazaki*

PANELISTS   *Dr. Shinji Tomita*
Dr. Katsuo Ikeda
Dr. Yoshio Oyanagi
Dr. Shoken Miyama
Dr. Malvin H. Kalos

9 Introduction

MASAAKI SHIMAZAKI[1]

I think there have been a number of related topics in preceding presentations, so let me sum up the important points in introducing the panelists who are going to give presentations. When we speak about supercomputing today, it seems that we take for granted its use in scientific computations. In doing computation, it is obviously very important that four elements, the hardware, system software, basic algorithm, and application, are well balanced, or in harmony, with one another. This importance, I think, is demonstrated by the fact that the Supercomputing Research and Development Center of the University of Illinois consists of three departments – hardware, software, and applications.

Nevertheless, as a long time has passed since computers came into existence, what is known as information engineering or computer science has come to make up an academic discipline of its own, distinct from the areas in which computers are applied, such as computational science, computational physics, and computational chemistry. So I imagine you very seldom have interactions with people in other disciplines in your everyday activities. Going back to the starting point of super-computing, however, I feel there may be some need for such interdisciplinary interactions.

The supercomputer is defined as a far faster computer than the fastest general-purpose computer in each age, but there is not definition as to the type of computer. This way of definition ensures flexibility as much as it involves problems. Looking back into the history of high-performance computers, the first generation of pipeline operating type supercomputers comprised CDC 6,600, 7,600, TIASC, and CDC Star 100, later followed by the famous CRAY-1, which achieved 160 MFLOPS peak performance. Then CYBER 205 emerged, and in that period Japan's HITAC S-810, FACOM VP, and NEC SX series also came into existence, marking the beginning of supercomputing in Japan as well. Now, Cray's latest products are CRAY XMP and YMP, and Japanese computers are entering the next generation. So far, the computation speed has been in the range of 500 MELOPS to 1 GFLOPS, but speeds of 10 GFLOPS will be obtained in a year of two. These situations are illustrated in Fig. 9.1 and Table 9.1.

---

[1] Computer Center, Kyushu University, Hakozaki 6-10-1, Fukuoka, 812 Japan

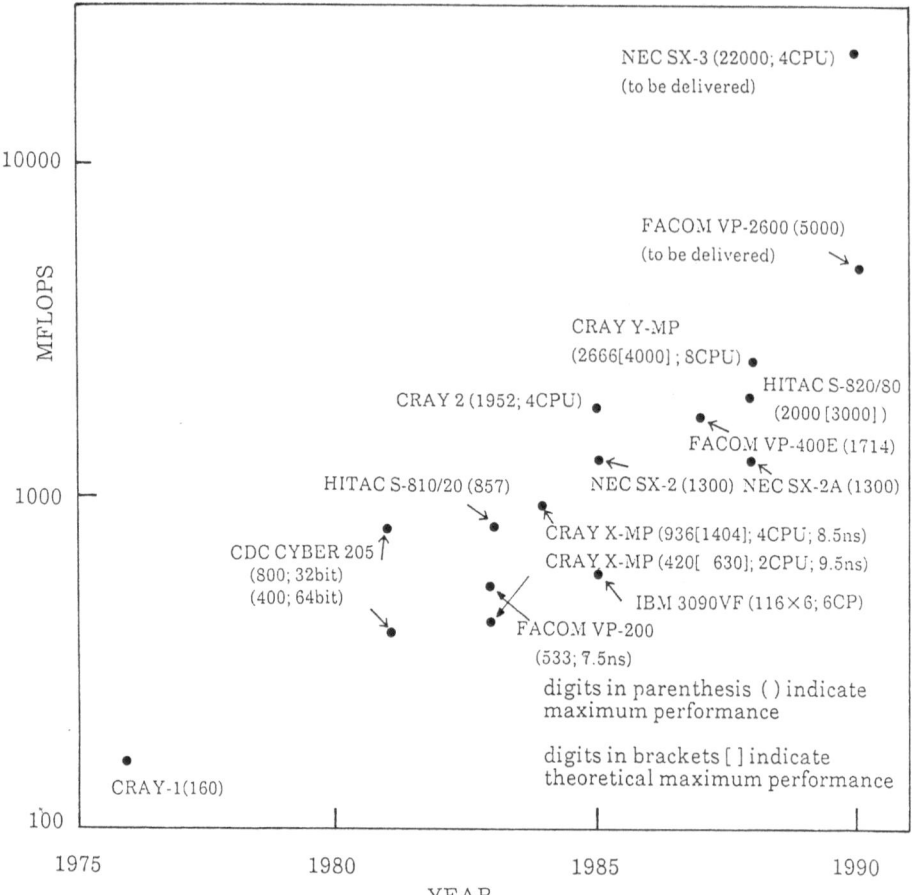

Fig. 9.1. High performance computers

As you see in Cray's specifications and elsewhere, the point is shifting from more vector processing to a parallel vector processing. When special purpose (dedicated) computers are entering an age of highly parallel processing, it is interesting to see how far general-purpose computers will advance in this highly parallel processing. Improvements in operational performance and expansion of memory space are also underway, and at the same time, the significant progress attained in information engineering or technology is bringing about remarkable changes in the environment of supercomputers. These, I think, are some of the notable trends today. In particular, an environment for distributed processing is being gradually realized in Japan as well as in the United States, and the issue of operating systems or networking seems to be exerting a heavy impact on the real world.

Another notable recent development is the progress in mathematical software: the integration of the symbolic (S), numeric (N), and graphic (G), or, as it were, the Trinity of SNG, is also becoming an important and feasible task. In the United

Table 9.1. High performance computers

Machine	Maximum performance (theoretical) MFLOPS	Number of CPUs	Pipeline multiplicity	Main memory (max)MB	Extended storage (max)GB
CRAY-1	160(240)	1	1	32	—
CYBER 205	400[64 bits] 800[32 bits]	1	1 2[32 bits]	64	—
CRAY-2	1952	4(max)	1	4096	—
CRAY Y-MP8	2667(400)	8(max)	1	1024	4
CRAY Y-MP4	1333(2000)	4(max)	1	512	4
CRAY Y-MP2	666(1000)	2(max)	1	256	1
HITAC S-820/80	2000(3000)	1	4	512	12
HITAC S-820/60	1000(1500)	1	2	256	6
FACOM VP-400E	1700	1	4	256	0.75
FACOM VP-2600	5000	1	4	2048	8
FACOM VP-2400	2000	1	2	1024	8
FACOM VP-2200	1000	1	1	1024	8
NEC SX-2A	1300	1(AP)	4	1024	8
NEC SX-3/44	22000	4	4	2048	16
NEC SX-3/42	11000	4	2	2048	16
NEC SX-3/24	11000	2	4	2048	16
NEC SX-3/22	5500	2	2	1024	16
NEC SX-3/14	5500	1	4	1024	16
NEC SX-3/12	2750	1	2	1024	16
NEC SX-3/11	1370	1	1	512	16

Except for CRAY-1 and CYBER 205, restricted to high-performance computers with a maximum performance over 1000 MFLOPS.
FACOM VP-2600 and NEC SX-3 are expected to be delivered in 1990. In the FACOM VP-2000 series, two scalar processors can share a vector unit.

States, "visualization in scientific computation," abbreviated to "ViSC," is an often talked-about term. The application of computer graphics, which is an area of computer science, to computational science is having a heavy impact on the real world in the form of the newly emerging field, ViSC.

So much for the general outlook and the introduction to important points; let me introduce the panelists. Our first speaker will be Dr. Tomita of Kyushu University (Chap. 10). He specialized in computer architecture, and is one of the foremost specialists in parallel computer architecture. For the type of computer architecture now known as VLIW (Very Long Instruction Word) computers, Dr. Tomita, in the early stages, designed a computer on his own and made significant achievements in low-level parallel processing. More recently, he has become actively engaged in research on another aspect of computer architecture, which concerns reconfigurable computers.

The second to give a presentation will be Dr. Ikeda of Kyoto University (Chap. 11). He specializes in such areas as the operating system, computer networks, image processing, and pattern understanding. Dr. Ikeda is a professor in the Department of Information Science, and concurrently has a joint appointment as the Director of the Integrated Media Environment Experiment Laboratory annexed to the Faculty of Engineering.

Dr. Oyanagi of University of Tsukuba will be our third speaker (Chap. 12). He is a specialist in numerical analysis, and has made remarkable achievements regarding parallel vector algorithms, among other things for Quantum Chromodynamics (QCD)-related linear calculation.

The fourth presentation (Chap. 13) will be given by Dr. Miyama of the National Astronomical Observatory. He is an active researcher in astrophysics using computer simulation. He will speak from the viewpoint of "needs" in this first half of our panel discussion.

Chapter 14 is contributed by Dr. Malvin H. Kalos, the Director of the Center for Theory, at Cornell University. He will discuss supercomputing as an interdisciplinary activity.

Lastly, extracts from the question-and-answer session are reproduced in Chap. 15.

10 Computer Architecture in the 1990s

SHINJI TOMITA[1]

In this panel discussion, I would like to discuss what types of computer architecture are expected to achieve more than one TFLOPS performance in the near future and clarify some key hardware technologies by which high-performance TFLOPS computers can be successfully built.

10.1 Needs and Seeds for Parallel Processing

Recently, parallel processing has become a hotter topic than ever before. The reasons may be attributed to the following needs and seeds:

1. Experiences of using supercomputers in a wide range of scientific application areas:
   - Research areas which require ultracomputers with more than one TFLOPS performance.
   - Research areas whose programs are irregularly structured so that they cannot be efficiently processed by supercomputers.
2. Appearance of new application areas such as artificial intelligence which deal with dynamic structures and are not suited to the vector-processing scheme provided by supercomputers.
3. Limitation of speed-up for general purpose computers.
4. Necessity for very large scale integrated circuit (VLSI)-oriented architecture:
   - design cost of VLSI is still so high that we must employ some repetitive hardware structures.
   - We should extend the reduced instruction set chip (RISC) architecture to a more powerful stage in an era of large integration (more than one million tracks/chip). RISC was born in an era of small integration (100,000 tracks/chip) and has been overwhelmingly used.

All these needs and seeds are combined to make us feel that parallel processing is the most promising direction for future computer systems. There are various kinds

---

[1] Department of Information Systems, Kyushu University, Kasuga, Fukuoka, 816 Japan

of computer architecture such as the array processor, pipelined processor, super-scalar processor, very long instruction word (VLIW) processor, multiprocessor, data-flow processor, neurocomputer, and so forth. Among these kinds of architec-ture, we pay the most attention to the super-scalar/VLIW processors and large-scale multiprocessor systems.

10.2 Super-scalar and VLIW Processors

As shown in Fig. 10.1, both of these processors utilize the parallelism obtained at the machine instruction level. If there are machine instructions which can be executed in parallel, they can be issued and executed simultaneously. They have an ability to issue more than one machine instruction per clock cycle. Since general purpose computers can issue at most one instruction per clock cycle, parallel-processing computers have an inherent possibility to exceed the performance of general purpose computers. A major difference between these architectures lies in the way of detection of parallelism and realization of compatibility. The super-scalar processor detects parallelism at run time. Program compatibility is guaranteed at the object program level. On the other hand, the VLIW processor detects parallel

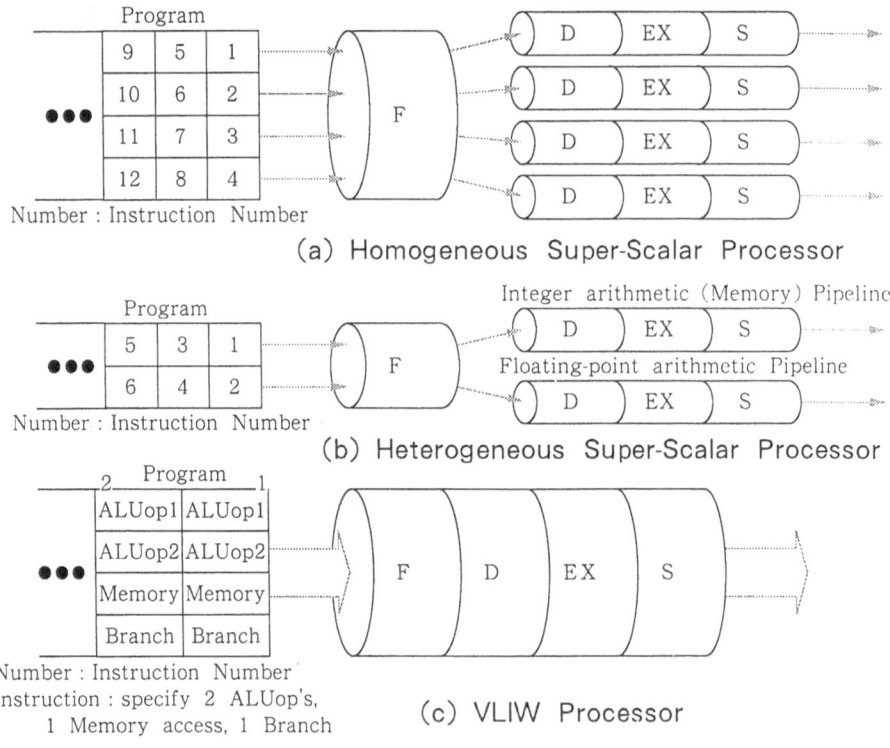

(a) Homogeneous Super-Scalar Processor

(b) Heterogeneous Super-Scalar Processor

(c) VLIW Processor

Fig. 10.1. Super-scalar and VLIW processors *ALUop*, arithmetic and logic unit operation

operations in a program and embeds them in a very long instruction word (VLIW) at compile time. Program compatibility should be kept at the source program level. The wise compiler can manage to detect as many parallel executable operations as possible by employing some powerful global optimization techniques. So, even a program with irregular structure which could not be vectorized on supercomputers may be executed at high-speed.

We expect these processors to run more than 10 times faster than general purpose computers [1, 2]. For the average work load, this speed-up rate is achieved by supercomputers. So, these processors may provide a performance comparable to that achieved by supercomputers. Furthermore, if we employ these processors as a processing element, we may build a high-performance multiprocessor system with a relatively small number of processing elements.

10.3 Large-scale Multiprocessor System

10.3.1. Pipelined Processor

Among various kinds of architecture, pipelined computers have kept the leading position in the field of scientific applications. The reason is the following:

1. Simple hardware structure
2. General structure to be usable in a wide range of applications as long as their algorithms are represented in some vector form
3. Program compatibility and speed-up by using a powerful vectorizing compiler
4. Speed-up by improving device and implementation technologies Supercomputers will extend their ability in the following three directions:
   - High-speed capability: reduction of machine cycle, multiplication and chaining of function units
   - Generality: list vector access, hardware to support vectorizing
   - Speciality: built-in application-specific hardware such as a logic simulation accelerator

However, the factors which limit their performance are the following:

1. A supercomputer consists of the arithmetic function units and memory units which share vector registers. Arithmetic function units are relatively easy to build because the information flow is one-dimensional in the arithmetic pipeline, and speed-up can be attained by reducing logic in each pipeline stage and inserting a latch between successive stages. On the other hand, memory units have a two-dimensional structure because memory units employ in interleaving scheme for fast access. Memory units are divided into many banks (for example, 256 banks) and must supply data in an aligned form. Memory units are constructed with a jangle of crossbar switches and their control logic is too complex. So, memory units become a severe bottleneck.
2. The basic elements by which supercomputers are built are ECL's (Emitter Coupled Logic). ECL power consumption is so great that the total system power consumption results in 50 ~ 100 kW/h. This rate would be too high to make a large-scale

multiprocessor system. The number of processors seems to be strictly limited to $4 \sim 8$. From these facts, it is obvious that supercomputers with 1 TFLOPS performance could not be build without some drastic modification of the present pipelined architecture.

10.3.2 Large-scale Multiprocessor System

The history of the multiprocessor system is divided into two eras. From the middle 1970s to the early 1980s, various kinds of experimental multiprocessor systems had been proposed but none had achieved commercial success. This is mainly because microprocessors at that time were too slow, even for a multiprocessor system using a full bucket of microprocessors to compete with a large-scale general purpose computer in performance. From the middle 1980s, however, the situation has drastically changed. RISC-type microprocessors have come to compete with a large-scale general purpose computer in both functionality and performance. Now the multiprocessor system has become a reality.

We now discuss the key technologies which led the multiprocessor system to success.

10.3.2.1 High-speed interconnection network (ICN). ICN plays an essential role in a multiprocessor system. For the purpose of attaining high performance, the gap between the physical topology of ICN and logical structure of an application should be as narrow as possible. To narrow or bridge the gap between them, there are two approaches taken:

1. Fixed ICN
Fixed ICN has a static network which cannot be changed. So, for a given problem, the compiler divides a program into subprograms and manages to map them onto the fixed ICN. The best fixed ICN would be the one to which the mapping from arbitrary applications can be done easily by the compiler. There have been proposed various networks such as the bus, ring, tree, torus, hypercube, cube-connected-cycle, multi-stage, and so forth. Among them, the hypercube is the most interesting. To each node of the network, a processor is connected. A node is represented by a binary number $(a_n a_{n-1} \ldots a_2 a_1)$ and is connected to its neighboring nodes, whose node numbers differ by Hamming distance 1 from its own node number: $(a_n a_{n-1} \ldots a_2 \bar{a}_1)$, $(a_n a_{n-1} \ldots \bar{a}_2 a_1)$, $\ldots$, $(\bar{a}_n a_{n-1} \ldots a_2 a_1)$. So at each node, there are $\log N$ link where $N = 2^n$ and data exchange is done by a crossbar switch among $\log N$ input and $\log N$ output links. So, in total, $N(\log N)^2$ switch elements are required. This network is very fast ($O(\log N)$), easily expansible, and has the ability to embed a wide range of ICN's, such as the torus, tree, and ring.

2. Reconfigurable ICN
In contrast with the fixed ICN, a reconfigurable ICN has a tailorability by which the physical topology of ICN is reconfigured to match the logical structure of an application program at hand. Two approaches are taken to utilize this feature. One approach is that the user defines his virtual topology of ICN and describes a program with explicit attention to the topology. In image processing, for example,

the user defines a torus topology and describes a space- filtering algorithm on that topology. Of course, the parallel language should support this approach. The other approach is that a compiler divides a program into subprograms, map them to processors, and defines processor interconnection patterns. Each processor interconnection is directly supported by the reconfigurable ICN. In neurocomputing, for example, 3-layered processing stages are interconnected by two connection patterns.

We are now building a reconfigurable multiprocessor system at Kyushu University [3]. As shown in Fig. 10.2, the machine consists of 128 SPARC microprocessors and a 128 × 128 crossbar network. The crossbar network works in two different modes. One mode is called demand-mode, where the crossbar network works asynchronously; interconnection requests occur at random so that some arbitration should be done at run time on each output bus basis. This mode is suited to

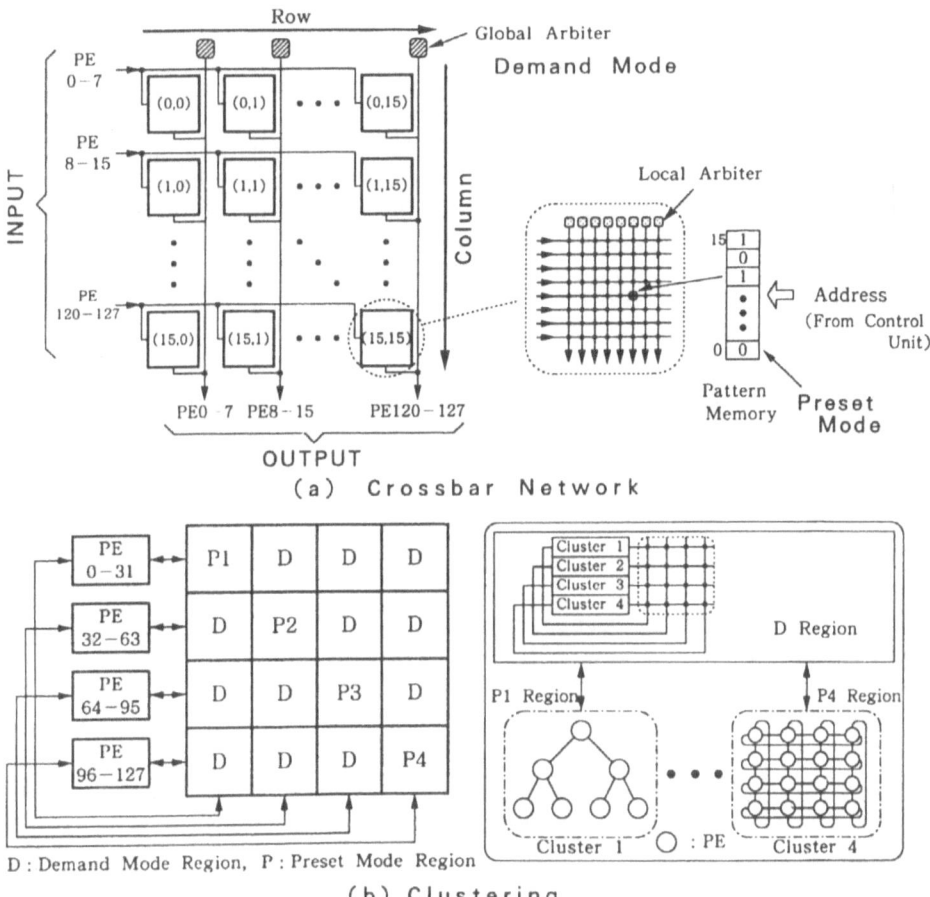

(a) Crossbar Network

D : Demand Mode Region, P : Preset Mode Region

(b) Clustering

Fig. 10.2. Kyushu University reconfigurable parallel processor

applications which are strongly irregular in structure. The other mode is called preset-mode. In this mode, each interconnection pattern is defined at compile time and stored in an interconnection pattern memory. In our case, 16 interconnection patterns can be memorized. Since the control unit of the machine can select any pattern at run time when necessary, the machine can provide any virtual topology. In addition, run-time arbitration is omitted so that high-speed interprocessor communication becomes possible. In our machine, several clusters, each of which can form a predefined intra-cluster topology, can also mutually communicate through a predefined inter-cluster topology. An example is shown in Fig. 10.2.

10.3.2.2 Processing element. It is very difficult to decide how high a degree of performance a processing element is designed to achieve. It depends on how much the inherent parallelism exists in an application program, how fast the ICN works, and how frequently intercommunications occur. Superscalar and VLIW processors will be promising candidates in the case where high-speed ICN is availble by using a full crossbar network, hypercube network, optical fiber network, and so forth.

10.3.2.3 Multi-read, multi-write memory system. Memory is always a bottleneck when we try to enhance system performance. Various high-speed memory systems have been devised. A 2-layered cache memory in a general purpose computer and an interleaved memory with a huge number of banks installed in a supercomputer are the typical examples. In the multiprocessor system, memory band-width poses a more severe limitation on performance than that in uniprocessors. A memory system which can support multi-read and multi-write capabilities is the most desirable thing. We may expect the three-dimensional device technology to provide such a memory unit. The three-dimensional memory has many layers, each of which holds the same contents and is dedicatedly used by a processor. The number of layers corresponds to that of processors. If write-operations are performed at several layers simultaneously, write-data can be simultaneously transferred to every layer through high-speed optical channels which provide parallel interlayered communication within the device.

10.4 Conclusion

There are many other important problems to be solved by the time parallel processing becomes commercially available. Parallel programming languages and operating systems are, of course, important. However, one of the most important things is to change the way of programming and thinking. The user is used to FORTRAN; but FORTRAN is a sequential language which is distorted to suit a general purpose computer. From a sequential algorithm, we can hardly extract much parallelism in using a multiprocessor. Today is a turning point, and from now we will pursue the parallel way and receive its fruitful results. A huge number of sequential programs should be rewritten some day – so let us start right now. This reminds us of the New Tokaido [railway] Line: this was a great success because it had completely departed from the Old Tokaido Line. The other important thing is to cooperate with other researchers who are working as application program writers (users), and operating systems and language designers. I think that the user and architect should communicate more frequently. A computer architect should know the real scale of application programs and real needs arising from the user, analyze them, and build computers which have a general structure to lend themselves to a wide spectrum of applications. Conversely, the users should make an effort to abstract their computations and classify them into several parallel-processing models. This kind of information is quite valuable to the architect.

References

1. Tomita S, Shibayama K, Nakata T, Yuasa S, Hagiwara H (1986) A computer with low-level parallelism. Proc 13th Int Symp Comput Architecture, ACM
2. Murakami K, Irie N, Kuga M, Tomita S (1989) SIMP-A novel high-speed single-processor architecture. Proc 16th Int Symp Comput Architecture, ACM
3. Murakami K, Mori S, Fukuda A, Sueyoshi T, Tomita S (1989) The Kyushu University reconfigurable parallel processor. Proc Int Conf Supercomputing, ACM

11 Computer-Aided Research and Engineering Network

KATSUO IKEDA[1]

I would like to talk about research and engineering networks which have become the essential infrastructure for the activities of researchers and engineers today. Many such networks have been constructed these days. One can access computing resources and various kinds of information required for scientific activities through these networks, at any time and at any place, overcoming distance and time limitations.

In this report, a brief introduction to computer networks, and the particular case of the computer-aided research network in Kyoto University, are presented.

11.1 Packet Switching Network

In 1969, ARPANET began to operate. This was the first experimental network that incorporated the packet switching scheme. ARPANET proved that packet switching is an efficient and reliable data transmission method.

In the same period, ETHERNET, which realized CSMA/CD (carrier sense multiple access with collision detection) on a wide-band short-distance data transmission channel, was developed jointly by DEC, XEROX, and INTEL. ETHERNET is a very flexible and easy-to-use transmission medium incorporating many-to-many simultaneous data switching, and has become a standard for the local area network (LAN).

In the beginning, the data transmission procedures between computers in ARPANET were implemented computer by computer, and were not standardized. In 1982, ARPANET was revised entirely using unified protocols, named Internet Protocol (IP) and Transmission Control Protocol (TCP). In 1983, DARPA adopted TCP/IP as the standard protocol of DARPA which became a de facto standard of wide-band packet data transmission. Today, TCP/IP is widely used in many types of computers, from main frames to work stations and personal computers.

The seven-layer reference model of OSI was developed by ISO in 1983, and some activities to develop standard protocols following this model have been continuing.

---

[1] Information Sciences, Faculty of Engineering, Kyoto University, Kyoto, Japan

These standards are expected to replace TCP/IP in the long run. However, for the wide range of computers available the repertoire of application software that conforms to OSI standards is currently smaller than that using TCP/IP.

As for codes for information interchange in Japan, the ISO 646 information interchange code, which is identical to the ASCII code, and the JIS X0208 Japanese character set with the JIS X020 code extension method, which is equivalent to the ISO 2022 method, are widely used. In some implementations, extended Unix code (EUC) or shifted-JIS are used.

Several research networks have also operating in Japan. One of such network is JUNET, which uses the public switching network. JUNET, which stands for Japanese University computer NETwork, has been operating for five years on voluntary contributions. Today, more than 200 sites including universities, research institutions, and private companies are connected to this network.

There is a trend toward the establishment of an organization which would act as a coordinating agent among networks and promote a virtual joint network system for the nonprofit research community in Japan. It would also act as an international agent to cooperate in world-wide networking activities.

11.2 Computer-Aided Research Network in Kyoto University

In 1989, Kyoto University began to operate a campus-wide integrated information exchange system – KUINS: Kyoto University Integrated Information Network System. KUINS consists of a digital telephone and data line-switching network and a wide-band optical-fiber looped local area network which connects to subnetworks in each department and in research laboratories as well as in many outside campuses. Fig. 11.1 shows the concept of KUINS.

11.3 Integrated Media Environment Research System: IMES

From 1985 to 1987, the Department of Information Science of Kyoto University instituted a computer-aided research network which consists of layered networks, several specially designed processing subsystems for various media such as images and diagrams, using special peripheral equipment, and two mainframe computing systems.

This system is utilized for both the research and development of, and the support of, multimedia information processing.

Later in 1989, an experimental laboratory called the Integrated Media Environment Experimental Laboratory, IMEL, was established, and the network was connected to KUINS. Since then, the Integrated Media Environment System (IMES) can be easily used from many places in the university, and has been operating as one of the gateways between outside and the campus. The layered network consists of a digital telephone and data-switching network to which we can gain access from all rooms in our department, and two segments of ETHERNET, one of which is mainly for carrying the usual data stream while the other is for

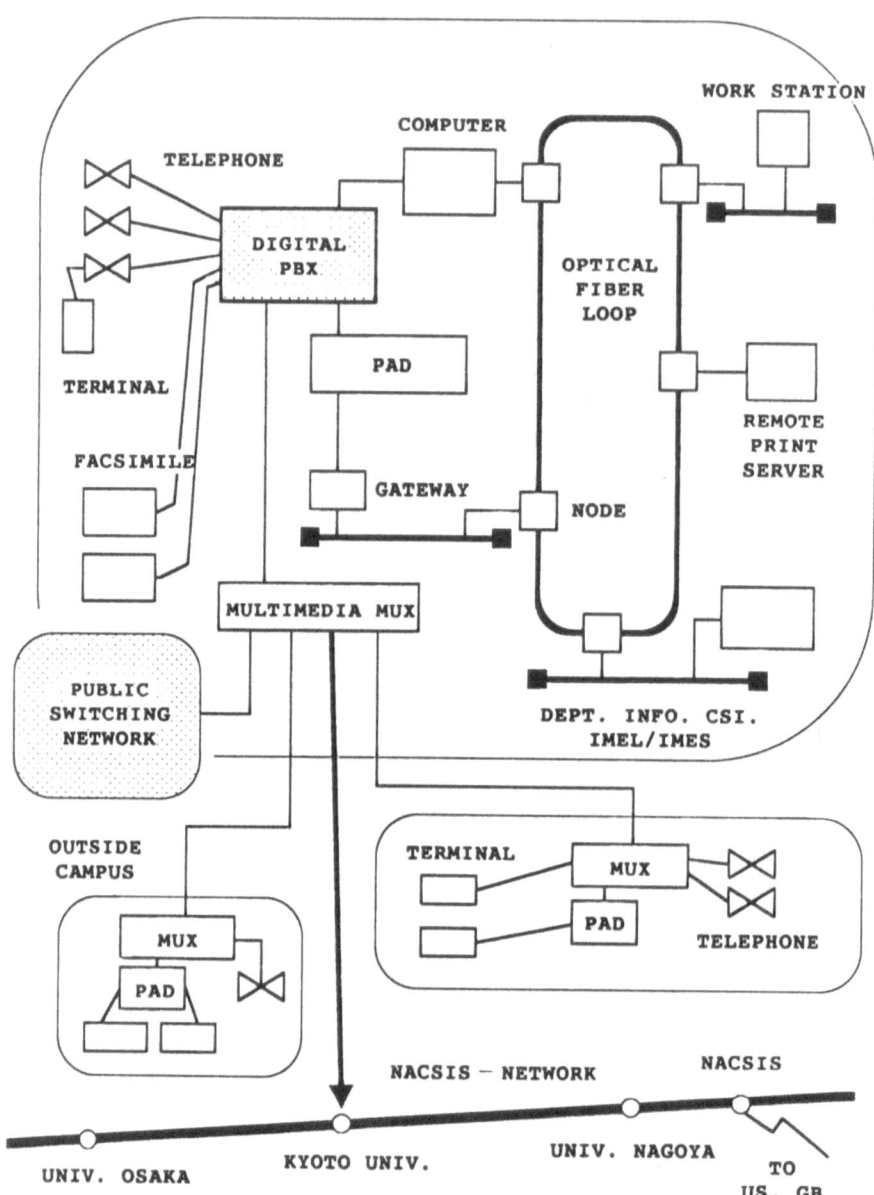

Fig. 11.1. KUINS system configuration

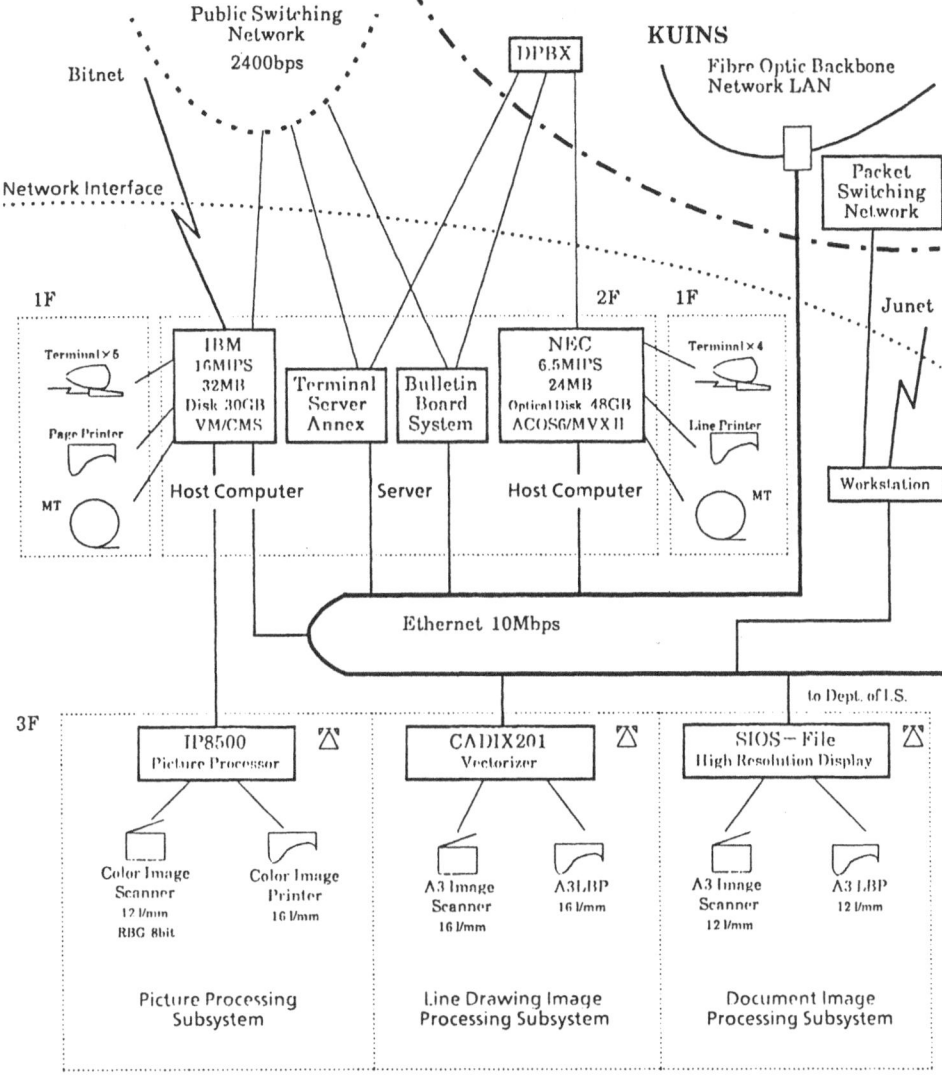

Fig. 11.2. IMES system configuration

carrying real-time data streams such as image and voice. Fig. 11.2 shows the system configuration of IMES.

A brief explanation for each subsystem follows:

11.3.1 Line-drawing Image-processing Subsystem

This system reads in line-drawing images, digitizes, vectorizes, and then extracts candidates of symbols, characters, and connecting lines. A software system, named FACORES, executing these operations, has been developed on this subsystem.

11.3.2 Document-processing Subsystem

Document-understanding systems are being developed on this subsystem. Some examples are the extraction of articles from newspapers, and the automatic data sheet and catalog database management.

11.3.3 Picture-processing Subsystem

Research on image understanding and an image database is being carried out on this subsystem.

12 *Supercomputing and Algorithms*

Supercomputing will be and already is based on parallel vector processing. Thanks to the development of hardware and novel architectures, people expect 1 TFLOPS machines will be available in the 1990s. However, more important is the software.

There are two strategies to provide software for new machines:

1. Implement OLD programs on NEW architectures.
2. Forget OLD programs and write NEW programs based on a new formulation of the problem.

The first strategy was adopted by Cray when it provided an automatic vectorization. Since scientific and technological programs in FORTRAN are very long-lived in general, we have already millions of lines of active programs. It is not realistic to convert all the programs for a new architecture. This strategy was quite successful for vector computers.

Can this strategy be extended to parallel computers? Automatic parallelization was partly successful for computers with low parallelism, such as the Cray X-MP, Y-MP, Alliant, Convex, Titan, etc. These machines provide compilers which can parallelize conventional programs more or less automatically. For highly parallel architecture, however, the distribution of tasks among processors is highly dependent on the nature of the problem, and cannot be done automatically.

In numerical simulation, the parallelism is in principle inherent in the problem. For example, partial differential equations, entail geometrical parallelism in them, and in particle simulation, Newton's law of motion can be processed in parallel. However, when we write a program in FORTRAN or another sequential oriented language, the inherent parallelism is no longer manifest. An automatic parallelizing compiler, if possible at all, should reconstruct the parallelism once hidden in the program. It would be much easier for the compiler if the program describes the inherent parallelism of the problem. This can be done, e.g., by DEQSOL (Differential EQuation SOLver), which compiles differential equations written in mathematical form into a program for vector supercomputers. The extension to parallel

---

[1] Institute of Information Sciences, University of Tsukuba, Tennodai 1-1-1, Tskuba-si, 305 Japan

computers will not be hard. Unfortunately, this strategy cannot utilize the vast accumulation of conventional software.

Which strategy is more productive in the near future? Both will be necessary, of course. In the long run, however, the second one will be more fruitful when highly parallel computers become popular.

13 "Needs" and "Seeds" of Computer Simulations in Astrophysics

Shoken M. Miyama[1]

Numerical simulation using recent supercomputers in astrophysics is considered to be a very important tool for analyzing astronomical phenomena, because that is the only experimental method to study these. The capability of the present supercomputer, however, is inadequate. For example, in the formation theory of sun and planets, we need very accurate computations because of the great mass difference between the sun and the planets. Hence, our need for the supercomputers of the next generation is very strong (we need new machines with a speed of several tens of GFLOPS and memory storage of several tens of Gbytes at least).

In the case of evolutional simulation of a globular cluster (an ensemble of about 10^5 stars), we need a machine with a speed of several TFLOPS. In order to be able to simulate this system, a new idea has recently been explored. Special hardware has been constructed to calculate the gravitational force, and this is connected with a host machine. Using this machine we will be able to calculate the evolution of the globular cluster in a few years.

13.1 Introduction

Because we would like to study astrophysical phenomena, we cannot perform our studies experimentally. For example, we cannot examine the formation of stars and galaxies, the expansion of the universe, or a supernova explosion. The astronomical pheonmena are very far from the human scale in length and time. Therefore, we have only observed many kinds of astronomical sources by telescopes and constructed some scenarios of the evolution by analyzing observation data. Now we can attack the analysis of astrophysical pheonmena more positively by numerical simulation using supercomputers. Numerical simulation in astrophysics is especially important because it is considered to be the only experimental method. That is, we can experiment with collisions between interstellar clouds, neutron stars, or galaxies, and we can also study formation of stars and galaxies, etc., only in a super-

---

[1] Division of Theoretical Astrophysics, National Astronomical Observatory, Mitaka, Tokyo, 181 Japan

computer. In this sense, we consider the supercomputer as the "telescope" of theoretical astrophysics, and we build up new astronomy using numerical simulations.

The most representative characteristic of the astrophysical phenomena is that they are governed by the self-gravitational force which is always neglected in the other areas of physics. For example, we solve the (magneto-) hydrodynamical equations with self-gravity in the case of the formation or the evolution of stars, or in the process of the supernova explosion, for example. We also study the evolution of the galaxies and the globular clusters as an ensemble of many stars which interact with each other by gravitational force, as an N-body problem.

Because the objects which we deal with are governed mainly by gravity, the evolution behavior is nonlinear and usually nonstationary. The spatial configuration is made very complicated by the gravity and the fluid is forced to be highly compressible (for example in the case of star formation, the molecular clouds in the galaxy have a mean density of 10^{-20} g.cm^{-3} but the mean density of the star is 1 g.cm^{-3}). Therefore, we must solve three-dimensional partial differential equations with the Poisson equation using as high a resolution as possible.

In the case of the N-body simulation for calculating the evolution of the globular cluster and galaxies, we need N^2-times computations at each time step for obtaining gravitational force. Therefore, the problem including self-gravity is very complicated and time-consuming for a standard computer.

In this chapter, we point out the need for supercomputers in simulating the formation of the solar system, and introduce a new concept, i.e., the "seeds" of new computer for computing the N-body problem.

13.2 Are We Selected People?

The interest of many astrophysicists is how the solar system is formed. From the age of the great Kant, many models and scenarios have been produced and discussed. Recently, a disk made from dusty particles was observed around β-Pictoris which exists near our solar system. Many scientists consider that the dust disk may be closely related to the formation of planets. So far, we have not been able to detect planets in other stellar systems. In the near future, however, we should be able to observe traces of the existence of such planetary systems.

By the way, we wonder whether the planet is usually formed around a star or not. If it is very common, there must be many planets in the galaxies and it is very interesting to imagine these. However, if our solar system is a special case, we (i.e., the human race) may be selected people. So to study the formation theory of planets is one of our basic interests.

In one modern scenario (the Kyoto model), the formation process is the following:

1. The sun is formed after the gravitational collapse of the molecular cloud which exists in interstellar space and consists of hydrogen molecules.
2. Around the proto-sun, a rotating gas disk is formed, called the primordial solar disk.
3. In the disk, the dust component sediments into the mid-plane and forms a dusty layer near the equatorial plane.

4. As the dust layer grows and the density exceeds the critical density, the layer becomes unstable because of the gravitational instability and fragments into many pieces (planetesimals) whose masses are about 10^{18} g.
5. The planetesimals collide with each other and grow. Finally, their masses reach the order of earth's mass (10^{24} g).

This is one scenario for the formation of planets, and the key point of this process is the initial structure of the primordial solar disk, i.e., the total mass, distribution of density, temperature, and angular momentum. In order to determine this structure theoretically, we must do computer simulations of the collapse of a rotating molecular cloud, and obtain the proto-sun and the primordial disk as the result of cloud-collapse. The numerical simulation of this process needs high accuracy, because the mass of the primordial disk is much smaller than the proto-sun ($\simeq 10^{-2}$ $M_\odot$). Hence we need a large number of grids, at least $(1000)^3$, because the scale of the molecular cloud shrinks by at least 10^{-3}. If we use these fine grids we can determine the structure of the primordial solar disk.

After determining the physical condition of the solar disk, we can investigate the evolution of the disk. If we simulate many initial conditions of rotating molecular clouds, we finally determine how rarely or frequently the planets are formed around the star. We must calculate at least one thousand time-steps for an average, then we need a machine of several tens of GFLOPS and several tens of Gbytes. Now this simulation takes about 1000 hours for one run and the main memory of the central processing unit is too small. We need the larger memory and the faster computer in order to determine whether we are selected people.

13.3 Gravitational Many-body Problem

As an astrophysical problem, we would like to analyze how an ensemble of many stars evolves. The globular clusters and the galaxies have about 10^5 and 10^{11} stars, respectively. Because the radius of the star is very much smaller than the radius of the cluster or galaxy, we consider one star as one particle in the evolutional calculation. Hence, the equations of the stars are simply written

$$\frac{dv_i}{dt} = -\sum_{j \neq i} Gm_j \frac{(x_i - x_j)}{|x_i - x_j|^3},$$

$$\frac{dx_i}{dt} = v_i,$$

where $i = 1, 2, \ldots, N$. We must calculate gravitational forces between each two particles for N^2 pairs. Then, even in the case of the globular cluster, the number is 10^{10} and the computational time for one time-step takes about 10^6 seconds using even the highest-level supercomputer now (1990). In order to simulate the evolution of the globular cluster, a machine capable of several TFLOPS, at least, is needed. Therefore, we must postpone that computation using the supercomputer for the time being.

Because the formulae as given, however, are very simple, it is a good idea to produce special hardware which can calculate the gravitational forces between particles. The special hardware is combined with a host machine which computes only the time integration in these equations. In order to calculate the gravitational force, for example, we only write a subroutine call as

$$call\ GRAPE(x, x_i, f_i, N)$$

where x, x_i, f_i, and N are respectively, the input array for all the particle positions, the position of i-th particle (input), the gravitational force acting into i-th particle (output), and the total particle number (input). Then, if we call this subroutine N-times we can calculate total forces.

Recently, Sugimoto et al. [2] made the prototype of the special hardware (a computer board) whose name is GRAPE (GRAvitational PipE). The speed of computation of the gravitational force is about several tens of MFLOPS, which costs only 3×10^5 yen (about U.S. $2000)!! They plan to make a several GFLOPS-machine during 1991, and finally in a few years the TELOPS-machine (about 10^8 yen) will be made. In order to compute the evolution of the globular cluster, the host machine must be also a GFLOPS-machine – a machine of supercomputer class.

13.4 Summary

For astrophysical problems, we cannot analyze the objects by experiments. Hence, we need computational simulation instead of experimentation. Among the astrophysical problems there are many which are currently unresolved for the reason that even the present supercomputer is inadequate. We need a faster machine and larger memory storage.

We pointed out two typical problems. One is the formation of planets, a problem which has been considered for many years. To solve how frequently planets are formed around a star can be done using a machine capable of several tens of GFLOPS.

The second point is the dynamic evolution of an ensemble of many stars. In the case of the globular cluster, the best way to simulate will be to perform the computation of the gravitational force by the special hardware, and the other part by a host machine. Two machines are combined with each other. This seed, a new concept for the simulation machine, will, I think, grow and succeed in the near future.

References

1. Hayashi C, Nakazawa K, Miyama SM (eds) (1988) Origin of the Solar System. Prog Theor Phys 96 (Suppl)
2. Sugimoto D, Chikada Y, Makino J, Ito T, Ebisuzaki T, Umemura M (to be published)

14 Comments on Supercomputing as an Interdisciplinary Activity

MALVIN H. KALOS[1]

I would like to discuss supercomputing as an interdisciplinary activity. It has always been true that computational science is a field that exploits the results of many others. Our computers are built by electrical engineers, usually produced by commercial companies. We use languages, compilers, and other software produced by computer scientists. So how is the situation changing? The answer lies primarily in the greatly increased pace of change and the greatly broadened scope of the disciplines and tools involved. It is no longer simply a matter of writing a program in some well-established language, debugging it, producing some results, and then writing papers about the results. First of all, we use hardware that is evolving very rapidly. Again two of the talks before mine have emphasized how true that is: we now exploit highly parallel computing, much more powerful vector computing, and combinations of the two. As the hardware progresses, we have to use still more powerful software, software that evolves while we use it.

Nowadays, we are usually obliged to, and find it very convenient to, present results in visual form. Computer graphics for scientific visualization is an intrinsic part of modern scientific computing.

Frequently we collaborate with other people, and so networking is equally an important part of our work. Some of what we do involves new areas of applied mathematics, including numerical methods. We rely on computer science to a much larger degree than ever before and again these issues are evolving. Our languages are evolving, the compilers are evolving, general kinds of techniques are evolving. As we do our work, the environment in which we do it is evolving and it is evolving much faster than ever before. That means that the work we do must involve close collaboration with people in other fields. This is simply the intrinsic work of scientific computing. There is one fundamental reason why this must be so: as our machines get faster, as they involve larger and larger resources, we must bring greater productivity of the scientists to bear on these problems and on these machines. We must match the productivity of the human to that of the machine. That again puts an increasing demand on the computer science infrastructure and we can no longer afford to be passive accepters of the computer science tools that

---

[1] Cornell Theory Center, Cornell University, Ithaca, NY 14853, USA

are produced. We must interact with computer scientists, and tell them what our problems are. The computer scientists of course have many other things to do but when we bring them new problems, and bring them in a spirit of cooperation, they often find them as important and as interesting as we do. Let me give one problem that I think is an outstanding problem in computer science that is created by the new machines we are talking about. Right now, the most effective supercomputers get most of their throughput from vector processing. There are many problems, important scientific problems, that are intrinsically very difficult to vectorize. My favorite example is radiation transport as solved by the Monte Carlo method. A similar problem arises in ray tracing which is a basic technique in computer graphics. How do you vectorize a complex ray tracing program or complex transport Monte Carlo? The answer is that it is possible, though very difficult. I invented a technique for this in the early 1970s when considering how to do radiation transport on ILLIAC IV. There is a systematic way of approaching the technique and later I realized that I had independently invented a kind of data flow organization of the algorithm. By now this has been exploited in a number of areas. The work I know best and which is extremely good is by Ken Miura who works for Fujitsu in San Jose, California. He and others have succeeded in restructuring this kind of program in FORTRAN. The new structure involves a basic kind of program transformation, one that I believe is capable of being done systematically through either new computer tools or new languages; I am not sure what is the best approach. This is an extremely interesting computer science problem: one must do the transformation in a systematic way because a FORTRAN program transformed manually becomes very intricate and inflexible. This is only one example of the challenges that arise when complex algorithms meet modern architectures.

Let me give two more examples, not exclusively in computer science. One problem that I have been interested in for a long time and whose difficulty has become much greater thanks to the needs of new computers is that of random number generation. For many years people used random number generators that came as part of a software library. If you understand it, it may work all right; if you do not understand too well, you may get wrong results and discover it too late. There is a certain amount of literature and qualitative knowledge about the design and testing of generators. Random number generators need to be better and they need to be more general. The other side of the issue is that as one goes to highly parallel computing, the demands put on random number generators are greater and it is much harder to solve them in purely empirical way, that is, through testing. Imagine that you have thirty thousand processors, each of which is capable of carrying out a different dynamic simulation. How do you create thirty thousand random number generator streams and prove that they are all independent in that sense needed by the application? We have not by any means solved the problem. It is a problem in the intersection of number theory, probability theory, and computational science. Very few mathematicians are worrying about it. So this is another area in which our computing power has created greater and more interesting problems. I think it is our responsibility to formulate these new challenges in clear terms and bring them to the attention of the widest possible community.

Finally it is clear that new methods in numerical linear algebra are needed. This can effectively be done on parallel and vector machines but each architecture poses new problems for each of the different kinds of things one needs to do. One needs to formulate this in general terms; one needs to be able to optimize the algorithms for individual machines. This is not a problem that has been entirely neglected: some of you may know about the LAPACK project in the United States.

As our environment in scientific computing evolves and it is now evolving very rapidly, we must solve the new challenges as a community of scientists from different disciplines. But that is not the whole story. I also want to emphasize that some of the most important computations that need to be done are themselves intrinsically interdisciplinary. A very good example is any large-scale study of global climatic change. Climate is not just the matter of atmospheric dynamics; it requires a knowledge of physics: the physics of cloud formation, the physics of radiation transfer, and so on. It also involves chemistry, particularly the knowledge of chemical reactions in the atmosphere; it involves biology, because the most important question will be the effects of global climatic change on crops, animals, and human beings. It is clear that investigations of global change require computer modelling. This is an example of a general paradigm: computer modelling is a very natural, a very direct way of doing quantitative interdisciplinary research. The results of chemistry, the understanding of biological effects, and the understanding of physics can come together effectively in a computer simulation. So we have the possibility, in this case, and hence the necessity, of attacking the problems in a truly interdisciplinary way. I think that now and in the future, important progress will depend on our ability to gather together interdisciplinary research that both contributes to and exploits the possibilities of supercomputing.

15 Panel Discussion 1: Questions and Answers

Member of the audience: Dr. Tomita discussed the future of supercomputer hardware in his talk. Given this, I wonder if you have any conceptions as to how software or languages should be developed around hardware. In other words, do you think anything needs to be done for the development of languages specific for hardware?

Tomita (Kyushu University): I think Dr. Oyanagi gave us a fairly detailed explanation concerning languages [summarized in Chap. 12]. From the standpoint of hardware, I think that in the future it will be absolutely necessary to develop parallel languages and for these to be adopted by users. Earlier, I said that the very long instruction word (VLIW) is a good method for the elements comprising multiprocessors, but at the object-code level this has virtually no compatibility with current general-purpose machines.

There is a very large gap between maintaining compatibility and making another big leap. Only when this gap is overcome will a high-speed processing environment become possible. This situation is often compared to that of old railway lines and the Shinkansen [bullet train]. I hope that users will soon make this leap and throw off the bonds of the past. If they do this, I think that we are now at the stage where we can provide them with excellent hardware. If we attempt to maintain current standards of compatibility with supercomputers, we are approaching the limits of performance. As a result, such moves are being made to a certain extent by the manufacturers as well.

Shimazaki (Chairman; Kyushu University): I think that Dr. Tomita just made several important points. When we look at the history of computers in information engineering, we find a trend towards avoiding the presentation of computer hardware in its natural form, or when memory space is limited, of making it as natural-appearing and as easy to use as possible in order to keep the programmer from recognizing this. With the advent of supercomputing, however, one of the demands is to use these machines to their theoretical limits. As a result, user-friendly design has, although we would not necessarily like it to be this way, been frequently discarded. This trend is also coming to a dead end, however, and in the future I think we will have to search out new directions.

As point out by Dr. Kalos [Chap. 14], the field of supercomputing deals with the most advanced technological problems, and there is a need for those in various fields to stop being passive accepters and become active participators in the search for new directions. Concerning this point, how is it from the standpoint of the users? Does the user to use computers in as passive a form as possible? Do you have any opinion regarding this?

Kalos (Cornell University): Architects must pay attention to the hardware support for operating systems, tools, languages, and all other issues that affect the productivity of users of their computers. It is not enough to produce a very fast numerical processor. This is especially true for highly parallel systems, particularly those aimed at a range of applications. That is another example of how supercomputing now and in future must be done in an "interdisciplinary" sense. Architecture is too important to be left to the architects.

Member of the audience: This may broaden the topic of discussion a little, but I would like to ask Dr. Tomita in particular about the following: 1-terabyte computers would easily be capable of producing 1-terabyte of data, or even a thousand times that amount. No problem arises when this data is to be thrown away after use, but sometimes it must be stored. From the standpoint of hardware, what could be done to deal with cases like this? Input/output-related matters have been left at a primitive stage of development. When computers this fact actually appear on the scene, corresponding data accumulation will also become necessary. Related hardware and language support are being ignored. In relation to this, what kind of concept is present behind the file processor being proposed by Dr. Tomita and others?

Tomita: To be honest, there is none. At present, I do not think we have a new storage medium capable of replacing disks.

Member of the audience: From the standpoint of languages as well, it would be difficult to consider languages without some such plan for hardware. It would be nice if you could incorporate this point in your concept.

Tomita: The area of input/output is a very "cluttered" one; everyone would rather ignore it. But we will try.

Member of the audience: In our case, about one-third of all computer costs are accounted for by disk usage fees. The use of three-dimensional computation would bring about a great increase in the amount of data being handled, and I am in perfect agreement with the previous questioner.

Kalos: At Cornell, we are right now faced with serious issues involving very large data sets. COCORP (the Consortium for Continental Reflection Profiling) seismic exploration of the earth crust accumulates a great deal of data; the Global Basins Research Network will be centered around a very large database of knowledge about one sedimentary basin. The intention there is to record everything that is known about the basin, a very large geological structure, and to do computer modelling of its chemical, physical, and structural properties. Very large sets of results will have to be stored. We know we have a major problem both in the sheer size of the basin data and of the computed results and equally in the software to retrieve them in an effective way. We are trying to start an initiative which we call "Super Storage" to address this problem. I believe that this will make some progress. The point is that we understand that this is a major problem. You are absolutely correct that as we do very large calculations we need to be able to store, retrieve, and manipulate the results. This merits serious research and implementation in its own right.

Ikeda (Kyoto University): I would also like to ask Dr. Tomita or Dr. Nakazawa one question. Computer access is very frequent in the case of database searches or when data is being rapidly extracted from a sparse matrix. So, if only this necessity for access could be disposed of, it would be extremely easy, because of a large locality, to compress data storage into a small space with a so-called virtual memory. If you try to do the job with hardware – although integrated circuits with content-addressable memory have been developed to some extent – it is not going to be enough. I think that if you cannot develop a large-scale device, the end result is no good. The question is one of practical realization. I think that such devices must be developed from the memory on up.

Nakazawa (University of Tsukuba): Dr. Ikeda's point is an extremely important one, and I think this a frequently encountered problem with current supercomputers as well. In a certain sense, I do not think the manufacturers have put enough work into this field. In the future, I have a feeling we may see a solution to this problem. The problem, however, is the great amount of money that is going to be required. This refers not to development costs but to the money that will probably have to be spent by the customer. In other words, a solution is possible, but it will be costly. Given enough money, I think the problem can be resolved.

There is one other thing I would like to point out. When data on the terabyte level is being handled as live information and used actively, I think that the data management or file-handling techniques used to handle this information will require the development of methods different from those used in the part. Just as various problems were pointed out concerning the use of parallel processing in super-computers, I think that there are various handling problems involved with the handling of large quantities of data input and output.

Panel Discussion 2

The Future of Supercomputing

CHARIMAN   *Dr. Masatake Mori*

PANLISTS   *Dr. Kisaburo Nakazawa*
Dr. Yasumasa Kanada
Dr. Katsunori Hijikata
Dr. Tadahiko Kawai
Dr. Noboru Kikuchi

16 *Introduction*

MASATAKE MORI[1]

The second session is entitled "The Future of Supercomputing," and I would like to begin the panel discussion. I think it would be fine if you considered this a continuation of the first session. As was mentioned in the keynote address of Dr. Kondo, words like "imagination" and "dreams" are among the keywords of the current symposium. In this sense, I would like you to feel free to discuss your opinions concerning the way you would like things to be in the future without so much concern as to whether or not these will be actually realized. This could cover hardware; operating systems, software, applications, the various problems of graphics, and also cooperation among different fields of science and technology.

I would like to begin with a brief introduction to our panelists. Professor Nakazawa, from University of Tsukuba, will give the first paper (Chap. 17). Dr. Nakazawa is a hardware specialist, and he will speak regarding his visions for the future of hardware and operating systems. Next is Professor Kanada from University of Tokyo. As you already know, the very active Dr. Kanada recently set a new world record for the computation of the value of π, and when that record is broken I am sure he will soon get it back. This area is covered in his talk (Chap. 18).

Next is Professor Hijikata, retired from the University of Electronic Communication and currently a member of the faculty at Meisei University, where he is working on atomic and molecular theoretical computation. Long ago I was also involved in this field, and I respected Dr. Hijikata as a man of great experience in this field, where he has been active for many years. He will talk about "supercomputing" in the earliest stages of the history of computers in Japan (Chap. 19). Next is Professor Kawai, who has retired from Tokyo University and is now teaching at the Science University of Tokyo. Dr. Kawai has been active in the area of structural analysis and was involved in work in Japan on the finite element method from the very beginning. Finally, we have Professor Kikuchi, who has already given us a fascinating contribution (Chap. 2). He has some extremely interesting things to bring up, and I am very much looking forward to his talk.

Although the topics are not necessarily so clear-cut, I would like this panel discussion to proceed in general from hardware to operating systems, software, and finally applications.

---

[1] Professor, Department of Physics, Faculty of Engineering, University of Tokyo

17   *The Future of Supercomputing*

KISABURO NAKAZAWA[1]

The recent progress of the supercomputer has been quite remarkable. Only a decade ago, the use of the supercomputer was limited to small academic or research communities; today, it is widespread used many people use supercomputers daily with as much ease as they used mainframes ten years ago.

Demand for more powerful supercomputer, say in a TFLOPS (tera (10^{12}) floating-point operations per sound) class, is accelerating. Today, "bleeding-edge" users are already looking at 100 to 1000 times more power than what is currently available in the market.

This article presents the author's personal views on the future of the super-computer from the perspective of hardware system development, rather than that of applications. As they are based upon the author's experience with the development of the commercial supercomputer, they may sound rather conservative in some senses.

17.1 Is a TFLOPS Supercomputer Really Possible? If So, When Will It Be Available?

No doubt there will come a time when there will be a TFLOPS supercomputer. However, the question and/or the answer is meaningless without the comments of availability (time-frame) and types of system. The argument here will be restricted to top-end and commercially available supercomputers.

1. Table 17.1 shows the rough growth of computers over the past 40 year (1949–1989). We can tell from the table that the speed of computer, the memory capacity, and the number of installed units all increased as much as $\sim 10^6$ times. The rate of increase, therefore, is around 5.6 times every 5 years, or 41% growth per year. Interestingly, the rate of growth in these measures coincides with the recent growth of 40% per year in worldwide shipped computing power.

---

[1] Institute of Information Science and Electronics, University of Tsukuba, Tsukuba, Ibaraki, 305 Japan

Table 17.1. 40 years' growth of the computer

	Processing speed	Memory capacity	Number of installed units
1949: [EDSAC]	~ms	~2 kB	~1 unit/year
Supercomputer			
1989: Mainframe	~ns	~2 GB	~10^6 unit/year
PC, WS			

PC, personal computer; WS, workstation

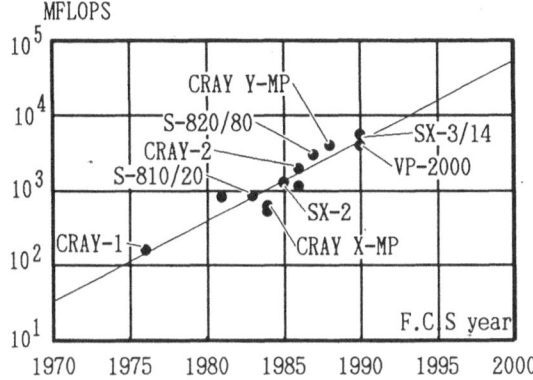

Fig. 7.1. Evolution of the supercomputer

On the other hand, high-end mainframes have recently scored a growth rate of roughly 3–4 times every 5 years (25%–32%/year) in terms of processing speed and memory capacity.

As shown in Fig. 17.1, the performance of a single unit (CPU) of high-end supercomputers is growing at a rate of about 4–5 times per 5 year at best, though various advanced features such as multiple pipelined arithmetic units, vector registers, chaining, and so on have been employed to increase the processing power.

The main factor determining these trends is the fact that the progress of hardware performance is primarily supported by semiconductor technology. For example, as to making the fine pattern on semiconductors, the minimum spacing width decreased by a factor of roughly $1/\sqrt{2}$ every 2–3 years, that is, 3 micrometer (μm, 64 kbit) → 2μm(256 kbit) → 1.3μm(1 Mbit) → 0.8 μm(4 Mbit) → 0.5 μm(16 Mbit).

Together with marking increasingly fine patterns on chips, the integration density has very much increased as shown in Fig. 17.2, and the circuit speed has also improved, but at a relatively slow rate of only 3 times every 5 years, as shown in Table 17.2, even though the improvement of circuit density contributes to speed increase. (It is worth noting, however, that the cabinet size and the power consumption of a single CPU system have remained pretty much the same for a long time).

All this implies that it is becoming extremely difficult to realize a TFLOPS supercomputer on a single engine, or relying only upon the progress of semiconductor technology, within the coming few years. Therefore, it is essential to introduce various forms of parallelism, as widely argued.

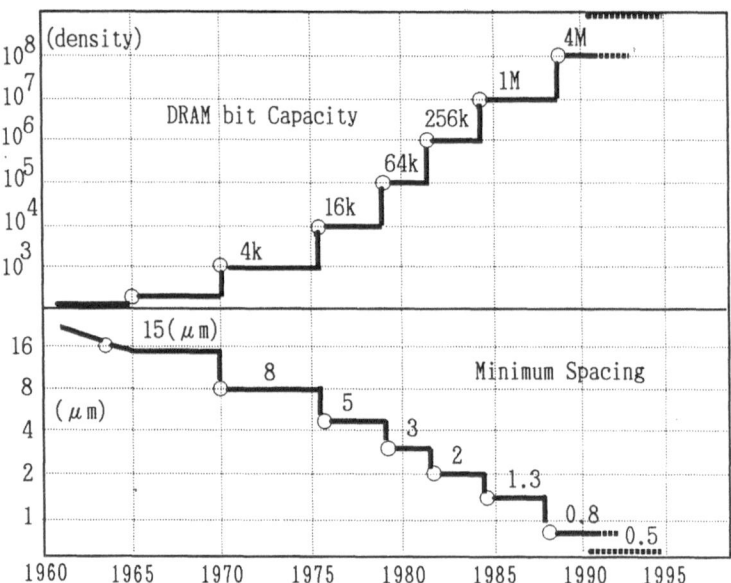

Fig. 17.2. Improvement in semiconductor technology

Table 17.2. Trends in semiconductors

Item	Trend
Speed	3 times/5 years
Density	6 times/5 years
Cost	−35%/year
Power delay product	1/7−1/8/5 years

Table 17.3. Forecast for development TFLOPS supercomputer

	Number of CPU units					
Year	1	3–6	10–30	~100	~1,000	~10,000
1989	~3 GFLOPS	~20 GFLOPS	~100 GFLOPS	~300 GFLOPS	(~TFLOPS)	
					? ? ?	
1997	~30 GFLOPS	~100 GFLOPS	~300 GF	~TFLOPS		
2005	~300 GFLOPS	~TFLOPS				

2. A rough forecast of performance is presented in Table 17.3, which is based on the fact that the performance of a single unit of a supercomputer in 1989 is around several GFLOPS (giga FLOPS, or 10^9 FLOPS), and the rate of its improvement is assumed to be 4.6 times every 5 years (3.4 times/4 years). The shaded zones in Table 17.3 will be feasible in the context of the author's fairly conservative projection.

Although in the time-frame of 1990–1994, the table shows the TFLOPS region, this will only be possible with a massive parallel array of more than 1,000 units of processors, which the author feels would be unrealistic on a commercial basis.

3. In the meantime, various kinds of features or improvements will be introduced properly into the high-end computers. The following are some examples:

- Integrated features on mainframe or supercomputer, such as IAP (integrated array processor), VF (vector facility), and IDP (integrated database processor)
- Minor modifications to supercomputer to make it fit for certain special applications other than just numercial computation will be expanded; an example is VELVET (logic simulation)
- Attachment of special features to a supercomputer for specific processing, such as Fast Fourier Transform (FFT), signal processing, sorting, and random number generation, etc.
  Problem-oriented special machines, such as the so-called XXXX-solver
- Hybrid systems, which have some coupled structured of several CRAY-1-like vector-scalar processors with a highly parallel array of processors.

17.2 High Barrier To Be Broken

The projection of the development of a TFLOPS supercomputer, presented in Sect. 17.1, has been based on the steady rate of technological progress and the tireless efforts made in industry. The challenge of the TFLOPS goal, however, faces a number of difficult barriers yet to be overcome.

17.2.1. Circuit Technology

Semiconductor devices
As high resolution in fabricating advanced semiconductors is coming closer to its limit, so the realization of 0.3 μm of minimum spacing will require a quantum leap from the current lithography technology. The shift from ordinary light processes to techniques such as laser (excimer) or X-ray (SOR) is much talked about. The development of such equipment itself, however, will require a huge investment. Other problems include those of hot electrons and wiring. In particular, extensive research and investigation into new fabrication processes and materials would be needed to form fine and low-resistance wiring free of open/short problems caused by atom migration.

New circuit devices
In recent years a number of new circuit devices have emerged as potential future elements of the computer. They include GaAs, optical devices, JJ (Josephson Junction), QFP (Quantum Flux Parametron) etc. None of these, however, are mature enough to find actual volume usage for supercomputer, even in a low-key way. No sufficient industrial basis has grown yet, and the area of their potential application is very much limited. This is in sharp contrast to semiconductors, which have

established a definite position in industry. Of course, top-end (experimental) super-computers will be allowed to utilize pioneer devices, but they are still a long way from making major inroads into the commercial market because of the far too inadequate level of industrial interest in base technology.

17.2.2 Packing Technology

In a parallel system consisting of several tens of CPU units capable of several GFLOPS each, one unit should have a size of ~ 1 liter/unit and should be able to cool at a rate of up to ~ 10 kW/liter to remove the heat from high-speed circuitry. Thus, very compact packaging, low power dissipation, and a powerful cooling technology are big barriers.

17.2.3 Algorithm Software

Whereas parallelism is essential as the future direction, the greatest barrier to be broken lies in the interrelation between hardware, system software, and application.

The programming language itself and the compiler for parallel processing are the areas which need some more exploration. As to the compiler, the experience of automatic vectorizing techniques for the current pipelined supercomputer will assist in developing a parallel compiler. As to the control program, efficient parallel resource assignment, scheduling, exclusivity control, and synchronization, etc., should be well managed in the context of the compiler's capabilities.

However, more critical than system software would be the issue of how to develop efficient parallel-processing algorithms for various kinds of applications, and this research is just about to take off. The parallel-oriented formalization of an application and the breaking-down to efficient programs are the greatest challenges in supercomputing in order to exploit the potential of parallel processing.

The top-end TFLOPS supercomputer may be difficult to mold as an all-round player, and it may be similar to current supercomputers, each of which has some strong and some weak points. Therefore, it is essential to have wide-ranging co-operating and close interdisciplinary discussions, which should cover such topics as characteristics of application, adopted algorithms, the programming language, operating system, architecture, hardware design, and device technology, in order to achieve breakthroughs. The objective is to overcome all these challenges and to crush the barrier. It is in this context that the author would like to call for close cooperation between people supplying systems and those on the application side.

18   The Supercomputer in Ten Years' Time

Yasumasa Kanada[1]

There are several things I would like to bring up. First, let me begin with a discussion of π, which was mentioned by Dr. Mori in his introduction (Chap. 16). Computation of the value of π required 12 years to go from 1 million places to 10 million places, 4 years to go from 10 million places to 100 million places, and $2\frac{1}{2}$ years to go from 100 million places to 1 billion places. Extrapolating from this pace, theoretically we ought to be able to achieve a precision of 10 billion places by next year, but things do not look good. In the stage from 1 million to 10 million places, the determining factor was the development of a way to use the $N \log(N)$ algorithm on a computer. The next advance, from 10 to 100 million places, was brought about by the use of supercomputers. The latest step, from 100 million to 1 billion places, was in fact due to competition with our American colleagues. I feel that we have already reached the peak of supercomputer performance, and that it will probably be the end of the 20th century before we can achieve 10-billion-place precision.

From the standpoint of records, this figure could theoretically be reached – given enough time – with a large enough memory and fast enough speed. By 1992–1993, for example, we could reach this figure if we wanted to, over a period of several months, but this would also depend on the reliability of the machine.

The greatest problem, though – and this was brought up in the first panel discussion – is how to go about perserving the results. The current figures of 1 billion places for π and $1/\pi$ and 1.6 billion places for $\sqrt{2}$ and $1/\sqrt{2}$ are world records, but they required a total of more than 5 GB in storage space. Since one cartridge tape is capable of holding 200 MB, that means more than 20 tapes are needed, and it is difficult for us to provide this many types to anyone. In order for these to become available to a wider range of individuals, we need a device that can put all of this onto one tape. This is one of the major hindrances to those attempting to set a new world record.

That is the present situation. Now I would like to talk a little bit about the most advanced computers, those that are capable of breaking world records for computation of π. A brief look at the history of computation in science and technology shows that in most cases the difference in results between the record holder and the nearest

---

[1] Computer Centre, University of Tokyo, 2-11-16 Yayoi, Bunkyo-ku, Tokyo, 113 Japan

competitor is only slight. Also, I think that most scientists, like myself, would like to win as comfortably as possible. In this sense, the problem becomes one of how fast a machine can be used, and of how to achieve access to it. The key should be to work in cooperation with the manufactures. Basically, as Dr. Nakazawa mentioned in his talk, technology is very hard to predict, and all we can do is to wait.

Today, therefore, I will speculate on the future. We could see a desktop audio-visual (AV) supercomputer developed within the next ten years. It should offer low power consumption and extremely high reliability. Since this type of machine will be used in the laboratory by turning on the power before leaving for home, letting it run for a new months, and then having a look at the results, reliability should be guaranteed for at least a year. It should also have an extremely largely memory capacity. At present, supercomputers capable of GFLOPS have memories of several hundred megabytes. As for processing speed, I would like to see speeds of from several hundred MFLOPS to the GFLOPS range. It should be a single processor if possible. I prefer a fast single processor, rather than a multi-parallel design with, for example, several hundred separate units, such as that described by Dr. Tomita. I think this kind of machine is very difficult to work with. Since experience is a key factor in the operation of these machines, I believe that a parallel processor with several units would be the easiest to use.

Next, it should have a graphic engine and the ability to show movies. It should be equipped with high-quality speakers – recall the quadrophonic stereos popular many years ago – and I think it would be excellent if movies could be easily projected on the high-definition (HD) television screen. In this sense it would be an AV supercomputer. Finally, it should allow easy connection to other networks and exchange of data with the host. I suppose that if the manufacturers really wanted to make a product like this, they could do it within ten years. I believe that the latest supercomputers are needed only by a very limited group of people. People such as the authors of Chaps. 1–8 often have to make special machines in order to keep abreast of the competition, but probably 95% of people would rather have extremely cheap, high-speed engines. I think they want to be able to make a movie easily.

If this kind of machine could be priced under 10 million yen – although the cheaper the better – and, since some will probably want to use it at home, if a price of several million yen could be achieved, I think a lot of people would be extremely grateful.

One other problem I see with the current situation is the great variety of machine – Sun, Alliant, and so on. Dr. Kikuchi suggested that the presence of various different types of machines indicates a difference in cultural maturity, but this is a major problem from the standpoint of the user. Rather than having to use a product from Company A when making movies and one from Company B when performing numerical computation, I prefer a single engine capable of handling all operations. In this sense, if there was an inexperience de facto standard supercomputer available, it would be very useful for an extremely large group of people.

Concerning the problem of competition, it is often said that in Japan manufacturers compete for a market with nearly the same basic products, while in foreign countries they compete with different products. This idea is probably at the bottom of my thoughts as well; I want manufacturers to compete for this type of de facto standard and produce high-quality products at low cost, just as has happened in the video cassette recorder (VCR) industry. I hope this will happen, and I think it can.

I predict that the use of this type of desktop AV supercomputer will make it possible, for instance, to compute the value of π to 100 million places in one or two hours. I hope the time comes when this type of problem is taught in the first or second year of a university course.

19 Computational Derivation of the Properties of Few-Electron Atomic Systems

KATSUNORI HIJIKATA[1]

The microscopic world is ruled by quantum mechanics. The effects of relativity and quantum electrodynamics are represented by the power series of αz, where α is the fine structure constant $(e^2/4\pi\varepsilon_0 \hbar c = 1/137.0)$ and z is the atomic number. If we admit an error proportional to $m_0 c^2 (\alpha z)^6$, the formulation is easily handled. In atoms and molecules, all the forces acting between particles are of electromagnetic origin and are completely defined. The theoretical derivation of the properties of atoms and molecules, therefore, is entirely a matter of computation.

In two-electron atomic systems we start from the Hamiltonian into which only electrostatic potentials are incorporated:

$$H = -(\hbar^2/2m)(\nabla_1^2 + \nabla_2^2) - (ze^2/r_1) - (ze^2/r_2) + (1/r_{12}) \tag{1}$$

where r_1 and r_2 are the distances of the electrons from the nucleus and r_{12} is the distance between the electrons. The wave function Ψ of the system satisfying

$$H\Psi = E\Psi$$

is expressed by the linear combination of nonorthogonal basis functions

$$\Psi = (1 \pm P_{12}) \sum c_{lmn}\phi_{lmn} \tag{2}$$

$$\phi_{lmn} = \exp(-\alpha r_1 - \beta r_2)r_1^l r_2^m r_{12}^n Y_{LM}(\cos\theta), \tag{3}$$

where P_{12} is the permutation operation, $+$ and $-$ correspond to singlet and triplet states, and Y_{LM} is the spherical harmonics. The coefficients C_{lmn} are determined so that the quantity

$$\langle \Psi, H\Psi \rangle / \langle \Psi, \Psi \rangle = E \tag{4}$$

is stationary. The non-linear parameters are fixed before the procedure of linear algebra, and the best pair is chosen to minimize the total energy E. Once the "nonrelativistic" wavefunction is known in this way, the terms omitted in the Hamiltonian H, the relativistic corrections, the spin-orbit interactions, the spin-spin interaction, and the hyperfine interaction, are calculated as perturbations. By

---

[1] Meisei University, 2-1-1, Hodokubo, Hino-shi, Tokyo, 191 Japan

following a similar method with 1078 basis functions, Pekeris [1] calculated the wavefunction of the ground state of He, and obtained the value of the ionization potential within the limit of the experimental error.

Theoretical calculation has been subordinate to experimental methods, and the main interest has been to calculate the values as close as possible to the experimental values. It seems, however, that the recent development of computers has changed this situation. The calculation is expected to be an independent effective method of investigating atoms and molecules, as we show in the following by the result of our calculation on the ^3P states of two-electron atomic systems. The complete detail of our treatment was published in 1988 [2].

19.1 The Fine Structure of the 2^3P State of Two-Electron Atomic Systems

In Fig. 19.1 the multiplet intervals of the 2^3P state of ^{4}He were calculated and compared with the experiment. For both the intervals the relative error is 0.02%. This triplet state of ^{4}He is completely inverted, that is, the energy is lower for the higher J-value. The same calculations were easily performed for the isoelectronic systems and the results were compared with the experimental values as shown in Table 19.1. Schiff's wavefunctions [3] contain more terms than ours. In view of the signs we note that from N^{5+} to Ne^{8+}, the orders of the multiplets are completely regular and that the process of transit from the inverted multiplet of He shows perfect agreement between the calculations and experiments. Among the experimental results, however, v_{10} is missing for Be^{2+}, and some are of poor accuracy. By analyzing this comparison we could gain a general idea of the accuracy of our wavefunctions. It was found that the order of the multiplets in determined by the relative magnitude of the spin-orbit and the spin-spin interactions.

19.2 The Hyperfine Structure

In view of the fine structure of the ^3P state of He, we note that the intervals are anomalously small and comparable with hyperfine structure splittings. In the investigation of the sublevels of the same state of ^{3}He (nuclear spin $I = \frac{1}{2}$), therefore, the fine and the hyperfine structures must be considered simultaneously. From the standpoint of computation, the two effects can be calculated to the same accuracy since they are related similarly to $(1/r^3)$. The result is shown in Fig. 19.2, where the numbers in parentheses are J and F, the electronic and the total angular momentum quantum numbers, respectively. As we had expected, $^3P_1$ and $^3P_2$ are strongly mixed with each other by the hyperfine interaction. It is regrettable that purely experimental data could not be found in the literature. Freize et al. [4] show the same diagram in which the intervals are different from ours by 0.1 MHz. Their values are, however, derived by mixing theory and experiment. Our results may have errors of the order of 1 MHz.

Table 19.2 shows the comparison of the calculation and the experiments for $^6Li^+$

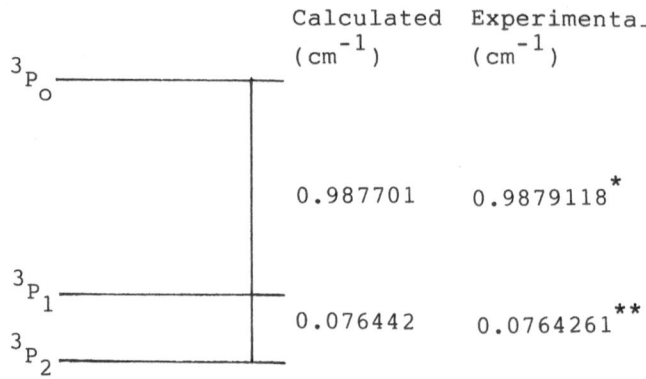

Fig. 19.1. Fine structure intervals of 2^3p of ^{4}He. *From [4], **from [8]

Table19.1. Fine structure intervals in cm^{-1}. Number in parenthesis is the mass number

| | Theoretical | | | |
	Present Paper	Schiff et al. [3]	Experimental	Reference
$Z(N)$				
ν_{21}				
2 (4)	−0.07644	−0.07637	−0.0764289	[8]
3 (7)	2.08893	2.08988	2.093	[9]
4 (9)	14.879	14.8829	14.8	[10]
5(11)	52.604	52.6134	52.3	[10]
6 (12)	135.612	135.632	136	[11]
7 (14)	290.493	290.525	290.8	[12]
8 (16)	550.357	550.394	551.5	[13]
9 (19)	955.25	955.26	956.6	[13]
10 (20)	1552.68	1552.57	1554	[13]
ν_{10}				
2	−0.98770	−0.9880	−0.987912	[4]
3	−5.19381	−5.19443	−5.179	[9]
4	−11.5580	−11.5586	—	
5	−16.1974	−16.1971	−16.0	[10]
6	−12.506	−12.504	−13	[11]
7	8.666	8.674	14.5	[12]
8	58.734	58.757	58.4	[13]
9	150.96	151.04	157.7	[13]
10	299.96	300.14	299.5	[13]

$\nu_{21} = E(2^3P_2) - E(2^3P_1)$, $\nu_{10} = E(2^3P_1) - E(2^3P_0)$

and ^{7}Li$^+$. Jette et al. [5] obtained their values by a linked cluster many-body perturbation method. In ^{7}Li$^+$, the expected coincidence is observed. In ^{6}Li$^+$, however, the agreement is worse. Since the calculations are quite similar, it is not expected that our results for ^{6}Li$^+$ would be worse than those for ^{7}Li$^+$, whereas the experiments are supposedly more difficult for the species with less natural abundance.

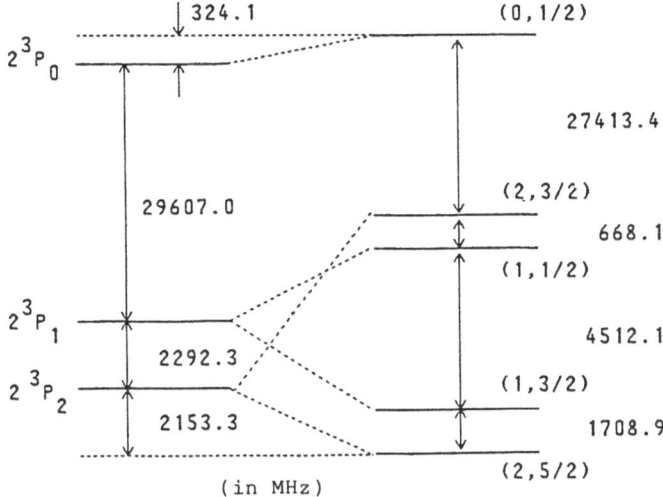

Fig. 19.2. Hyperfine structure of 2^3p of ^{3}He

Table 19.2. Hyperfine intervals of 2^3P state for ^{6,7}Li$^+$ in GHz

$(J,F)-(J',F')$	Theoretical		Experimental	Reference
	Present paper	Jette et al. [5]		
^{6}Li$^+$				
$(0,1)-(2,3)$	90.326	90.320	—	
$(2,3)-(2,2)$	4.1267	4.127	4.091	[14]
$(2,2)-(2,1)$	2.8580	2.857	2.858	[14]
$(2,1)-(1,2)$	57.108	57.15	—	
$(1,2)-(1,1)$	2.8876	2.88	2.856	[14]
$(1,1)-(1,0)$	1.3173	1.3314	1.302	[14]
^{7}Li$^+$				
$(0,3/2)-(2,7/2)$	82.738	82.733	—	[15]
$(2,7/2)-(2,5/2)$	11.7744	11.77	11.7758	[15]
$(2,5/2)-(2,3/2)$	9.6078	9.606	9.6087	[15]
$(2,3/2)-(2,1/2)$	6.2032	6.204	6.2036	
$(2,1/2)-(1,5/2)$	41.752	41.801	—	[15]
$(1,5/2)-(1,3/2)$	9.9641	9.941	9.9652	[15]
$(1,3/2)-(1,1/2)$	4.2380	4.223	4.2378	

19.3 Prospects

Entirely similar calculations were performed on the hyperfine splittings of the same state for the isoelectronic series He to Ne^{8+}, and the table was completed for the species having $I = \frac{1}{2}$, 1 and 3/2 [6]. If we succeed in performing an accurate calculation for a system, we can straightforwardly extend the same treatment to similar systems and can claim the same degree of accuracy for the results, no matter how difficult the experiment is in practice. This is the definite advantage of computation.

The same treatment has already been extended to 3-electron atomic systems [7]. In the calculations given here for the 2-electron systems, we took the basic functions satisfying

$$l + m + n = w \leq 8,$$

totalling 165 terms. For the 3-electron system, the basis functions have the form

$$\exp[-\alpha r_1 - \beta r_2 - \gamma r_3] r_1^a r_2^b r_3^c r_{23}^d r_{31}^e r_{12}^f$$

and the number of the terms satisfying

$$a + b + c + d + e + f = w \leq 8$$

is 1716, and so the optimization of the three parameter (α, β, γ) is not easy. Moreover, in our experience it happens that the $(n + 1)$th basis is almost linearly dependent on the preceding n functions. The extension to the larger systems, therefore, is not straightforward. The accumulation of considerable known-how is required, just as in the history of orbital methods.

For the atoms which larger z, the higher relativistic and quantum electro-dynamical corrections must be taken into account. For the time being, however, we have to be constrained to the first-order corrections as described in this article. The problems are still innumerable.

References

1. Pekeris CL (1958) Phys Rev 112: 1647
2. Hijikata K, Ohtsuki K (1988) J Phys Soc Jap 57: 4141
3. Schiff B, Accad Y, Pekeris CL (1973) Phys Rev A8: 2272
4. Freize W, Hinds EA, Hughes VW, Pichanik FMJ (1981) Phys Rev A24: 279
5. Jette AN, Lee T, Das TP (1974) Phys Rev A9: 2337
6. Ohtsuki K, Hijikata K (1988) J Phys Soc Jap 57: 4150
7. Larsson S (1968) Phys Rev 169: 49, and several other articles by the same author
8. Lewis SA, Pichanik FMJ, Hughes VW (1970) Phys Rev A2: 86
9. Herzberg G, Moore HR (1959) Can J Phys 37: 1293
10. Edlén B, (1952) Ark Fysik 4: 441
11. Edlén B, Lofstrand B (1970) J Phys B3: 1380
12. Bockasten K, Hallin R, Johanson KB, Tsui P (1964) Phys Lett 8: 191
13. Elton RC (1967) Astrophys J 148: 573
14. Berry HG, Pinnington EH, Subtil JL (1974) Phys Rev A10: 1065
15. Kowalski J, Neumann, R, Noehte S, Scheffzek K, Suhr H, Putlitz G (1983) Hyperfine Interactions 15: 159

20 Comments on Supercomputing from an Engineering Point of View

TADAHIKO KAWAI[1]

First of all, I was very much impressed by Dr. Kalos' talk (Chap. 14). Indeed, the computer will change and reconstruct all fields of learning in the near future and play an important role in their development including both life sciences and social sciences.

Professor Kikuchi gave a very interesting overview on the development of super-computing techniques achieved by leading scholars in the field of finite element methods (FEM) (Chap. 2).

Lectures given by Japanese scientists working in the field of modern physics, chemistry, and material sciences were also stimulating. The majority of participants might have gained the impression that supercomputing will solve all the interactive problems in science and technology. Let me give my comments on this point from the engineering point of view.

1. I cannot have an optimistic view on the future of supercomputing. This is because I am a structural engineer challenging nonlinear problems of solid mechanics such as collapse or crash of structures, slope stability of foundations, liquefaction problems of soils, etc., with computers. Nature has a hierarchical structure of numerous particles of different sizes – or in terms of FEM, nature is a multilevel substructure system of infinite dimensions. The macroscopic approach, on which FEM is based, is only a crude approximation of nature.

Therefore, it is clear that material nonlinear problems cannot be solved by supercomputing FEM, no matter how powerful the hardware becomes or how effective the software may be. The difficulty in such nonlinear analysis relates to matching the continuum model with the behavior of the actual particles (such as crystalline, molecular structures). In other words, the refinement of the constitutive law which relates the material behavior of particles of different sizes plays a key role to the better understanding of nature. Based on this point of view, I have developed a new discrete element model, which is especially useful in studying the mechanics of discrete element systems such as concrete, and granular and composite materials.

---

[1] Department of Electrical Engineering, Science University of Tokyo, Kagurazaka Shinjuku-ku Tokyo, 162 Japan

2. The supercomputing method is very successful in physical science and technology. But they form only a small portion of all the fields of natural sciences. Innovative development will be expected in the application of supercomputing methods to medical and life sciences, and to many other unexplored fields of computer sciences. I have a feeling that the development of a physical model which represents the essential features of human organs or biological structures, and computer simulation using such models, is only one possible way to develop computer applications in these fields.

3. I consider that solving the following problem is currently very important for achieving breakthroughs in areas of bottlenecks in high technology and frontier sciences:

  a) Development of the method inverse analysis, which is especially useful in failure or risk analysis, prediction of volcano eruptions and earthquakes, or medical diagnosis
  b) Establishment of methods for the long-term prediction of global, environmental, and geophysical problems
  c) Development of approaches to coupled field problems of transport phenomena in solid, fluid, and gas mixing systems
  d) Development of solutions to three-dimensional (3D) solid contact problems which play a vital role in the study of tribology
  e) Application of computer simulation to studies of chaotic, fractal, and catastrophic theories

Finally, I would like to propose to found a kind of national research institute where a problem can be solved interdisciplinary from science field, engineering field and technology field and related computing soft wares are also developed.

21 Some Comments
on Hardware and Software
for Science and Engineering

NOBORU KIKUCHI[1]

I would like to make just one comment concerning both hardware and software. I think that in every case, a difference emerges between science and engineering. Involved as I am in engineering, everything is located at the farthest point downstream, so to speak. In the case of science, whether you are dealing with software or hardware, everything is done once, used one, and published once.

In the field of engineering, however, something may be used 1,000 or 2,000 times; it may be applied to something completely different; a paper may be written many times. In this sense, although computers are becoming more and more specialized and extremely high-density parallel processing is being adopted, I think that if these designs can really only be used for special applications, then they are of little utility. No matter how fast and how specialized, unless hundreds of thousands of people can freely use the machine 1,000 or 2,000 times, the computer has little value. This is particularly true in the case of software.

Our biggest problem with software is that from the standpoint of engineering, supercomputer software and PC software, for example, should be the same. If it is not, it will not sell. Take the example of NASTRAN, which is used in structural design. NASTRAN runs on general-purpose machines, it runs on engineering work stations (EWS), and in some cases it may have to run in a more compact form on PC's. On top of all this, it has to run on supercomputers, and when it does, it must take advantage of the unique characteristics of supercomputers to perform faster calculations. Unless a package can do all of these things, it cannot truly be called software, at least in the field of engineering. So what we are asking of the people "upstream" is very simple: we want them to provide products which can handle a wide variety of applications and which are flexible, fast, inexpensive, and large in scale. Without these characteristics, repeated use by a wide range of individuals will not be feasible. From our standpoint, such a product is of no use, since it makes it impossible to recover the initial investment.

There is one other point that I would like to make. As was mentioned by Dr. Kalos (Chap. 14), the reason we are focusing our attention on supercomputers is

---

[1] Computational Mechanics Laboratory, College of Engineering, The University of Michigan, Ann Arbor, Michigan, 49109 USA

not for their use as single units, but rather to determine their possibilities as integrated units for comprehensive research by people in a variety of fields.

For example, take the case of a polygonal elastic plate. When the angle of this polygon exceeds 180°, proof of existence work in mathematics shows that no solution can exist. When we take away the area surrounding this point, however, we can see a solution in the interior. This can be seen when you apply an adaptive method to solve this problem. The solution converges until midway through. It appears as if it were converging. In fact, however, it jumps about from midway on. In other words, if the problem is solved carelessly using the finite element method, it becomes impossible to solve midway through, and it becomes clear that, in mathematical terms, this problem is not well-imposed. From a physical, or engineering, standpoint, this problem is nonsensical from the very start. When an angle exceed 180° and a bend is made in an extremely small region, the upper part contracts, and the lower part opens up. In other words, at this point in time, the dynamic process of a flat plate has already been broken. Despite the fact that it has already been broken, we are trying to solve a 4th-order equation and force it into a solve form. In conclusion, this kind of gap between mathematics and physics can now be tracked down using numbers and pictures. I would like to emphasize that it is the appearance of supercomputers, with their extremely high capacity for con.putation, which has made it possible to picture this gap.

If we proceed further along this path, it should be possible to preserve, in an abstract form, things learned with mathematics, and to express abstract symbols using concrete pictures and numbers. I have limited the discussion to contact between mechanics and mathematics, but the possibilities of computational mechanics should allow the same for chemical engineering and chemistry, for example, and to allow more concrete representations of various points of contact between fields. Herein lies our role.

22 Panel Discussion 2: Questions and Answers

Nomura (RIKEN): This is for Dr. Kawai. I do not want to force you to commit yourself, so please feel free to answer informally. My question concerns the future national research institute; could you give us a few more specifics as to what you would suggest for such a center?

Kawai (Science University of Tokyo): First of all, I would like to say that this is only a vision, only a dream. At present, we are all carrying out research and development at our respective campuses. What I envision is a comprehensive system under which – there are a large number of hardware specialists here todays as well – experts are provided with the state of the art in hardware and allowed to develop software on the same exacting level.

At the same time, the field of engineering contains an extremely wide range of problems. As was mentioned by Dr. Kikuchi, I think that in order to be able to solve these problems, software must possess great variety and, in the area of functionality, gradually move towards single-function designs. This in turn will make necessary a large investment. I believe that government, academia, and industry should pool their funds and work jointly to develop large-scale software. The resulting software should then be used not only by companies across Japan but in the universities as well, thereby leading to subsequent developments. I think it would be wonderful if we could establish this kind of system. But again, this is only a dream.

Kanada (University of Tokyo): I would like to make one comment on Dr. Kawai's idea. I have nothing against such a system, but I think there would be one problem. Although this is probably true at corporations as well, in order to "move up on the totem pole," in most cases one must write papers documenting one's work. If you create such an organization, in many cases the person who brings in the most money, or in the case of a corporation, the person who is able to get the most money out of the plant's headquarters, is going to be the one who "gets ahead." Unless we can create an atmosphere in which workers are routinely rewarded for their efforts, in the form of improved benefits or promotion, I do not think this kind of system would work.

Mori (Chairman; University of Tokyo): Fields involved in developing applications are extremely interdisciplinary in nature, and I do not think this type of work will necessary involve individuals in specialized fields getting all the attention. Dr. Kanada's talk of the need for "evaluation" is also felt by us, for whom receiving such evaluation is very important. At present, however, I think this would be very difficult. One solution might be the establishment of the suggested joint cooperational body or research institution. Does anyone have any good ideas concerning this point?

Kikuchi (University of Michigan): I am afraid I cannot agree with you. When we are talking about the development of software for use in science, I think a national research institute would be fine. When it comes to software that is to be used in engineering or industry, however, I do not think you can develop a good product unless you have got individuals who are staking their capital, and their corporate existence, on the product.

When you compare the available software for supercomputers and PC's, for example, you find that the PC software is far better made. The reason? Simply because if it is not, it will not sell on the market. I think that if you forget this point when talking about software, you will never got a good product, no matter how much money – taxpayers' money – you spend. This kind of thinking is probably due in part to my time spent in the United States, but one thing is certain: software must come from "downstream." Without people who give their all to produce and sell a good product, you are not going to find good software. I am constantly reminded of this whenever I compare the software available for supercomputers and PC's.

Nomura: I am in agreement with what Dr. Kikuchi just said, but the universities and government agencies do not spend money on software. As a result of the lack of software, they have fallen far behind the private sector in Japan, and this has resulted in a variety of problems. Also, with the development of parallel processing, government and academia are simply borrowing machines made in the private sector without really understanding them. In this sense, I think it is important that we establish some kind of system to respond to the new age of computing in government as well. I would like to see some kind of national organization.

Mori (Chairman): Are there any other opinions concerning this point? I think that in the end Dr. Kikuchi and the others are actually saying the same thing. Specifically, it is important that the software be evaluated. I think that they were speaking of two possible methods of evaluation, and I do not think their views necessarily conflict.

Kikuchi: For example, projects like LINPACK and EISPACK were probably undertaken with government assistance from the National Science Foundation. The results of that work were then used to produce and sell software like MATLAB. Without that kind of system, the resulting good software goes to waste. If it stays in government, it will definitely go to waste. In order to make use of it, I think it is necessary for university professors to leave academia, form their own companies, and stake themselves on it. In our field, at least, virtually all of the programs in general use originated in government; but the originators have all left government. I-DEAS was made based on work done at Cincinnati University, and NASTRAN was made based on NASA software.

At NASA, however, NASTRAN is no longer in use. It survives in the form of MSC's NASTRAN. I think that we have to remain very aware of this point. Unless we are well aware of it when developing software, we are going to come out on the losing end, no matter how much money we spend.

Mori (Chairman): Based on Dr. Nakazawa's talk as well, I think that the hardware situation will gradually move in the direction of your vision, but from the standpoint of those of us on the application side, the main problem definitely lies in software development, the type of thing we are discussing right now.

Doyama (Nishi Tokyo Science University): Without question, I think that from the standpoint of technology, the fact that a variety of people are going to use the product is an extremely important point. For those of us in science, however, only 'one' is necessary for each problem. Use of it for some other purpose does not lead to any recognition. I think that we scientists and computers are on a honeymoon. Computers for us are a tool. If there is a problem that we would like to solve, supercomputers allow us to solve it at the fastest possible speed. We have no concern about other uses for it. I hope that you will keep this in mind.

Mori: (Chairman): Dr. Doyama's is a new opinion, and I think it brings up a very important point.

Kanada: Why is that, Dr. Kikuchi? I think there is a sizeable gap between Japan and the United States on this point. As I understand it, the status of teachers at American universities is determined not so much by their employer as by their income. Thus, I expect that there are those who, upon tiring of the academic life, form their own companies, make a lot of money, and end up looking down their noses at their former employers. This could never happen in Japan, though. In my experience – although this is a personal opinion – I do not think it would be possible for a teacher at a national university to start his own company and survive for 20 or 30 years. I think there are a lot of people staying in the universities because that is the only place they have. It would be extremely difficult to do things the American way. Furthermore, I think the fact that these people are civil servants also complicates any joint efforts with the private sector.

Kikuchi: I think exactly the same thing can be said of the situation in the United States. The majority of teachers are incapable of that kind of mobility; but I think it is important to have an environment in which those who try, can.

Kanada: If that is the case, I think the same could probably be said of Japan as well.

Ikeda (Kyoto University): It is possible to carry out software development for computer manufacturers, given the authorization. This was brought up by Dr. Kondo, but problems such as the global warming effect cannot be solved by academicians alone. Corporations are providing some financial aid – Keidanren [federation of economic organizations] has offered some back-up, and recently there was the chair donation support. The problem is, we need someone, a well-known, respected professor if possible, who will take the lead. If this happened, I think something could be done to generate a third sector. What is your opinion?

Kawai: In relation to this, I would like to bring up the earlier topic of a national research institute. I envision a center provided with the best available equipment in the world – and I am sure you all have some specific ideas regarding this – backed by the government, and staffed with leaders in the field to solve some of the large-scale, fundamental problems we now faced. There is no reason why Japan and all of its newly-found wealth could not set up such an institute. Even assuming an investment of, say ¥100 billion, this would be nothing compared to the money that could be saved by predicting a major earthquake in the Tokyo area that could reduce the city to ashes. I think it is now time to consider spending money for projects like this.

I am sure that are various opinions concerning this in America, but in science today you cannot understand something unless you actually try it. The number of fields in which computer simulation offers the only possible foothold is rapidly increasing.

In this sense, this type of national research institute – take the space development work in the United States and the Soviet Union, for example – has made an irreplaceable contribution to the world in the 20th century. In this sense, I wonder if Japan and its vast wealth could not begin a new and unique enterprise in this field to do work that will benefit mankind in the 21st century. This is where my motivation lies.

Kashiwagi (Kyushu Institute of Technology): I could agree more with Dr. Kikuchi. I wonder, if it would be better to break down the large organization into several small ones. I am often taken by the feeling these days that national universities are not very good. I also think it might be better to divest huge companies like IBM and Hitachi.

Member of the audience: The research institute envisioned by Dr. Kawai appears to have its focus on the development of hardware and software. I wonder if a section for the absorption of young, talented people in math-related fields might not also be provided.

Dr. Kawai always makes it a point to write pure mathematics and applied mathematics and has given us excellent evaluations from these standpoints, and I am very grateful. Earlier the words "upstream" and "downstream" were used. In the upstream areas, I think that Japanese mathematics has made a very important contribution to the supercomputing field. When viewed very broadly, however, I think you will find that very few young people are being brought into these central problems. I wonder if a place could not be provided for these people to work.

Kawai: I think that science and technology from a pyramid of related fields, with pure mathematics, as well as applied mathematics, applied mechanics, and applied physics. I think that this kind of pyramid-like structure is only natural, and if this is a central problem I think it should be attacked from a variety of angles. We have no contact with our colleagues in pure mathematics. At best, there is some contact with those working in applied mechanics and applied physics.

One of my dreams is to establish a single closely-knit national organization to allow more interdisciplinary contact. I have heard that France has now established such an organization and is ready to overtake the United States in this respect. I sincerely hope that an integrated national research institute can be realized in Japan as well.

Index